PHOTOGRAPHS
WRITTENLIGHT

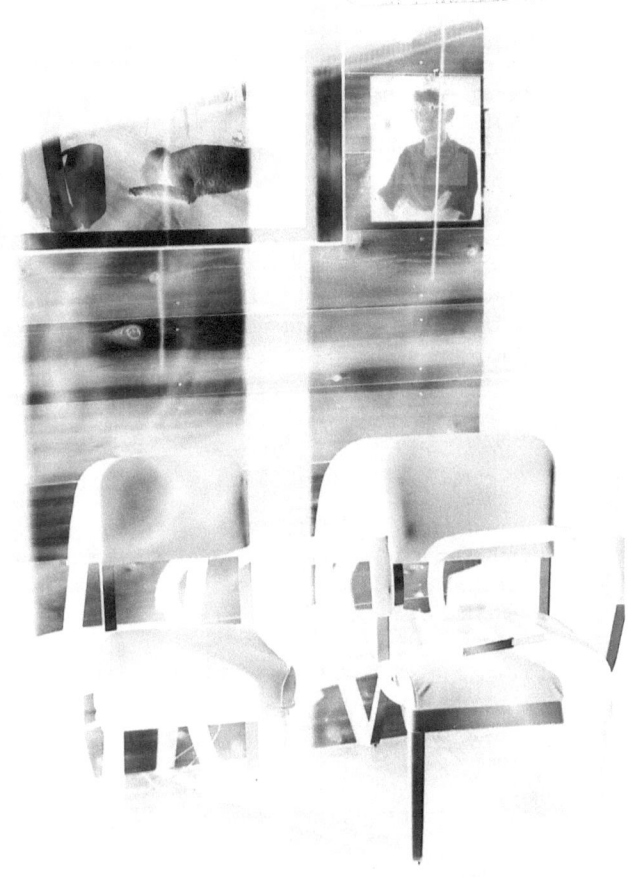

Mikesch W. Muecke

Obvious Press
918 5TH ST
Ames, IA 50010
USA

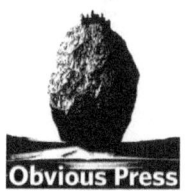

First published in the United States in 2005
Revised edition published in 2015 and 2023
PHOTOGRAPHS: WRITTEN LIGHT
© 2023 by Mikesch W. Muecke

The moral right of the author has been asserted.

All rights reserved. No part of this publication may be reproduced, stored in a retrieval system or transmitted, in any form or by any means, electronic, mechanical, photocopying, recording or otherwise, without the written permission of the author.

ISBN 978-1-941892-09-1

Obvious Press books are available at special discounts when purchased in bulk for sales promotions, premiums, fund-raising, or educational use. For details contact: Obvious Press Special Markets, 918 5TH ST, Ames, IA, 50010 or editor@obviouspress.com

Discover more at obviouspress.com

Book cover and interior design © 2023 by polytekton.com

To my parents,
who taught me to be curious...

TABLE OF CONTENTS

Introduction   6
Categories
     Advice   9
     Animals   15
     Contrast   31
     Details   49
     Films   57
     Hybrids   69
     Landscape + Architecture   91
     Memory   115
     Metamorphosis   149
     Mobility   173
     Observations   181
     Scale   243
     Textures   255

Introduction

"Beauty must be seen; this requires light."
                                    Karsten Harries, *The Broken Frame*

"Who needs sight when we got vision!"
                                    Herb Gardner, *I'm Not Rappaport*

When taken literally, a translation of the word 'photograph' means 'written light'.[1] In this book I offer the reader/viewer a collection of 'textual illumination' divided into categories. The accompanying short short-stories—in some cases no more than a few words—are literary counter weights to the visual text.

Rather than pretend to be a technophile and focus on how each image came about (aperture setting, focal length, lens type, film, etc.)[2]—which is a conventional means of augmenting photographic images—I borrow instead Roland Barthes' take on photographs, and treat what the camera captured as something that cannot be repeated. In other words, the *how* of the photograph is not as important to me as *what* is made visible with light.

Continuing with Barthes, conceptually these 'things written with light' are all *punctum* rather than *studium*. They represent what caught my eye over the years. Sometimes I framed my subjects consciously, at other times I only realized later the significance of a particular frame.

---

[1] From the Oxford English Dictionary Online. Photo-: Before a vovel properly phot- (but often in full form photo- in Eng. Compounds), repr. Gr fwto-, combining form of φῶς, φωτ- light.
-graph: repr. F. *–graphe*, L. *–graphus*, Gr. -γραφος. The Greek termination was used to form adjectives, sometimes in the passive sense of 'written', e.g. αυτογραφος written with one's own hand, χειρογραφος written with the hand; sometimes in the active sense, 'that writes, delineates, or describes', chiefly used absol. as ns.; 'one who writes, delineates, or describes': e.g. ζωγραφος a painter from life, βιβλιογραφος a writer of books, γεωγραφος a delineator of the earth, a geographer. Many of the passive formations in –γραφος have been anglicized, being for the most part used both as adjs. And ns., as in *autograph, chirograph, holograph*. These words have been imitated in a few modern ns. formed on Gr. types, as *lithograph, photograph*; and these in turn have been imitated in hybrid formations, such as *pictograph*; jocular nonce-words, like *hurrygraph* for 'a hurried sketch', are occasionally met with. The Gr. active formations in –γραφος,

In another reference, Jean-Michel Rabaté writes that Barthes' *Camera Lucida* was "a very moving autobiographical disclosure of his love for his mother under the guise of a study of photography."[3] Not to disparage the love of my mother but this collection of images is a disclosure of my love for my late father—a journalist for most of his life—under the guise of a collection of photographs.

I recall that on many weekends I would go with my dad to the newspaper, where he worked, and keep myself busy in the darkroom learning how to develop black-and-white film, dry the negatives without scratching them, and make enlargments on light-sensitive paper.

Photography taught me to look carefully at the world, and to respect, to take a second look (photography is that as well) across the scales from details to landscapes. Finally, taking photographs is always possessive, and I gladly admit to the taking of all the images in this book (with one exception, which is duly noted)—like a prowler in search of beauty—over a time span of about twenty-five years.

Mikesch W. Muecke
Ames, IA, March 2023

---

where they have been anglicized, take in mod. Eng. the ending –GRAPHER, which is used also for new formations denoting persons (exceptions, such as *calligraph*, are rare). The great bulk of the words in *–graph* is composed of technical terms of very recent invention, mostly formed on Gr. elements, and expressing the general sense of 'that which writes, portrays, or records', as *actinography, heliograph, hygrograph, ideograph, phonograph, seismograph, telegraph*, etc.

[2] For those who need to know, I used a number of different cameras to assemble this collection. Among my tools were a Rolleiflex 2.8 (inherited from my father), a Ricoh XR-1 SLR (borrowed from my partner), a Nikomat SLR and a Contax (borrowed from my partner's father), a Minolta AF SLR (my first camera), a 4.1 MegaPixel Minolta (my first digital camera), and a 6.1 MegaPixel Kodak DX7630 (my second digital camera).

[3] See http://www.press.jhu.edu/books/hopkins_guide_to_literary_theory/roland_barthes.html, accessed May 17, 2005.

ADVICE

For a great spatial experience visit the Law Library in the Iowa Capitol building in Des Moines. And—if you need some excitement in your life—when the librarians are not looking you can climb through a trap door in the north-west corner of the top floor into the attic of the capitol, dodge the cobwebs, and walk around the exterior interior of the dome, peer down through the skylights into the chambers, and worry about what might happen if you get caught.

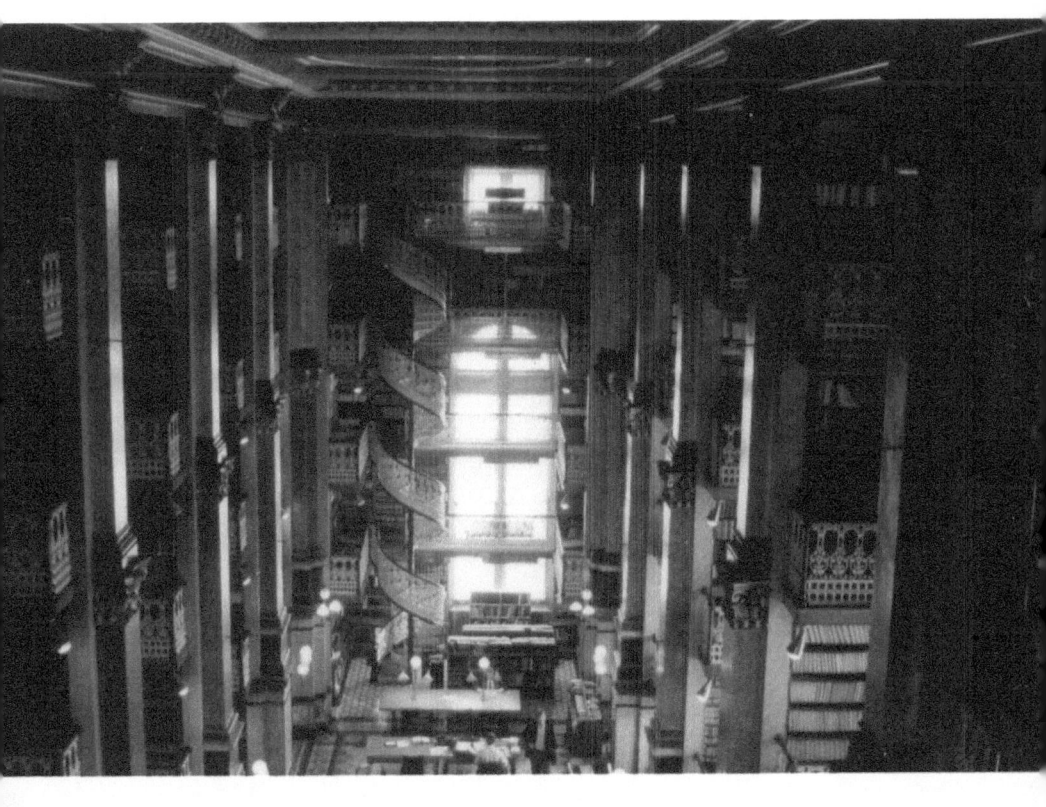

Advice 11

After the customs station has closed down for the evening—and if you're lucky and a smuggler—you may be able to cross the very old wooden bridge over the Rhine between Stein, Aargau (Switzerland) and Bad Säckingen (Germany) without getting caught by the border police agents. But be aware that they perform unannounced checks.

One day when we were staying with our friends Emmy and Georges on the Swiss side in Stein, I observed two boys who had tied a rope to one of the bridge's support pilings. They were hanging from the rope and used the river's current to watersurf; the freedom of youth...

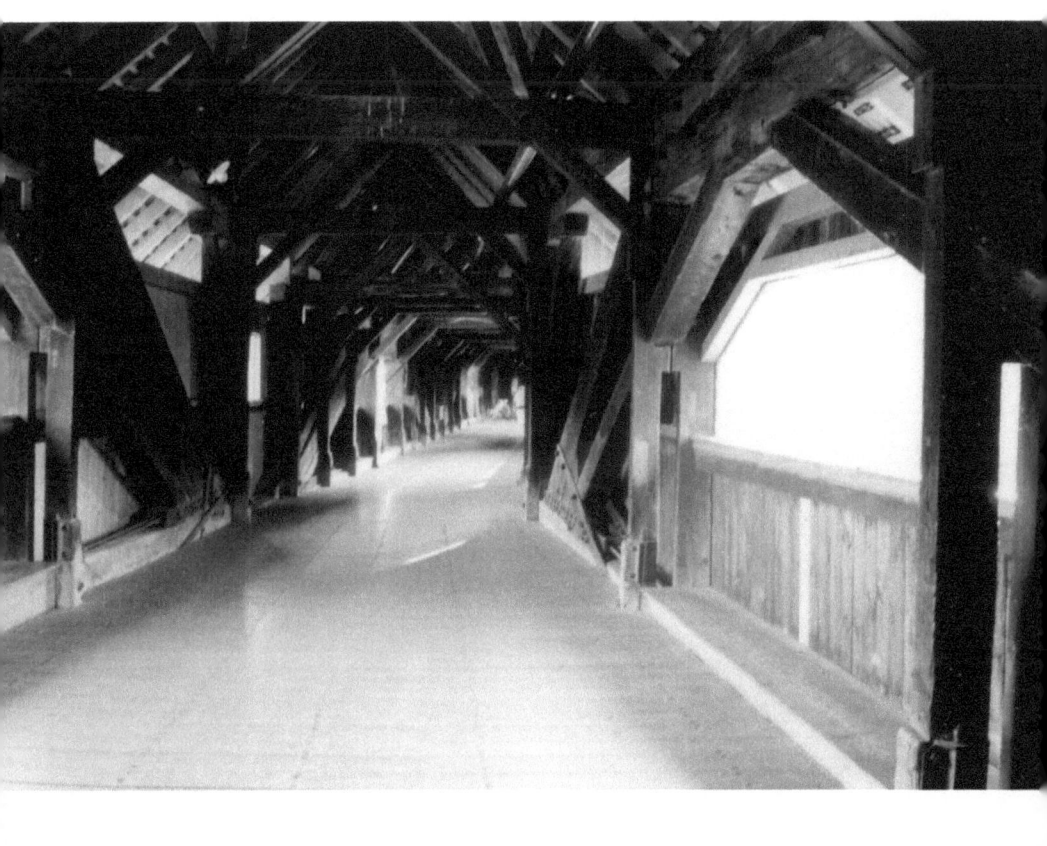

ANIMALS

Rabbits in the backyard.

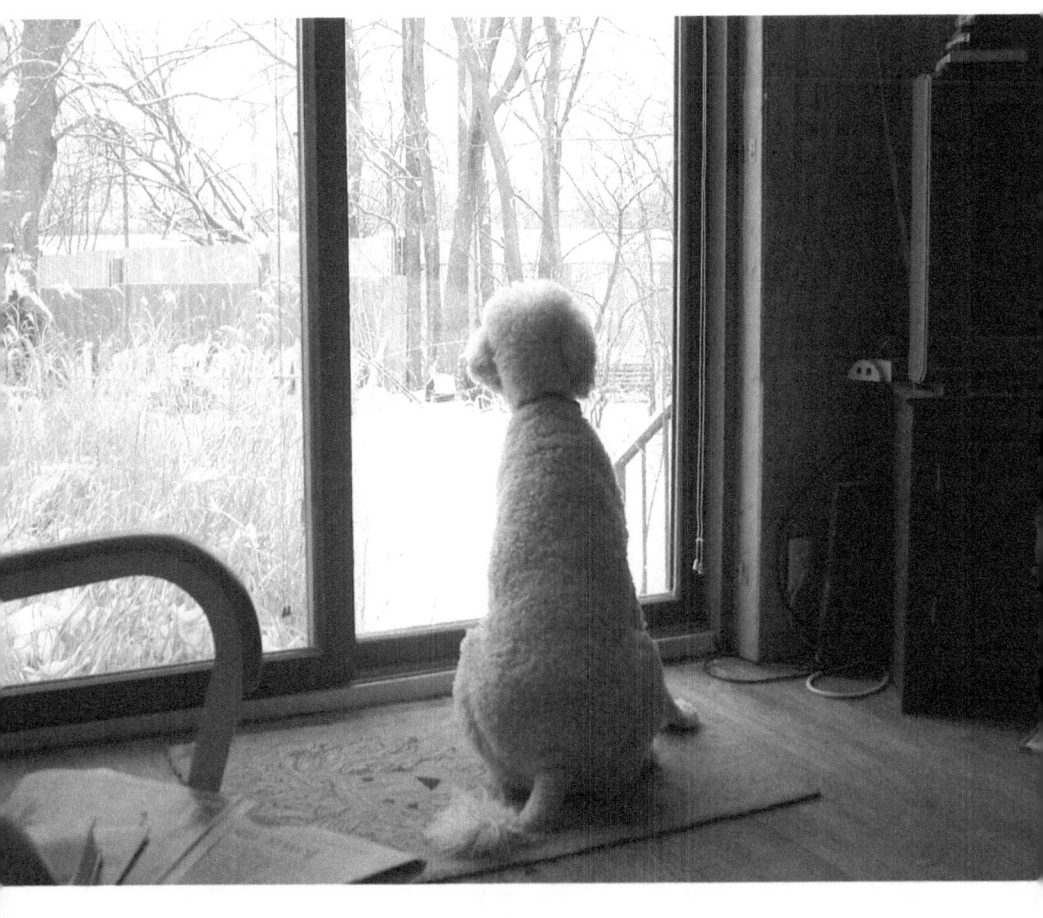

Storks, the masters of top-of-the-line design-built roosting places, have made a comeback in northern Germany, nesting not only on the provided poles but also on house chimneys.

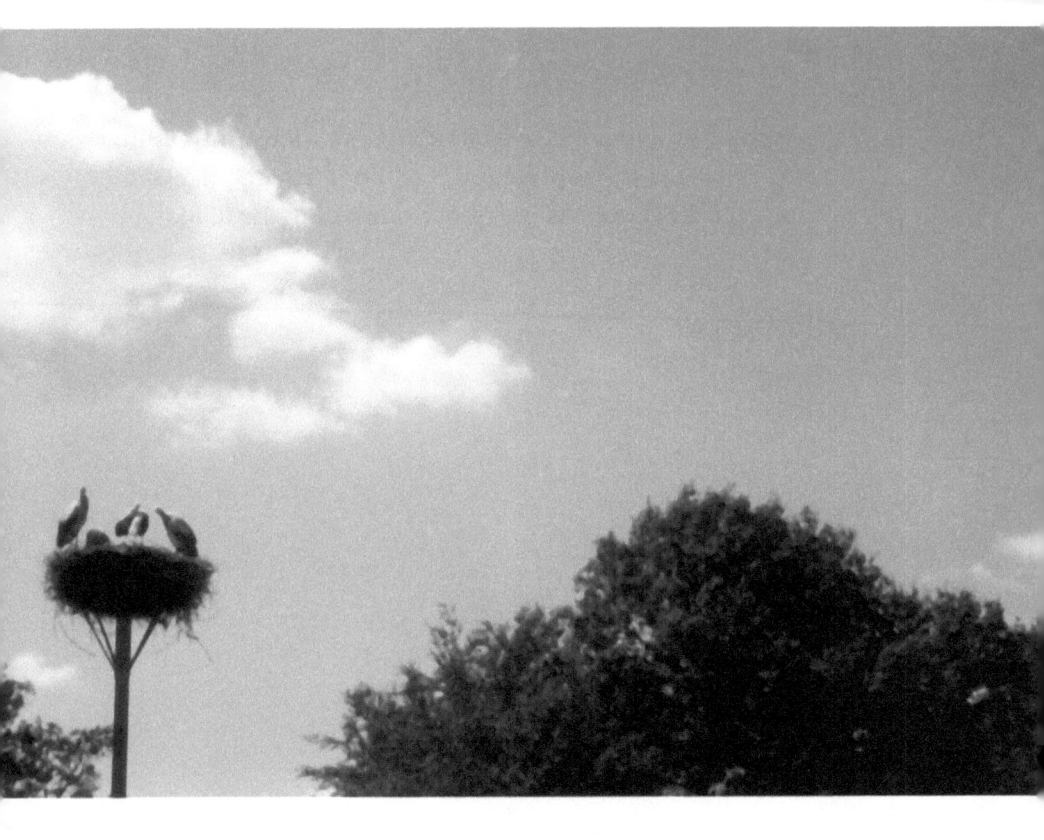

Whenever I walk down the *Unter den Linden* street in Berlin, I imagine what the sculptures on Karl Friedrich Schinkel's bridge near the *Museumsinsel* might think of us as we look up to them.

We are animals.

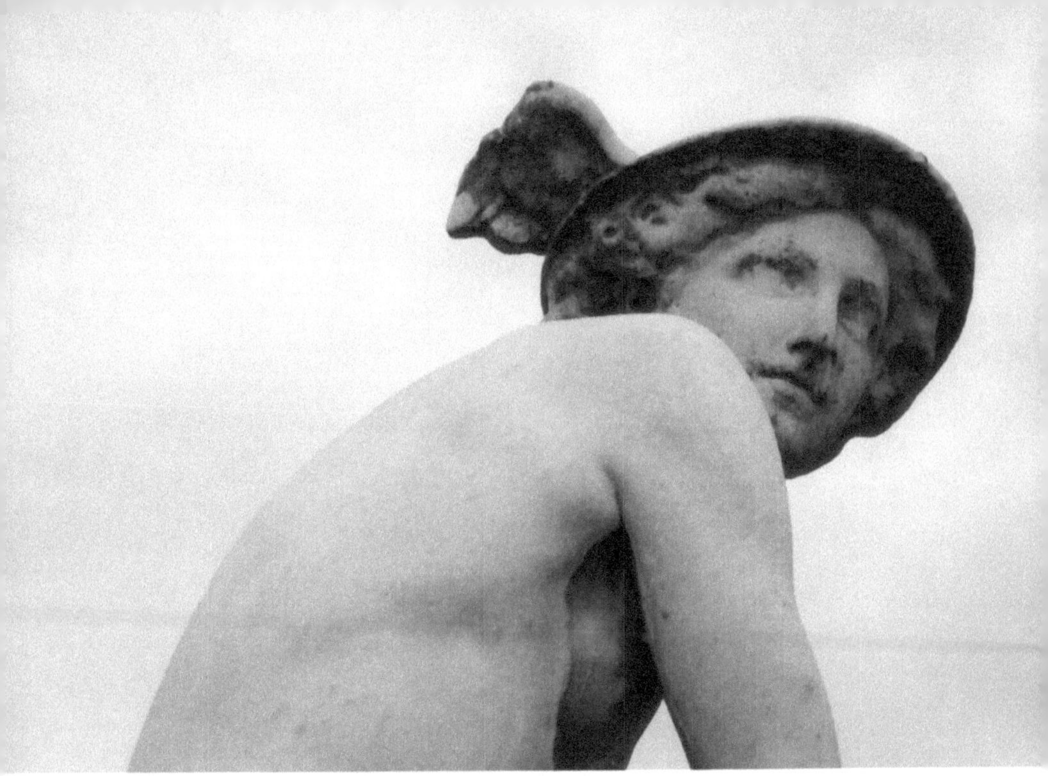

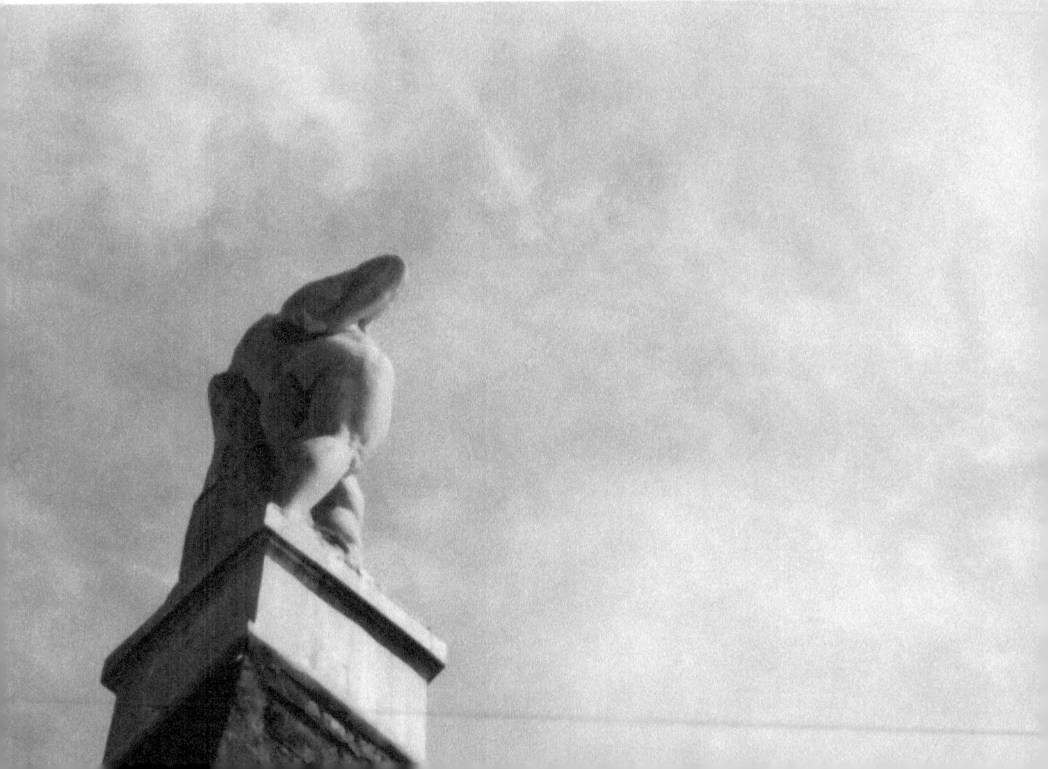

I have always admired donkeys (and elephants). This one did what donkeys do, i.e. meditate about being a donkey, and stand on the street that leads up to Mount Rushmore, stopping traffic.

Notice the elegant position of the right rear leg.

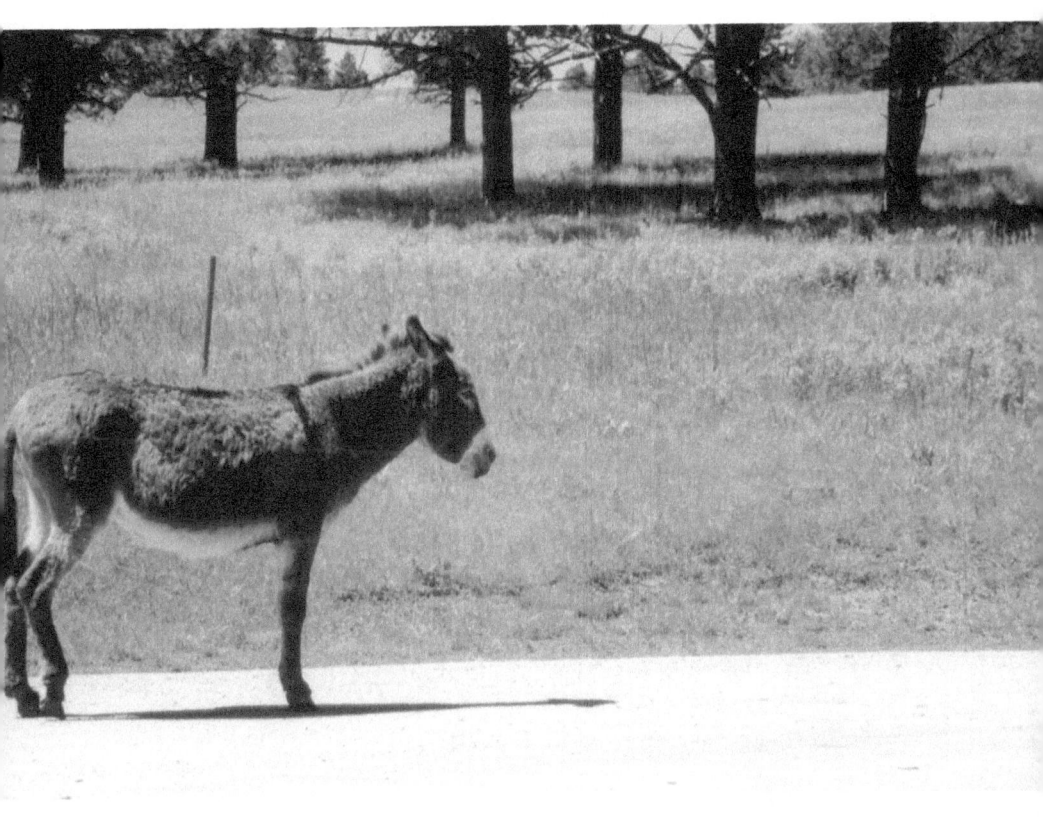

At the San Diego Zoo polar bears tread water like dogs, but with bigger paws.

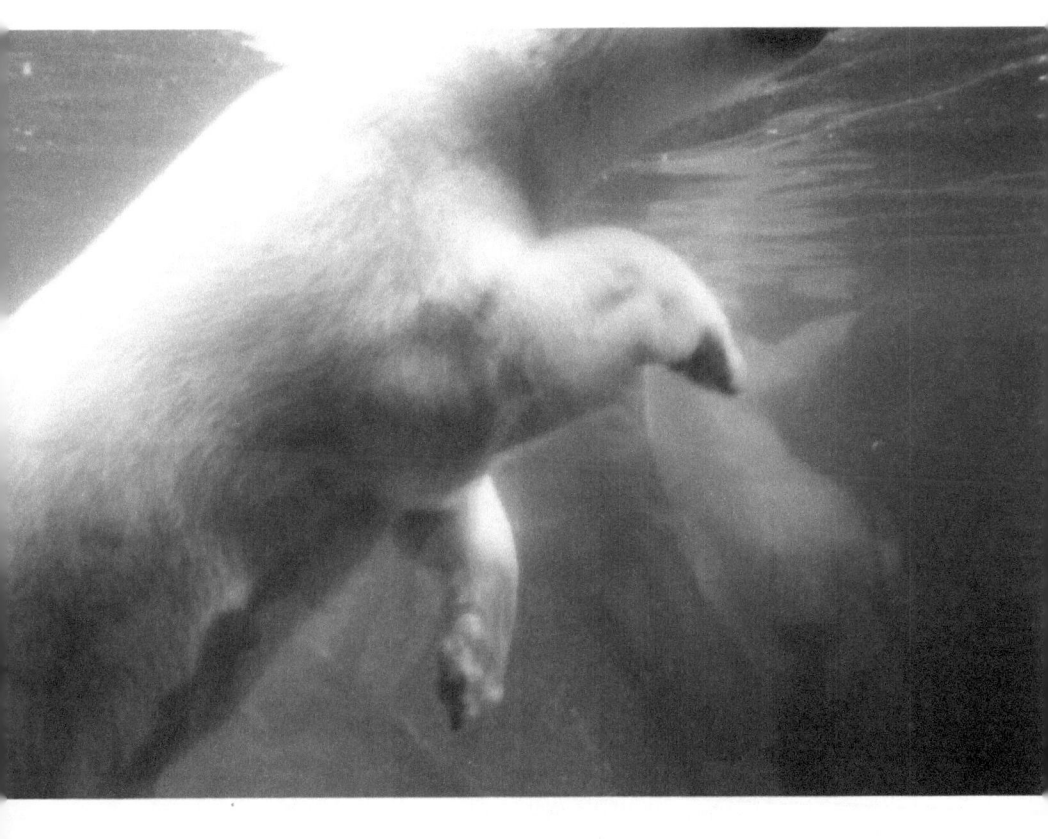

This primate in the San Diego Zoo was not interested in looking for the rest of the day into the lenses of chattering tourists' cameras.

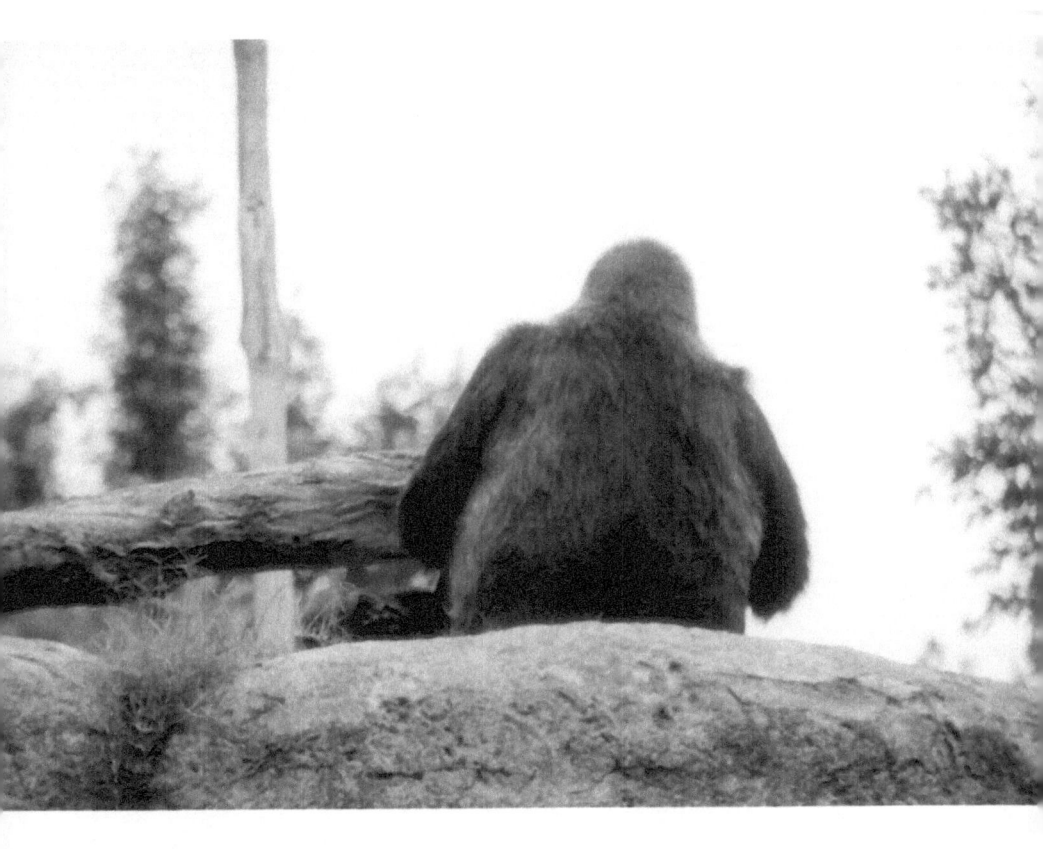

An animal odalisque times two: In memoriam Lambchop and Zsa Zsa.

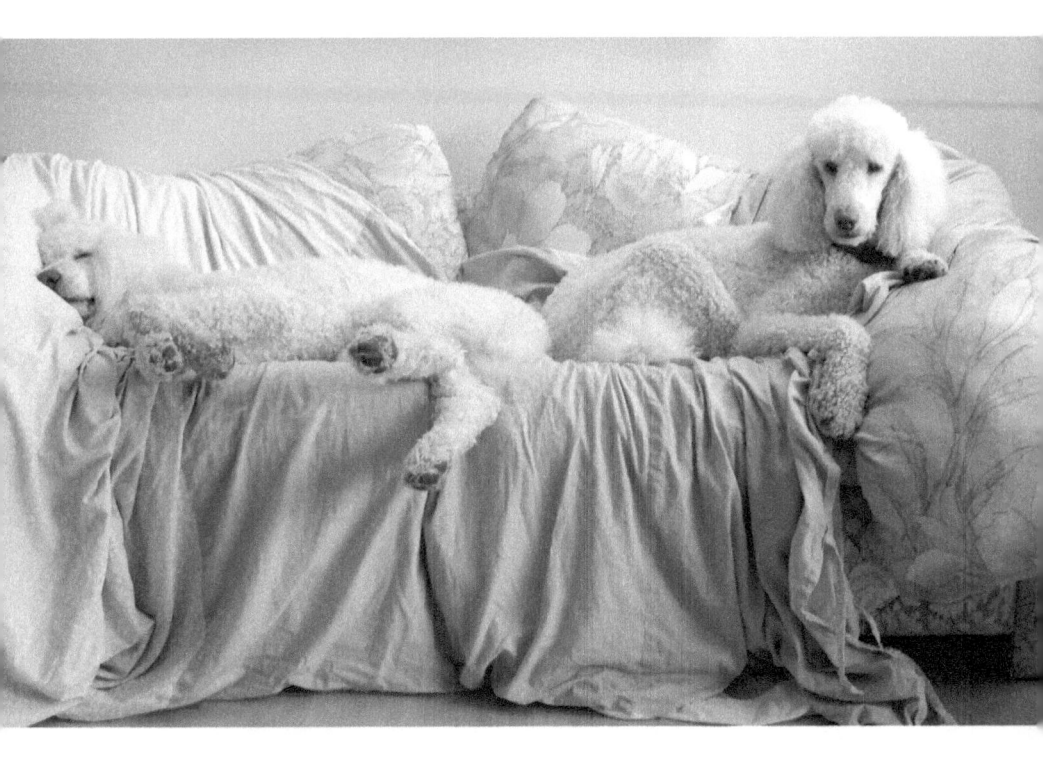

Contrast

I'm not sure why, but the second-year architecture studio would always take its fieldtrip to Chicago during one of those cold February weekends. In 2001 we stayed in the Congress Hotel on Michigan Avenue. I was waiting in the lobby to go out for dinner when I noticed the Native American on the horse. Then I learned that the word *Chicago* means 'wild onion'.

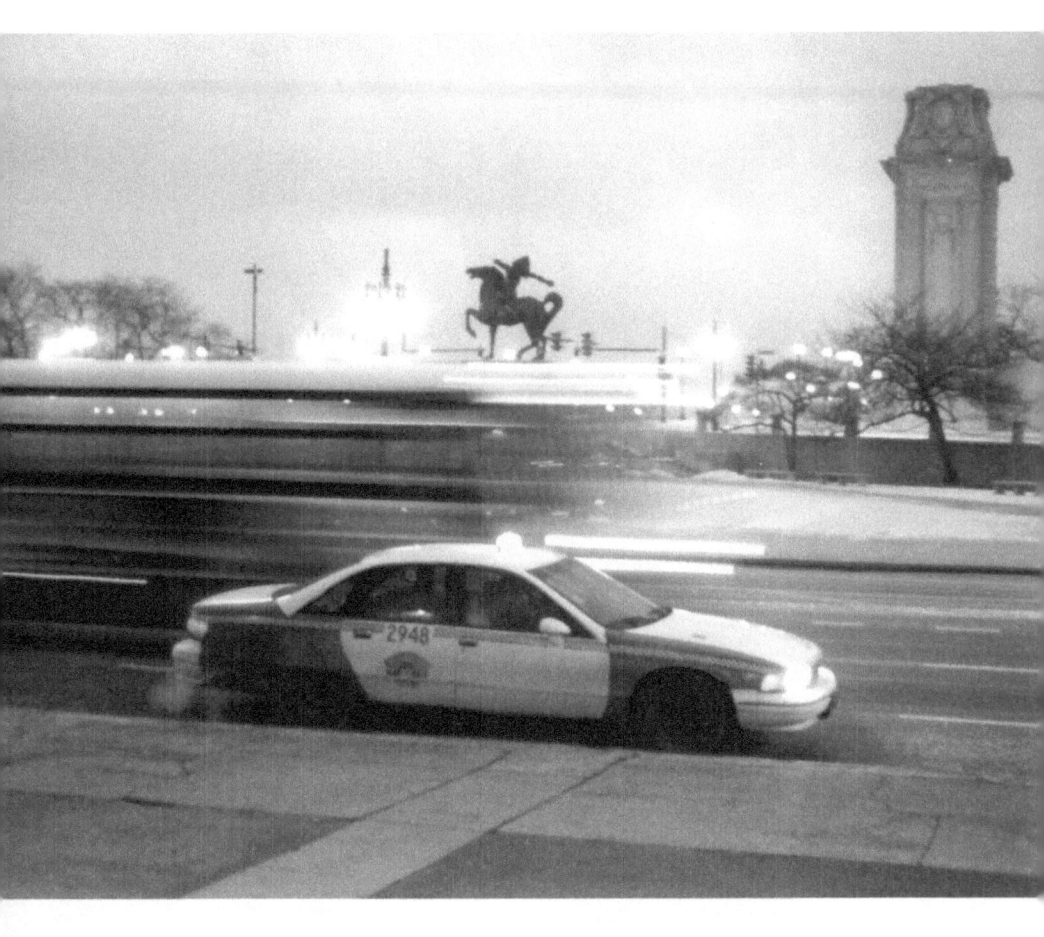

Contrast 33

It's only a twenty-minute ride by car between the best and the worst of Germany: Cultural Capital Weimar and the Concentration Camp Buchenwald.

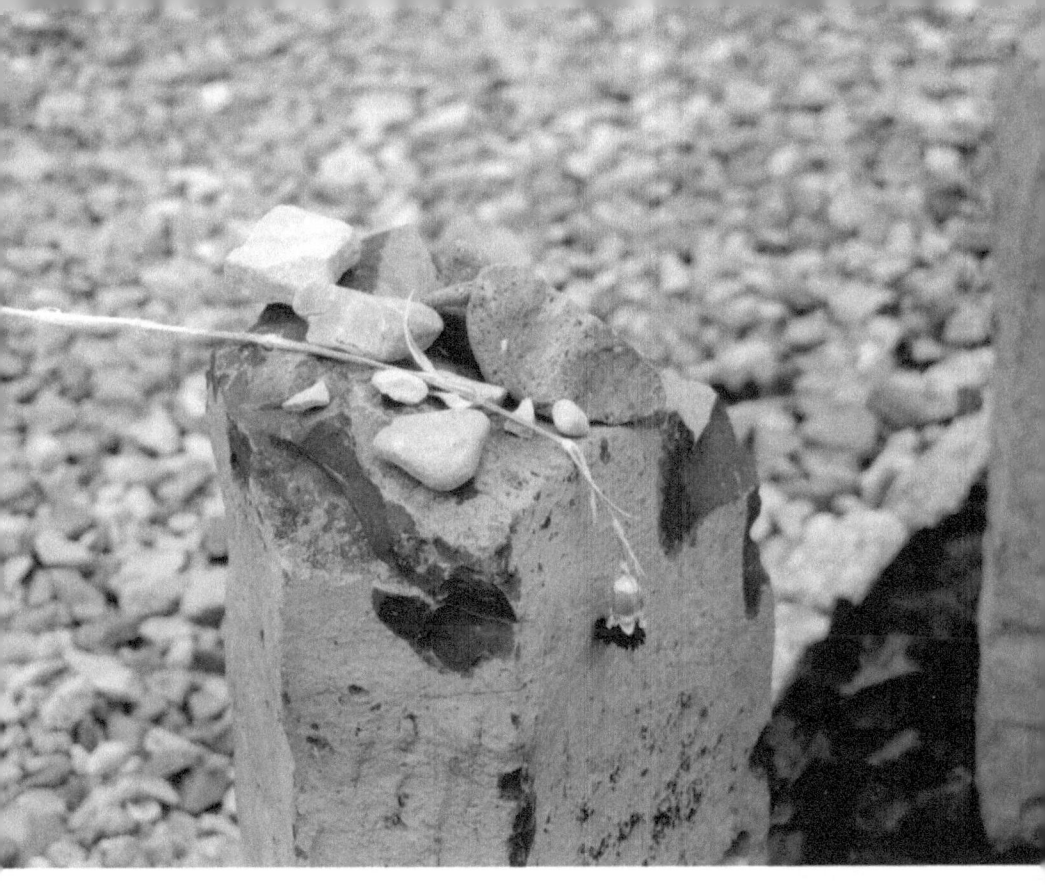

The Jewish Museum in Berlin by Daniel Libeskind was still under construction when I visited it with my students, but the skin was already in place, and the contrast to its neighbors appropriately emphasized.

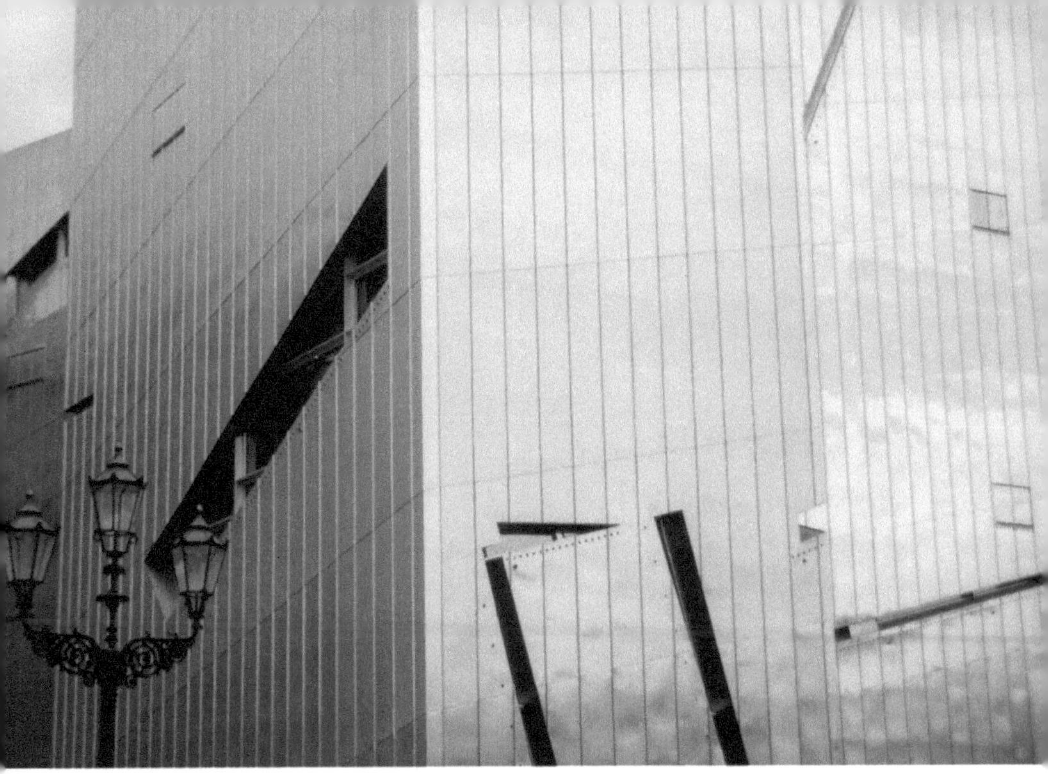

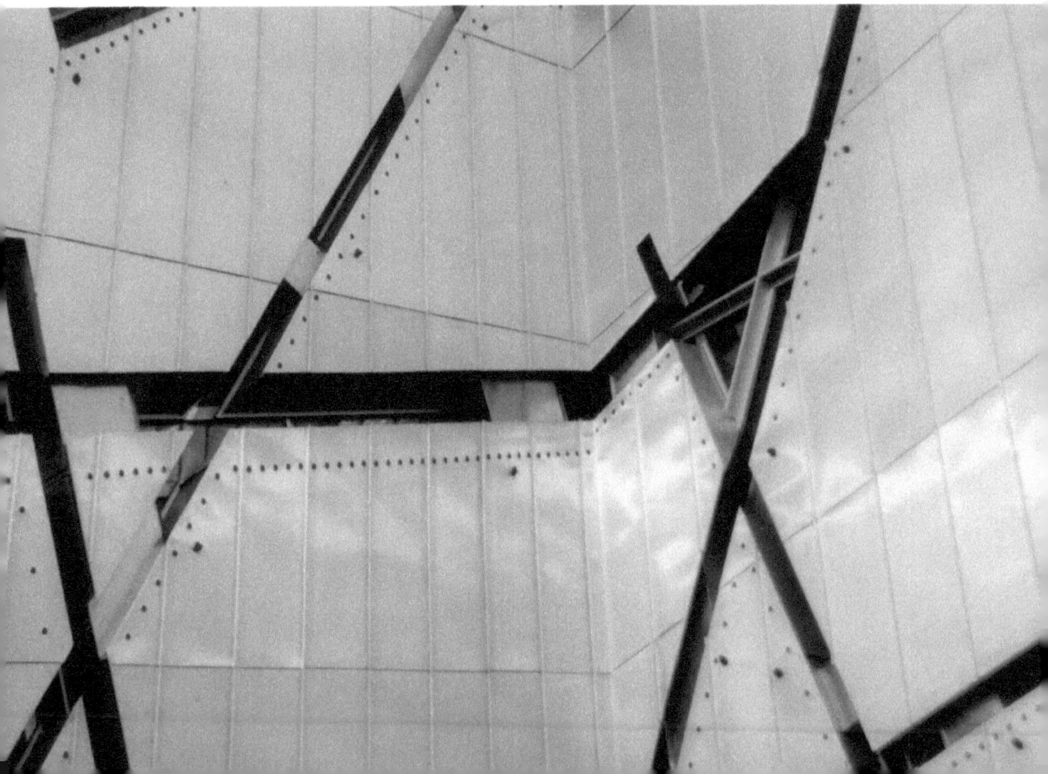

The Atlantic coast near St. Augustine can be at certain times as tranquil as the usually much quieter Gulf coast.

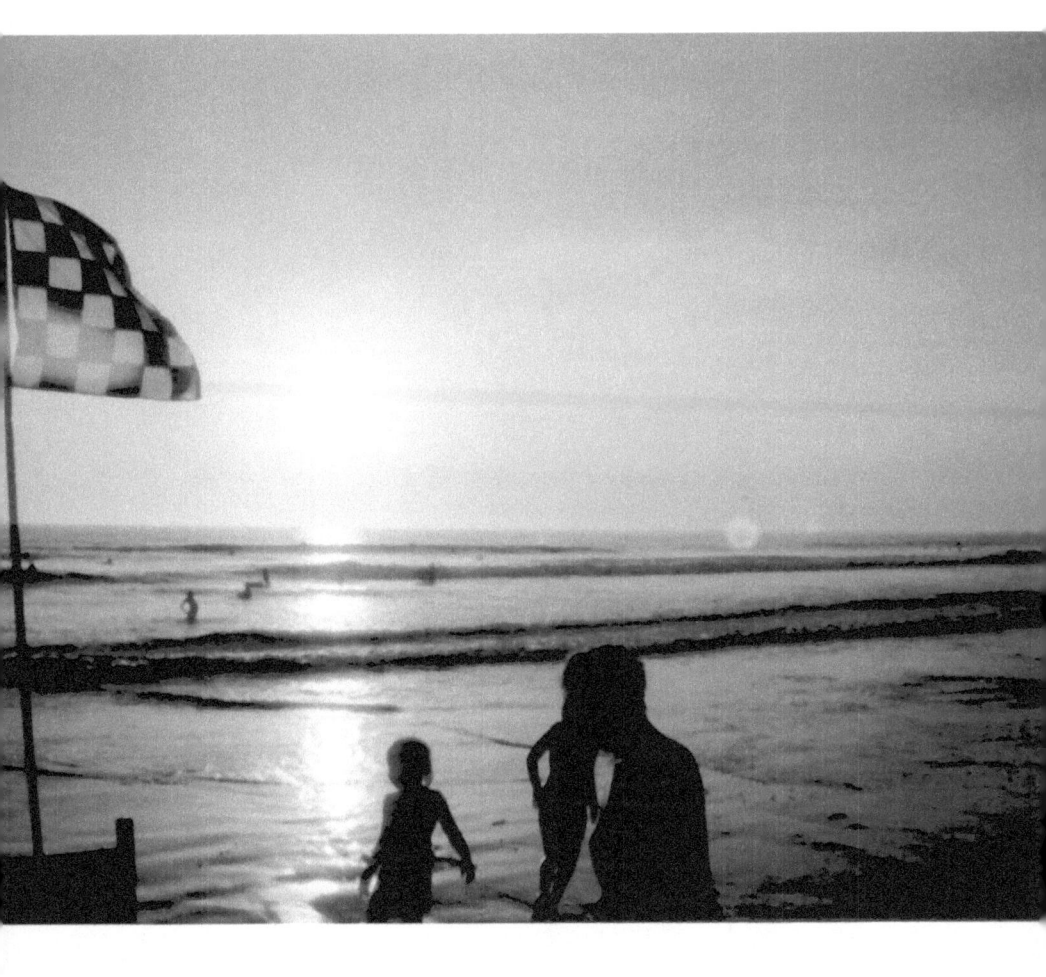

The very old and the not so new meet in Switzerland.

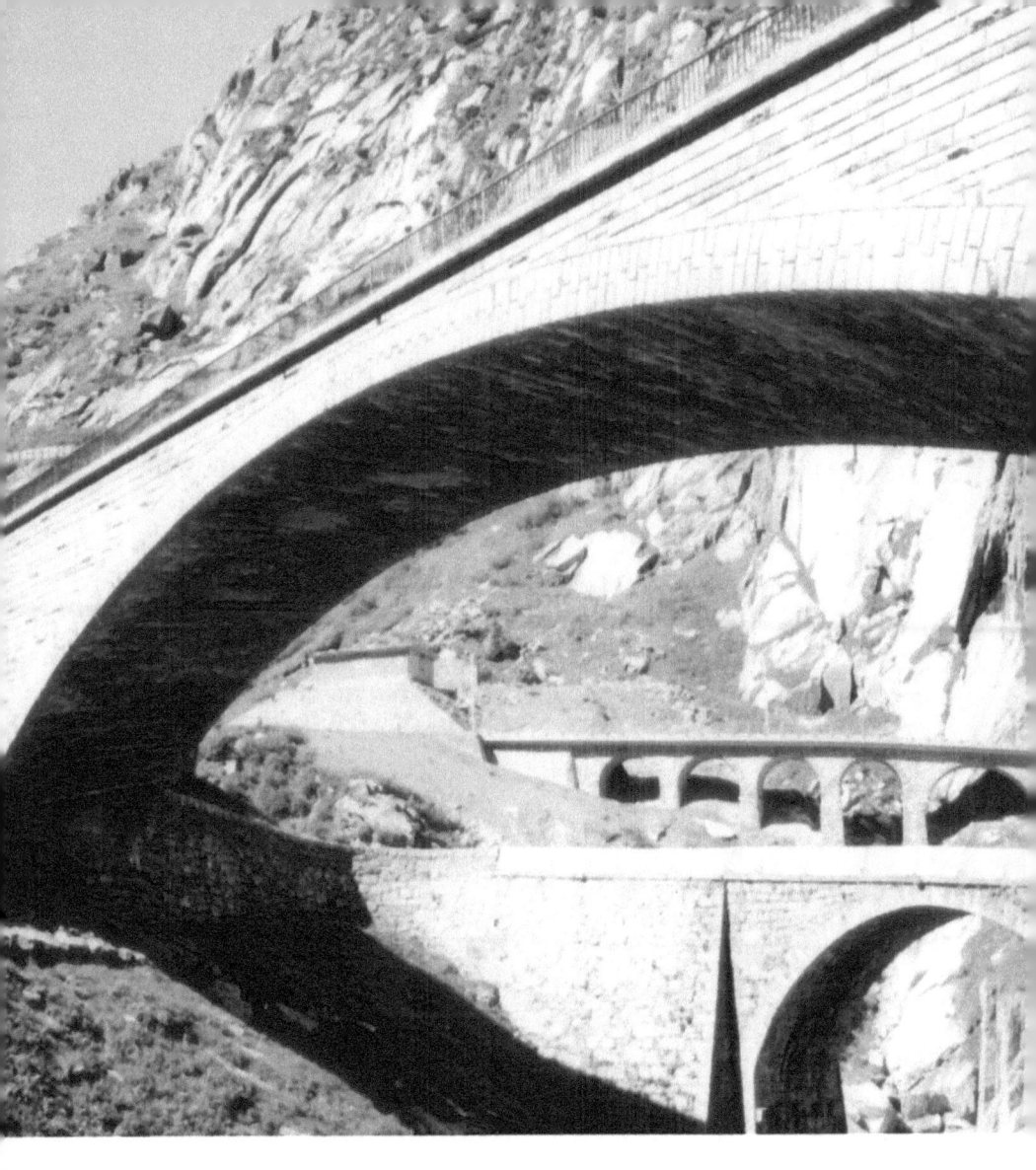

Aside from the light and shadows the only interesting part of Zaha Hadid's building for the *Bundesgartenschau* (Federal Garden Exhibition) is the men's bathroom which is located on the other side of the sloping wall next to the entry.

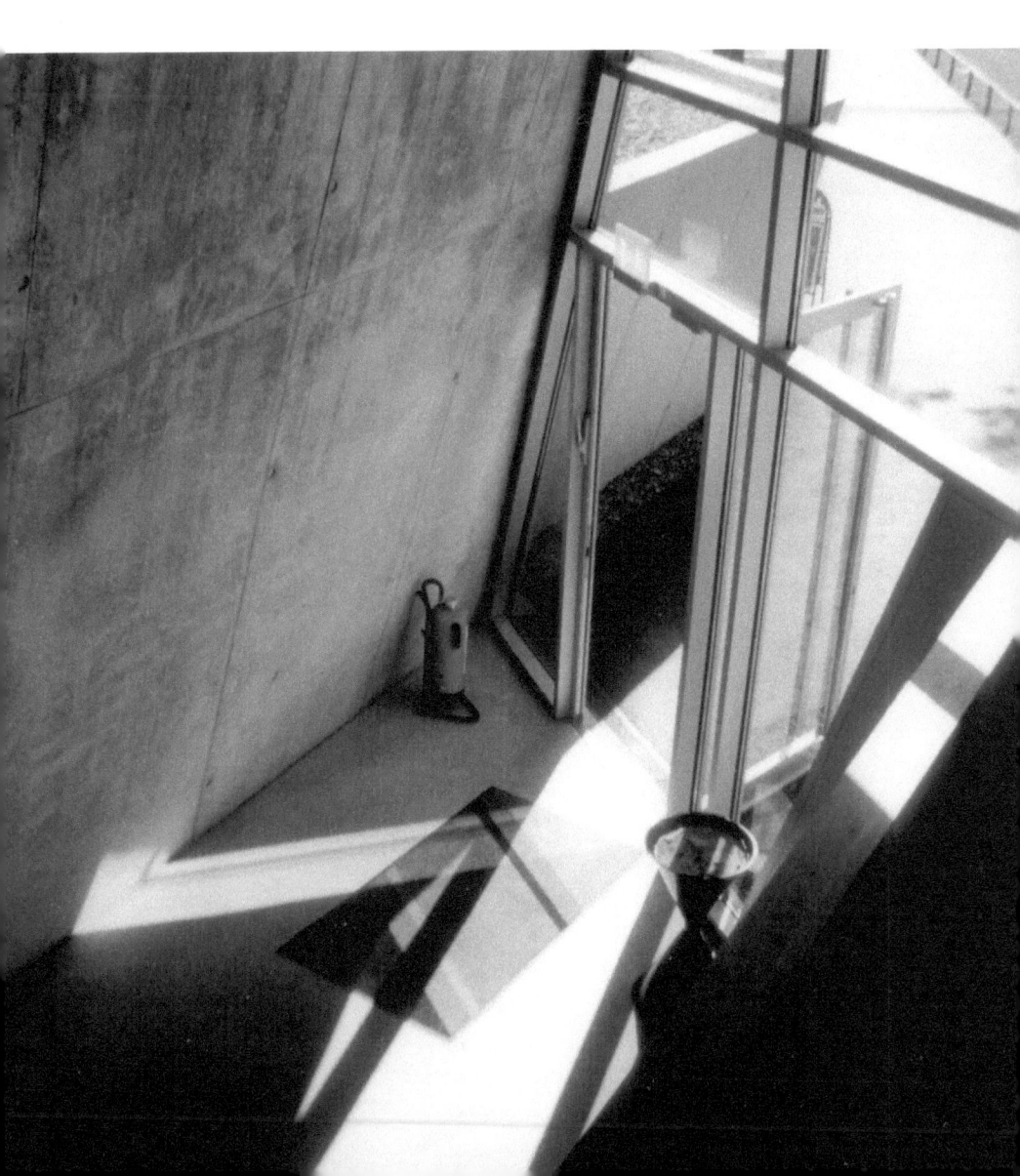

In Cedar Key the textured-metal siding panels appear to enjoy their proximity to the palm trees.

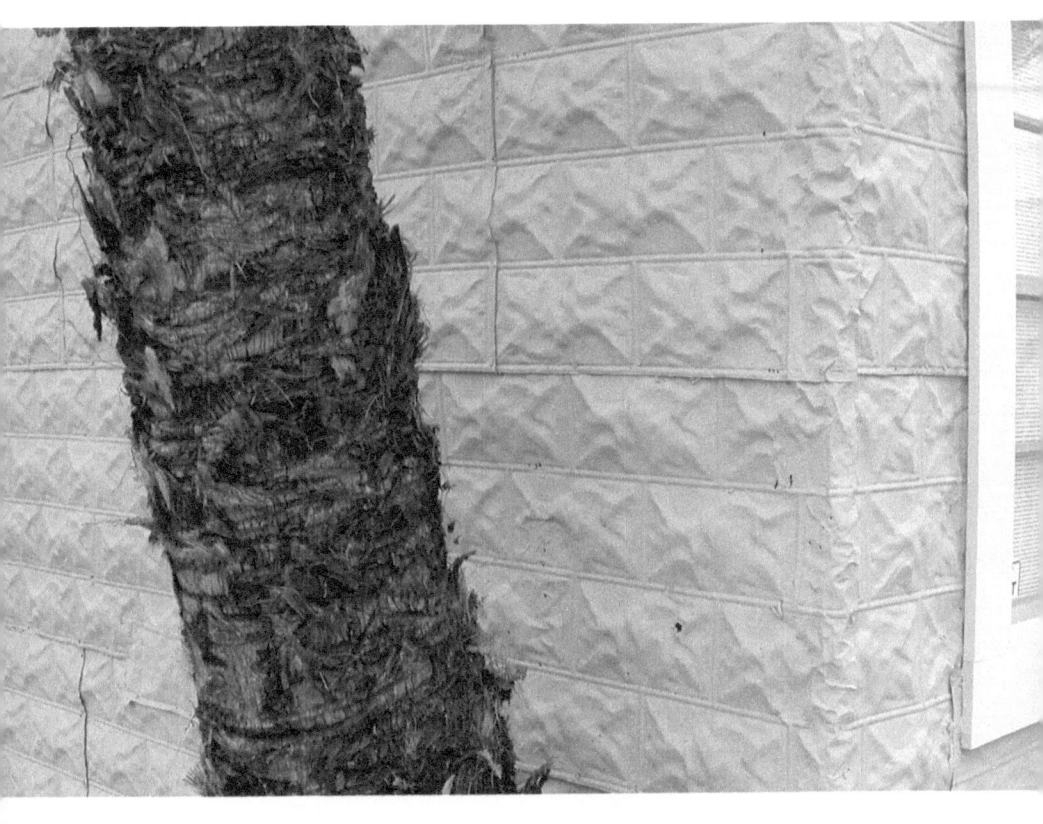

Someone decided to prop up a bright red sofa in one of the skylit niches of the Tadao-Ando-designed Conference Pavilion at the Vitra Design compound in Weil am Rhein.

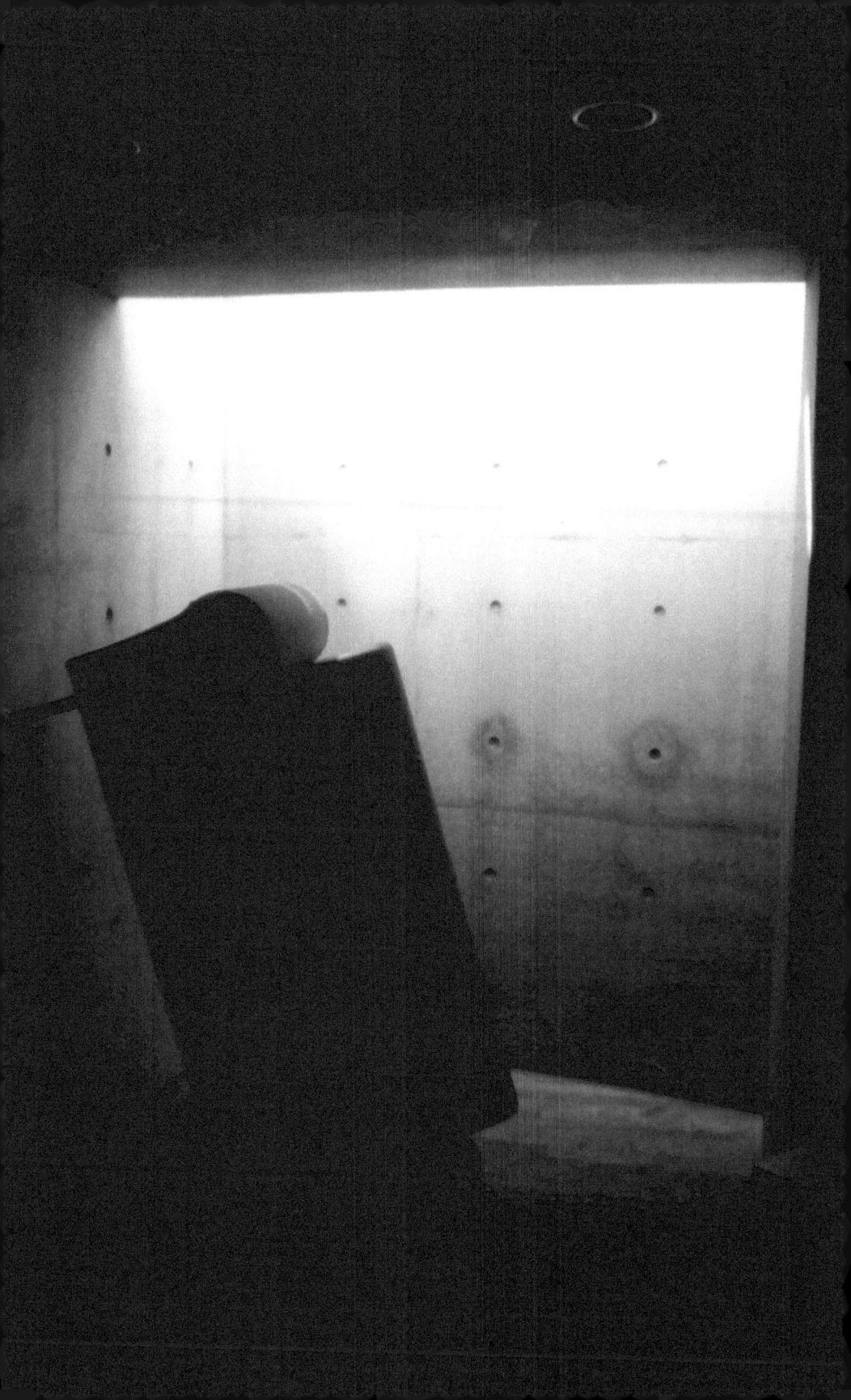

DETAILS

There is often an articulated gap between the structural supports and the attached surfaces in Frank Gehry's designs, as here in the Weisman Art Museum's handrail facing west toward the Mississippi River in Minneapolis.

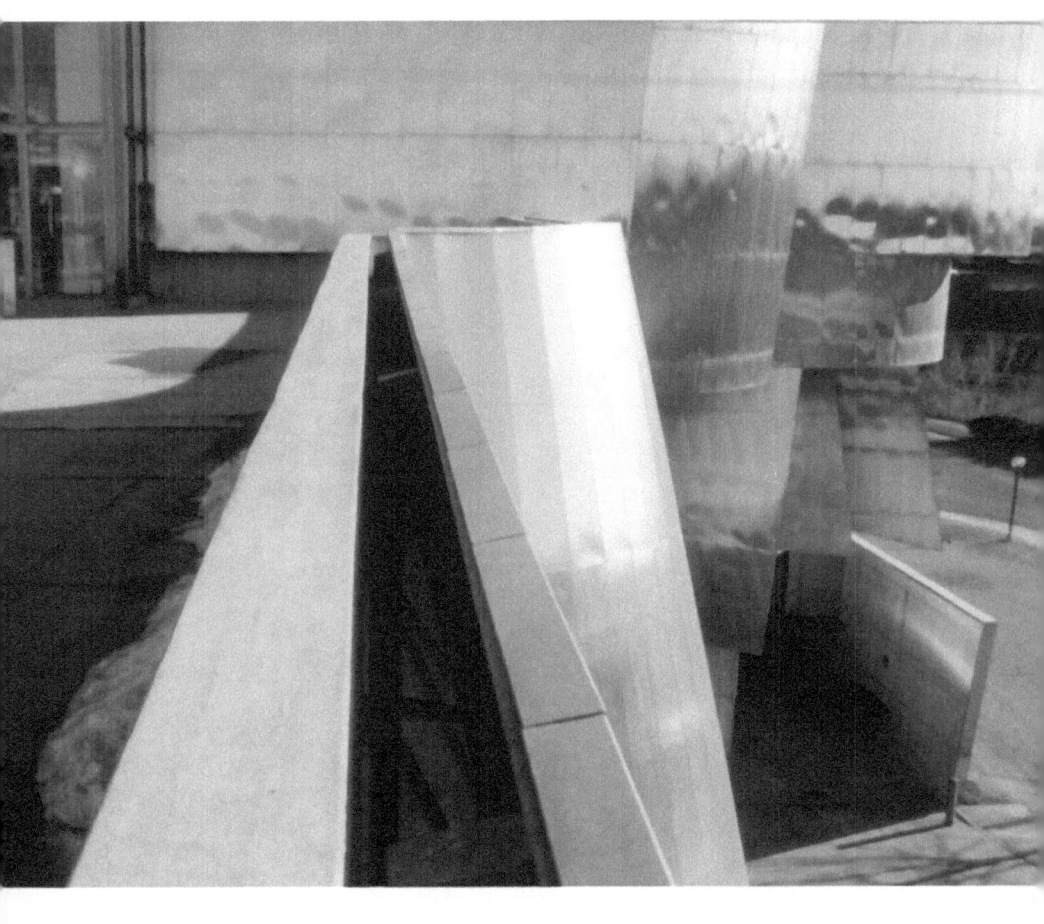

Cast aluminium (yes, with the appropriate European 'i') pendant lights in Christ Church Lutheran (1949) by Eliel Saarinen in Minneapolis. Gorgeous space, and great acoustics.

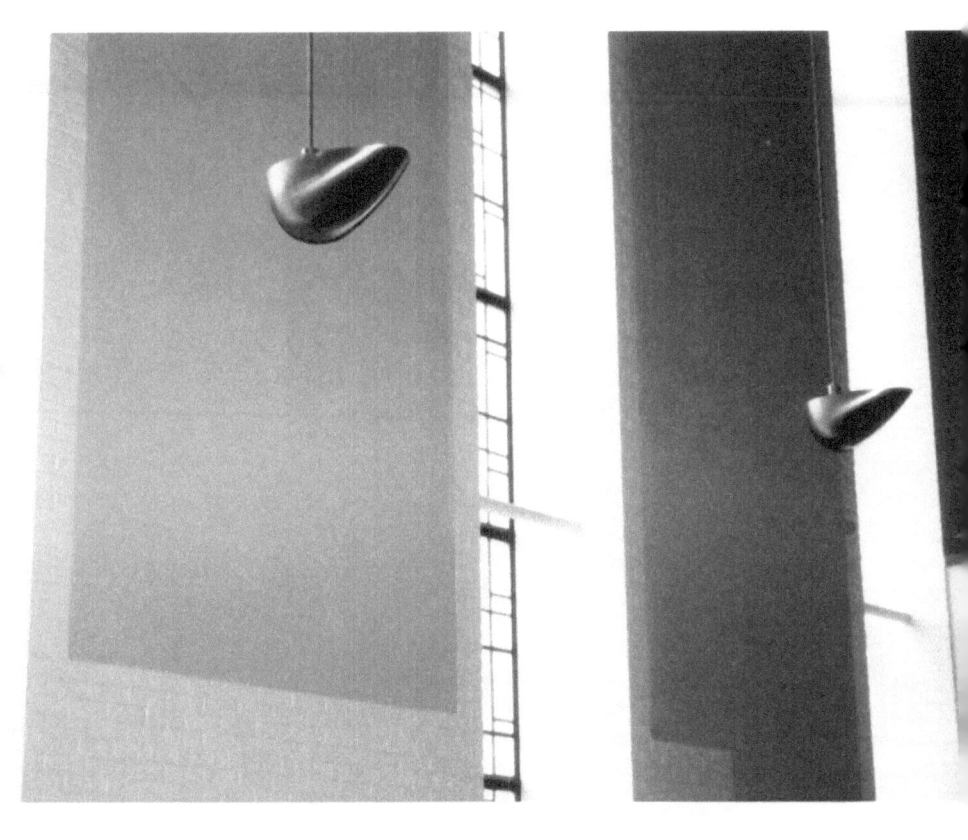

Details 53

Two of the steps in the old Seahorse Key lighthouse in Florida. It's reassuring to find beautifully designed everyday-objects now and then.

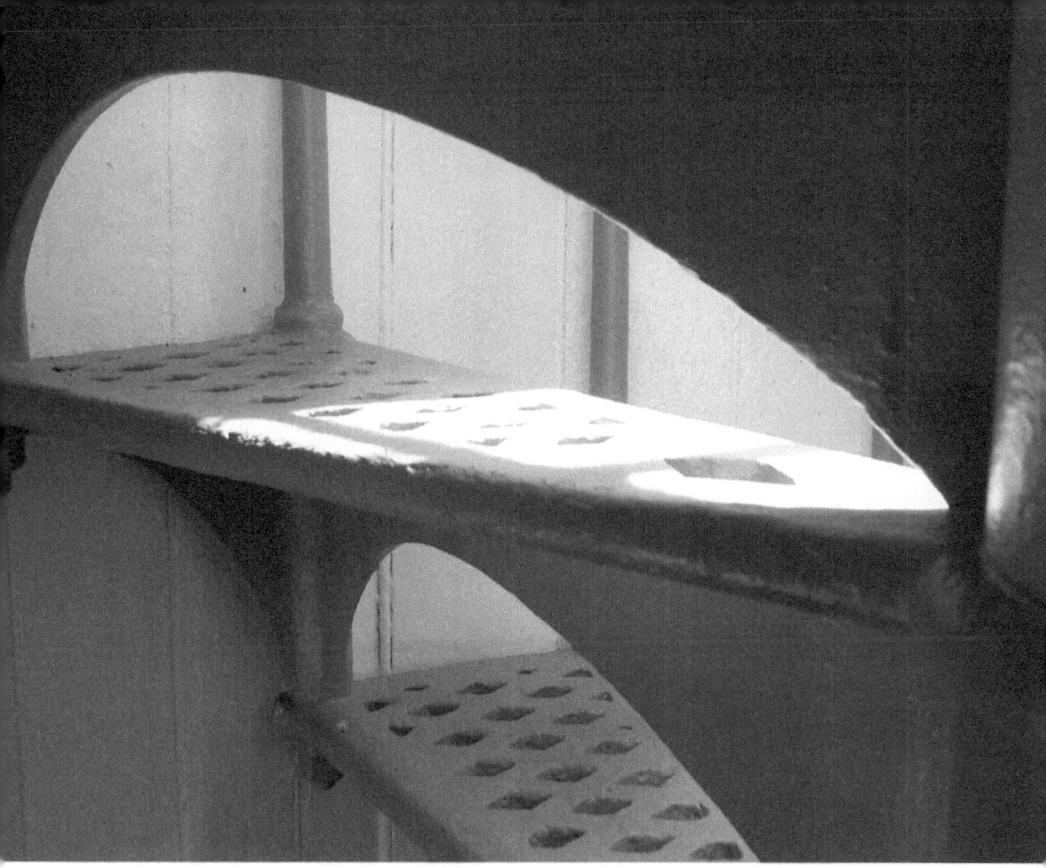

FILMS

It's difficult not to think about Wim Wenders' movie *Der Himmel über Berlin* (Wings of Desire) when walking through the *Nationalbibliothek* (National Library) which was designed by Hans Scharoun.

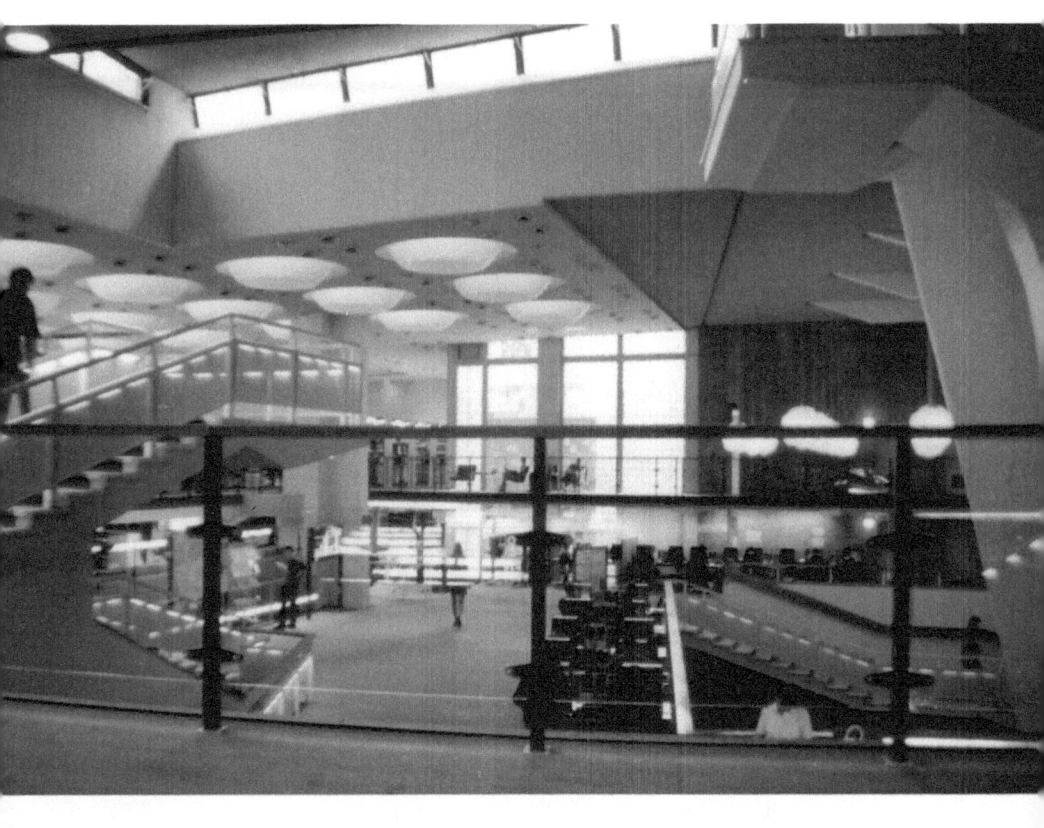

Films 59

A few times every year I would drive through Memphis, Tennessee on my way to Florida, and every time I remembered the opening scenes from Jim Jarmusch' movie *Mystery Train* which showed this very bridge with a slow-moving freight train crossing the Mississippi. For me there is gravity (perhaps attraction would be a better word) to this river, as there is to trains and bridges.

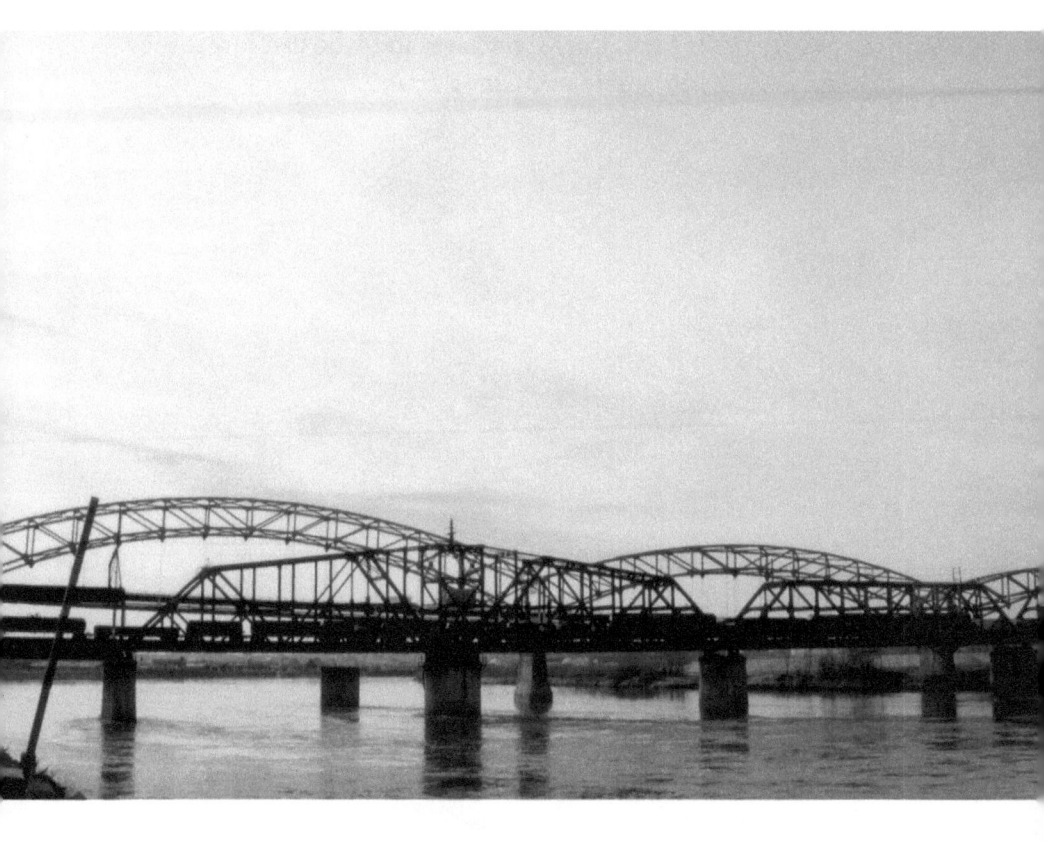

Sun Studio in Memphis, Tennessee; and who can forget the fast-talking tour guide in *Mystery Train*?

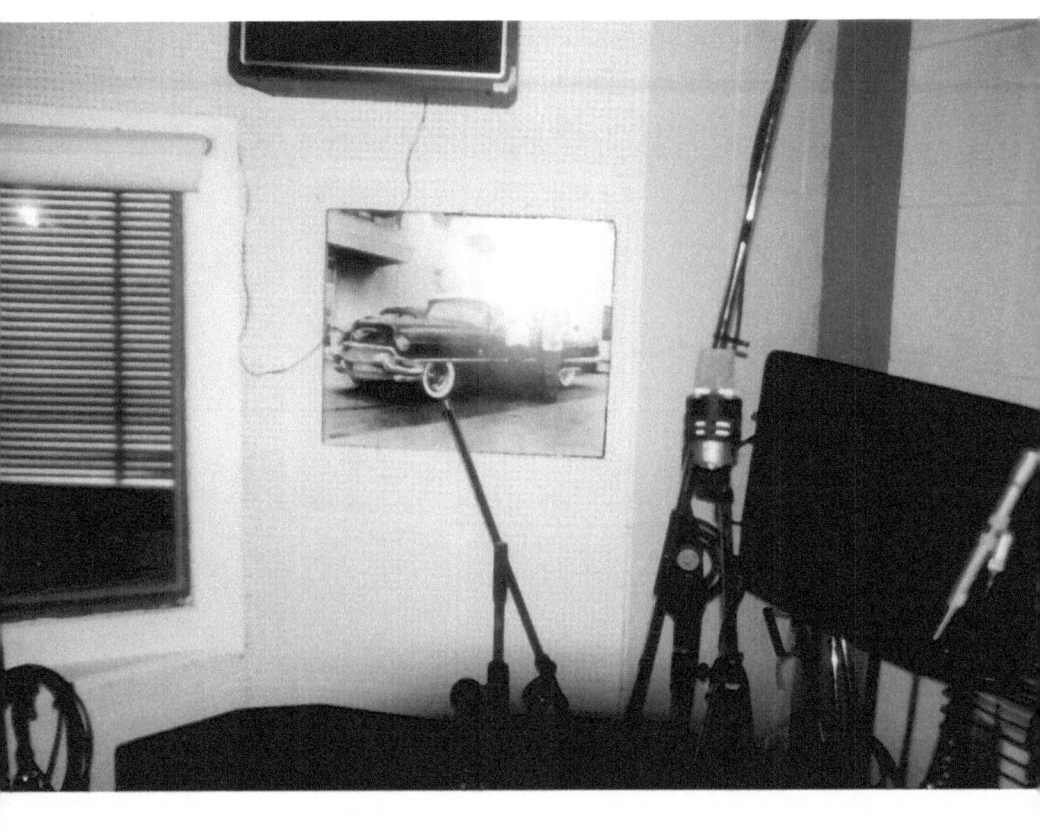

This is not the Casa del Fascio but the Museum of Contemporary Art, San Diego, in La Jolla (by Venturi-Scott-Brown) where you can check out hilarious video shorts by William Wegman and his obedient pack of Weimeraner dogs.

North by Northwest (from Ames, and certainly from Gainesville), sadly without Hitchcock, Cary Grant, and Eve Marie Saint.

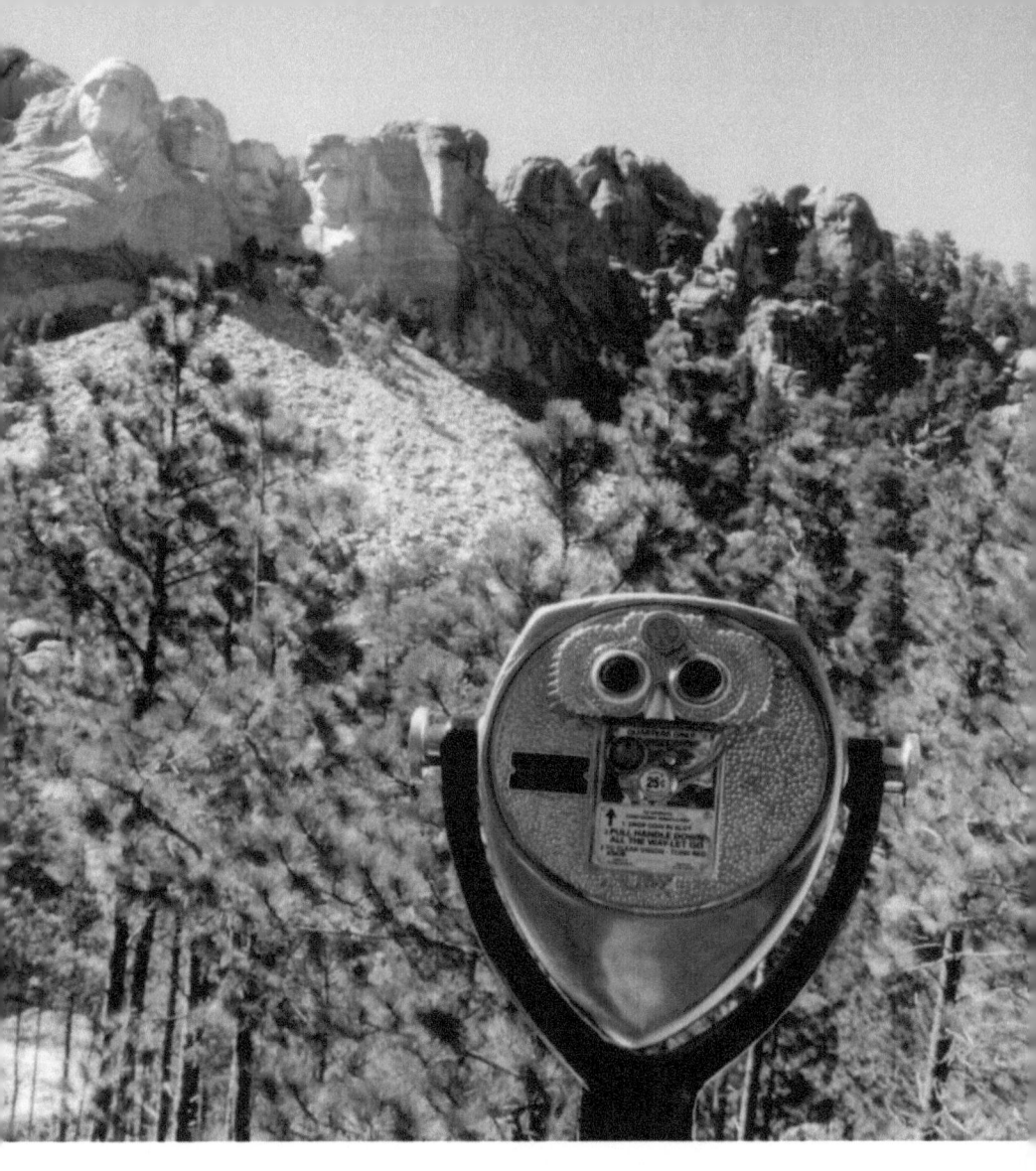

HYBRIDS

Within easy driving range of Gainesville, Florida, necessity continues to be the mother of adaptation.

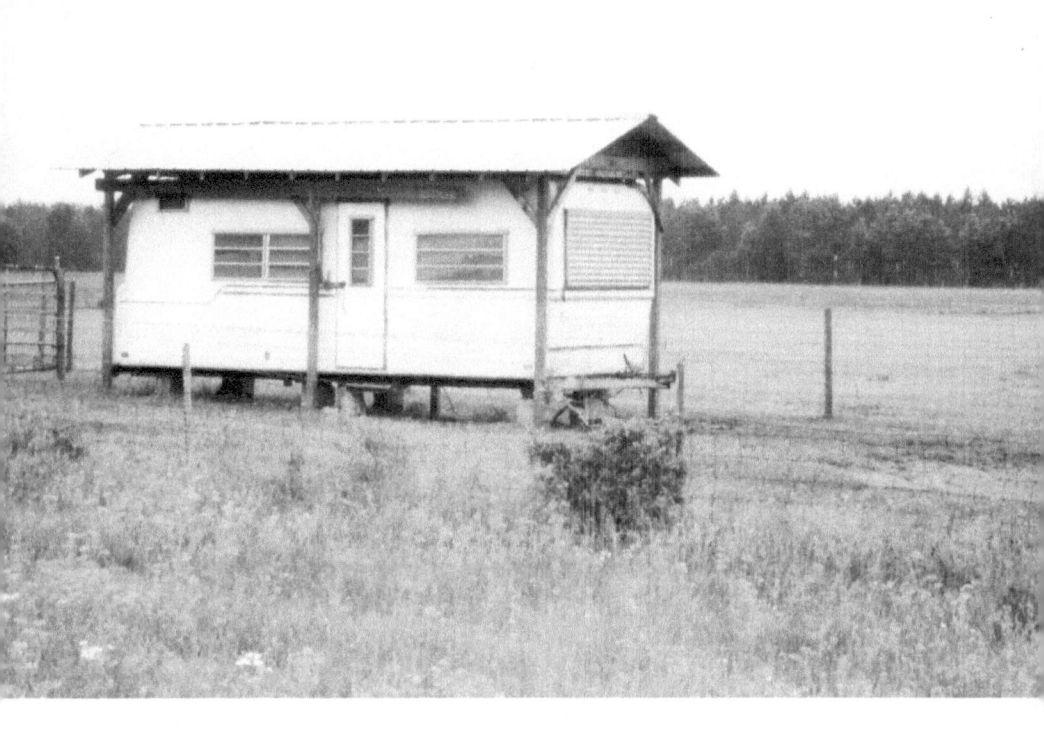

The perching-chair (to the right in front of the desk) in Johann Wolfgang von Goethe's house in Weimar always struck me as exuberant, as did the 'nosy' stove on the left.

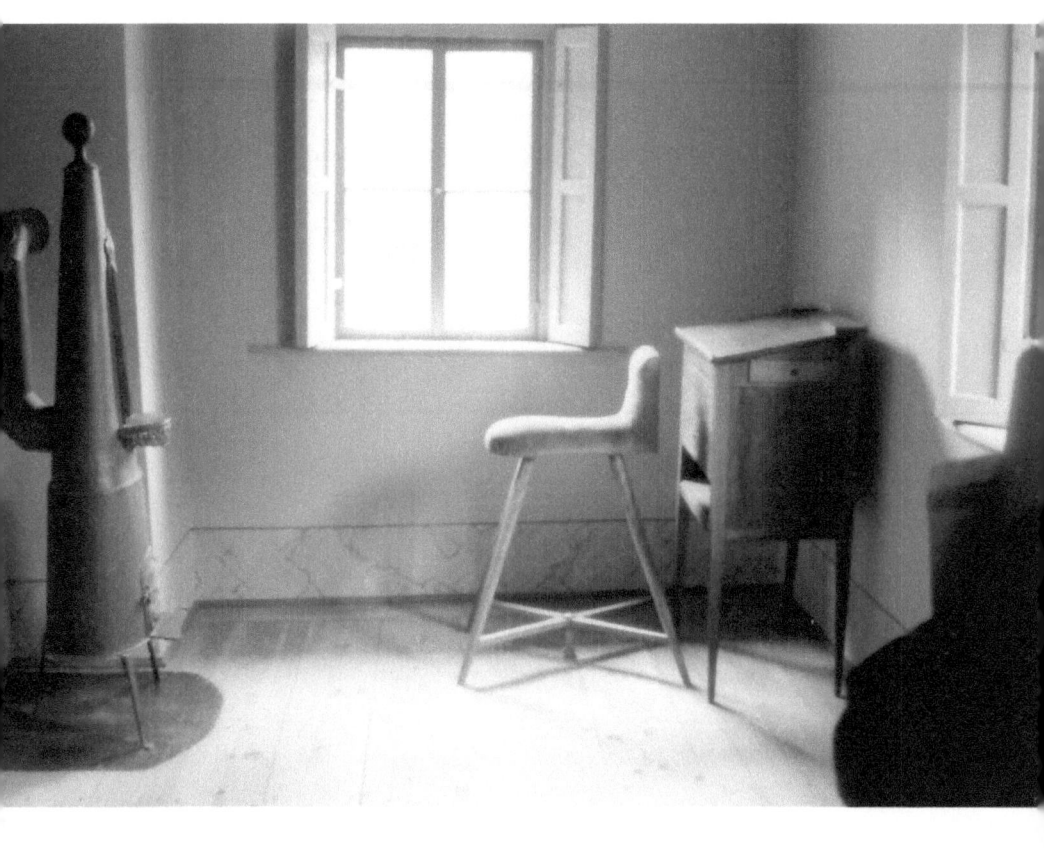

Some things I only do once. In 2001 I went to the Gator-Nationals, the annual drag-racing event in Gainesville, Florida, and I was struck—once more—by the American capitalist ingenuity of bringing the mountain to Mohammed.

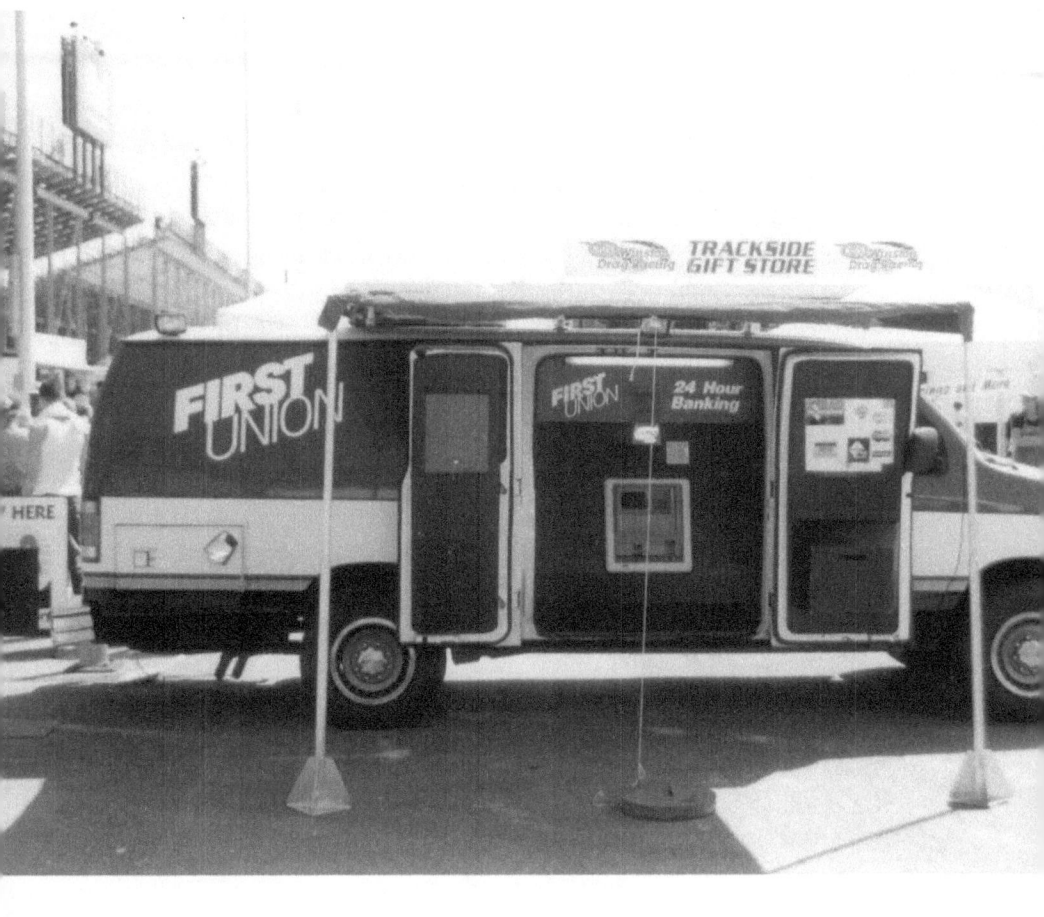

It was a clear blue day that turned warm and sticky late in the afternoon. The sun cast the electric transmission lines against the dam's concrete surfaces. The structure and the rugged rocky landscape around it seemed to exude beautiful necessity crossed with analogue utility.

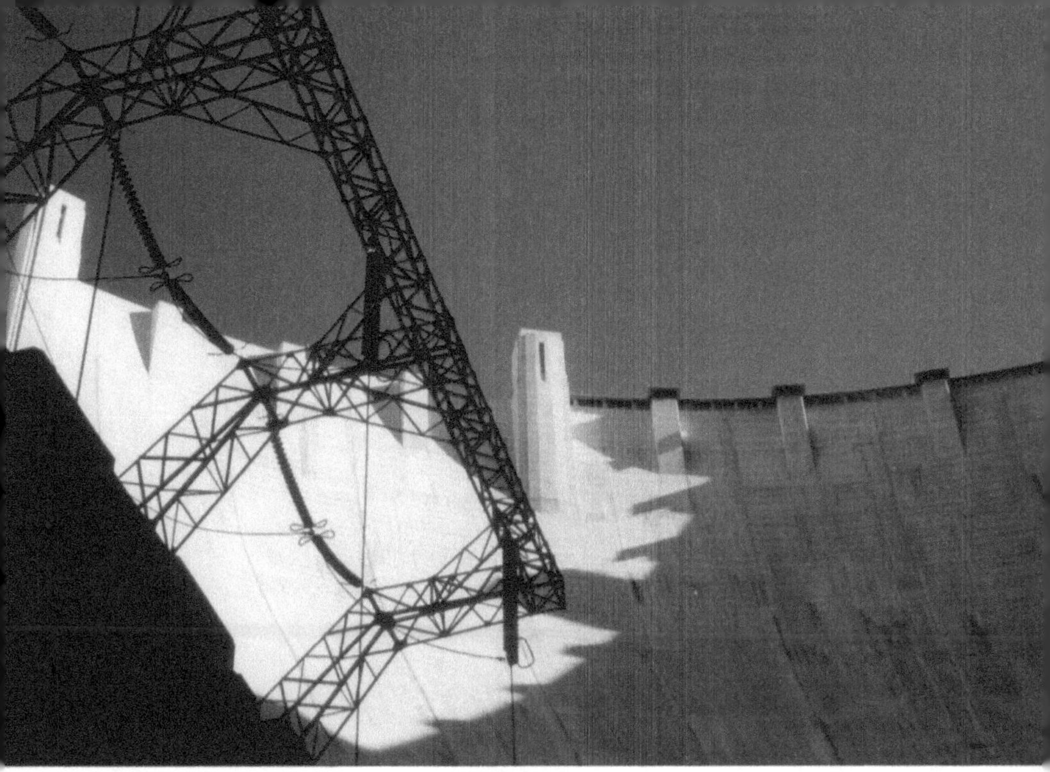

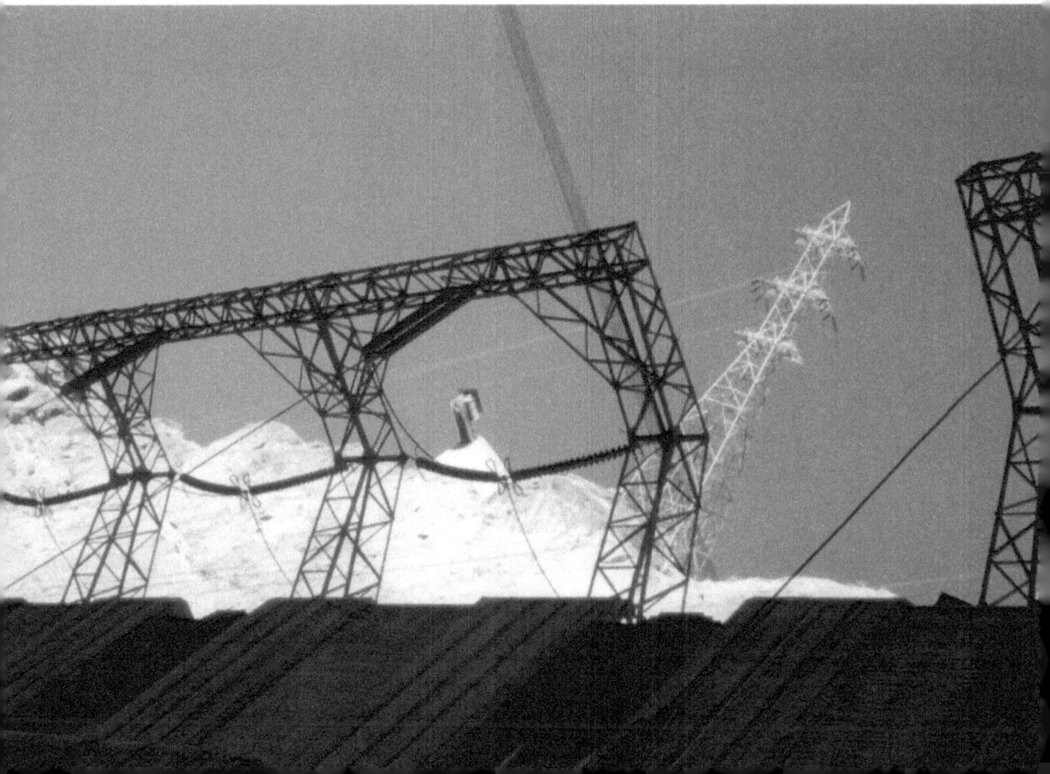

The Swiss have an uncanny capacity to join the artificial with the natural, as in this case of a highway embankment meeting the Alpine rock face.

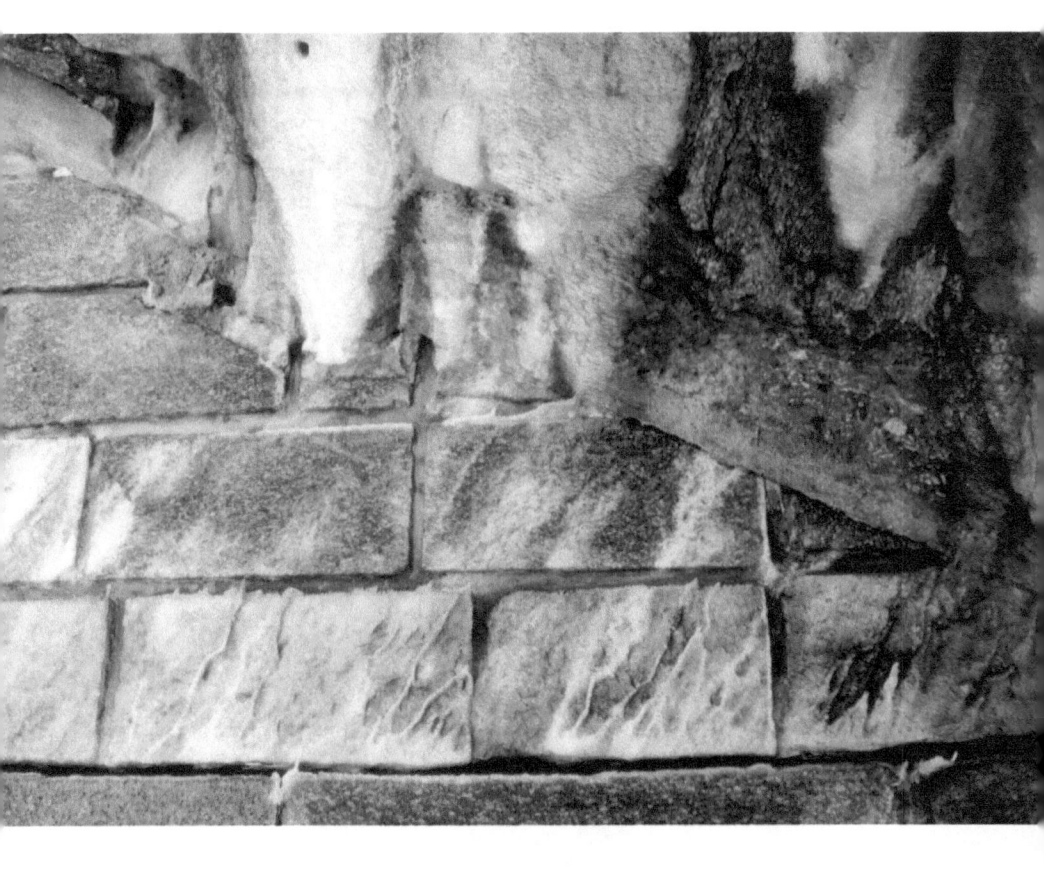

Sir Norman Foster's designers did something beautiful with the difficult space of the German *Reichstag* renovation in Berlin. They mated democratic transparency with a light-reflective thorn, a rotating leaf-shaped diffuser that tracks the sun to keep out glare, a spiral path that allows citizens access to the top of the dome, and a supervisory view into the governmental chamber below. It's a symbol—if not necessarily the actual working—of democracy.

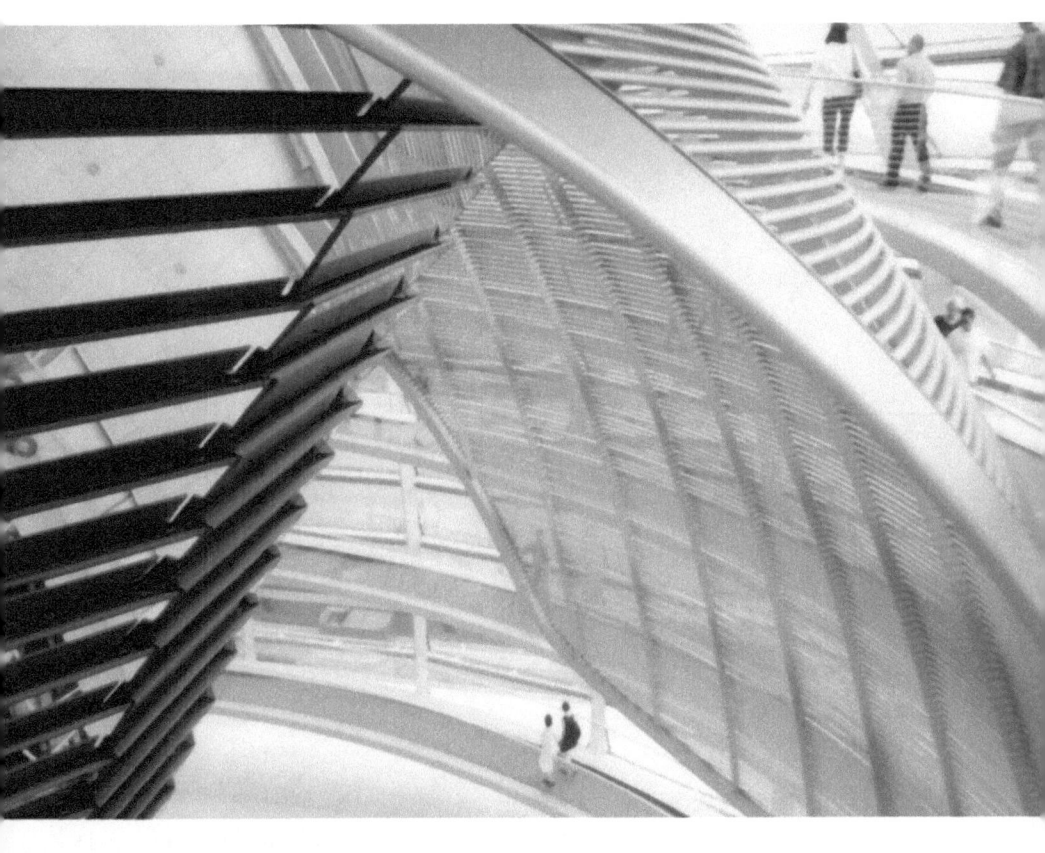

Hybrids

On special occasions there will be weight-headed people walking across the piazza in front of St. Peters in Rome, in this case a photographer operating the end of a camera boom.

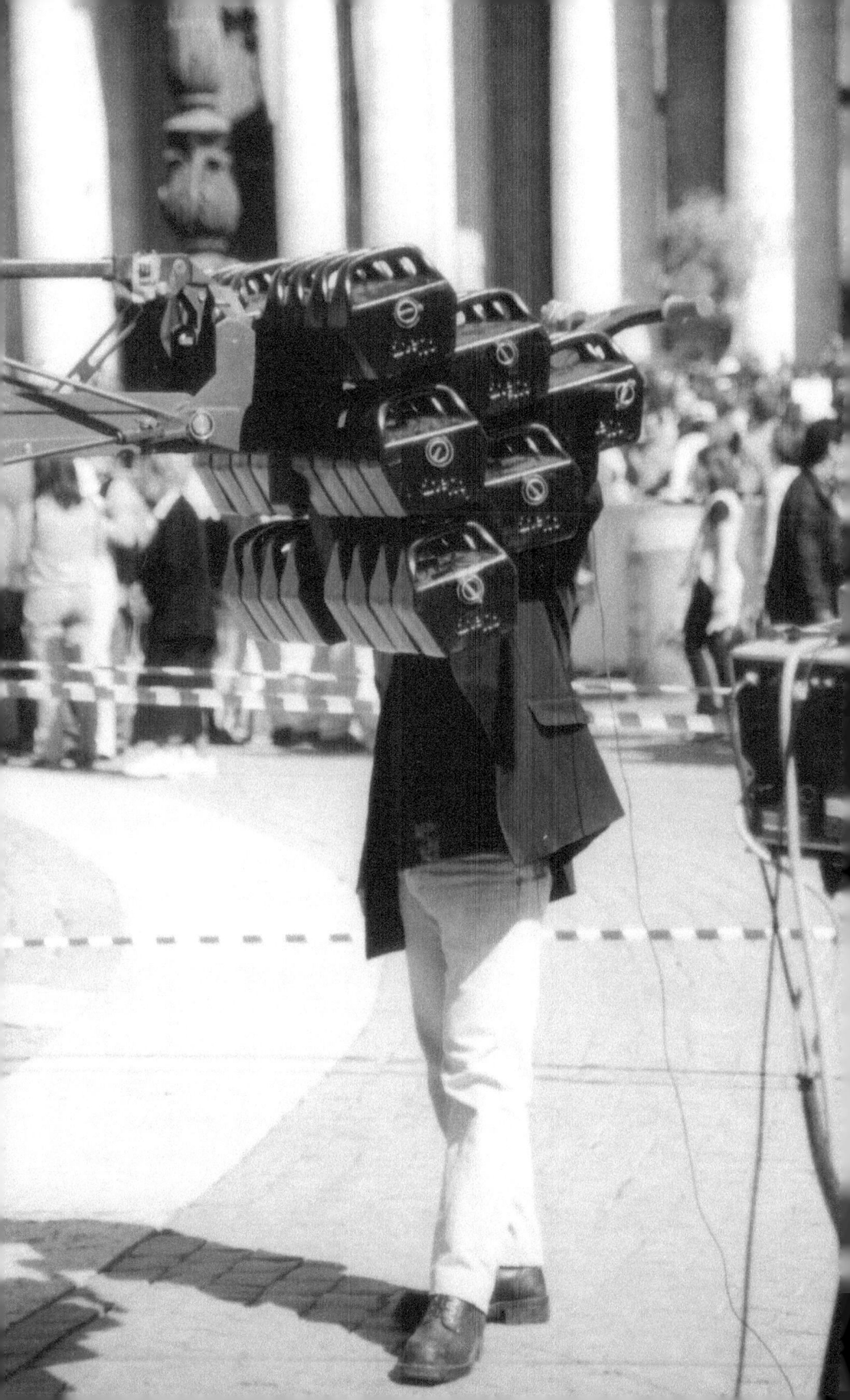

Floridians know how to create hybrids between an exterior living room and a boat in front of a bar near the pier in Cedar Key.

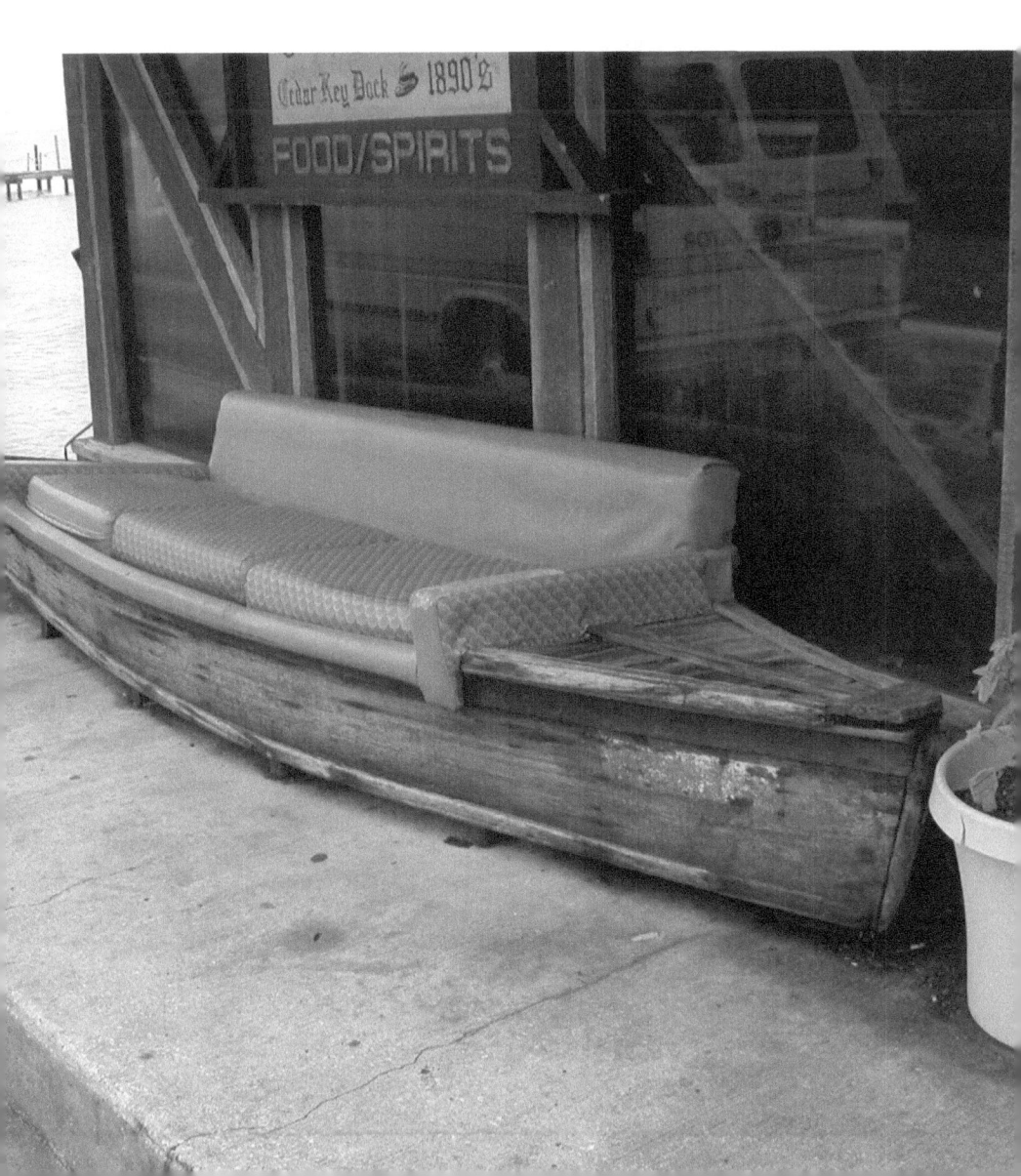

I found this sign across from a gas station in Cottondale, a small hamlet in Florida's panhandle. I regret to inform the reader that, on my recent return, Emma's place was closed down for good.

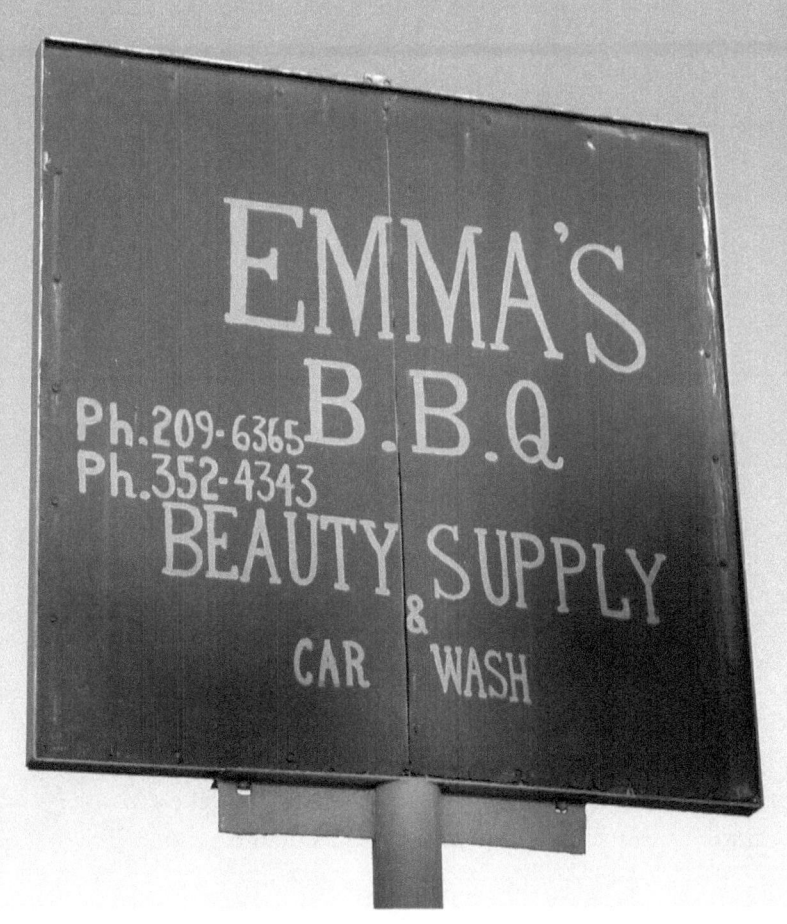

Looking out from my south bedroom in Ames, Iowa. There is a time toward evening when the internal illumination levels approximate the external light intensity. When you take a photograph at this time, the inside and outside merge.

Landscape + Architecture

While traveling south with my Bambi trailer in tow, I stopped somewhere in Georgia to take a rest near a lake with cypress trees. It was balmy outside, almost too warm.

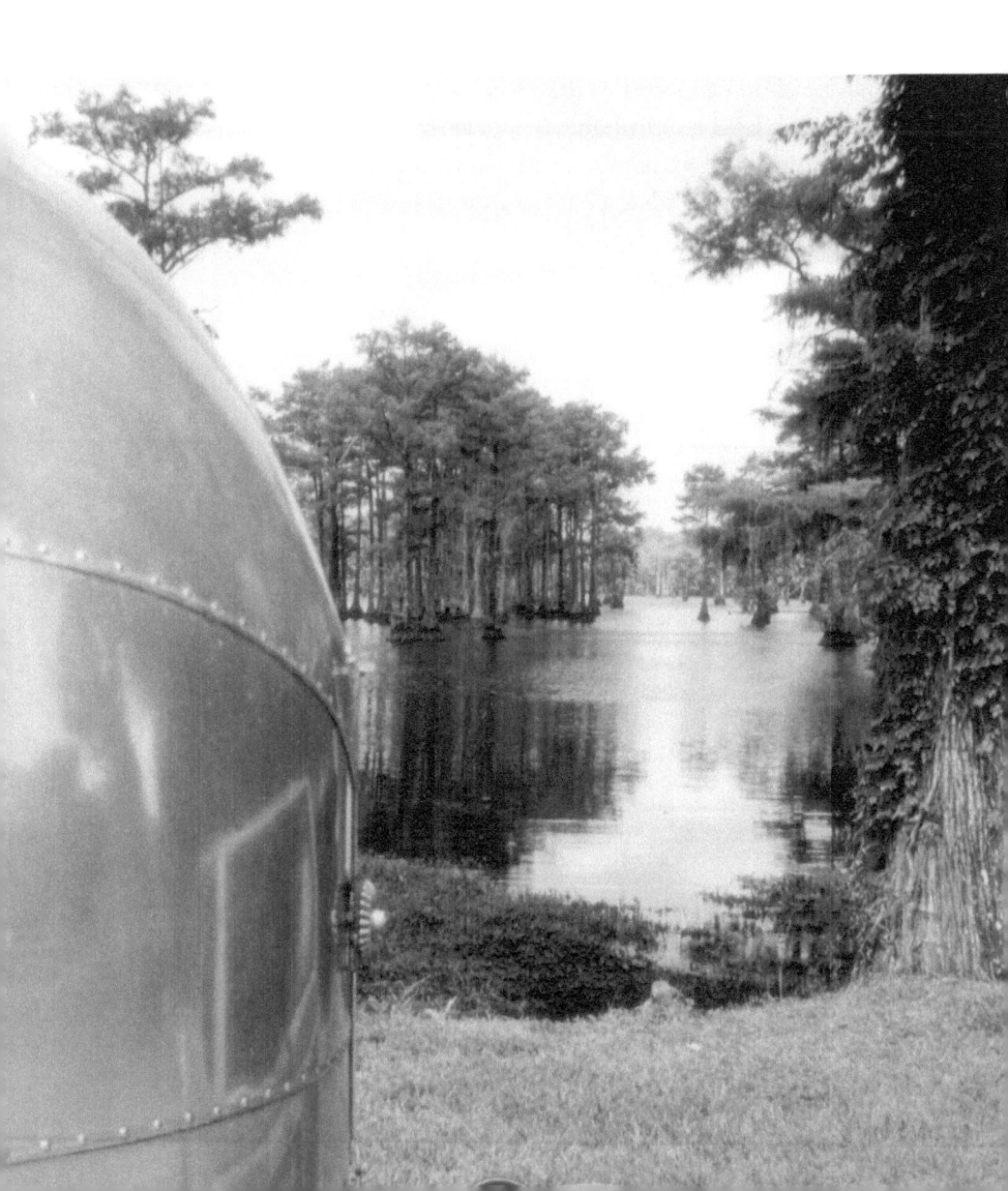

In 2000 we stayed in the Hotel Capucini in Amalfi on our south field trip in Italy. The view from my hotel room was serene, and perhaps scary for hotel guests with acrophobia. In the evening I took a bath, and watched the fireworks near the harbor.

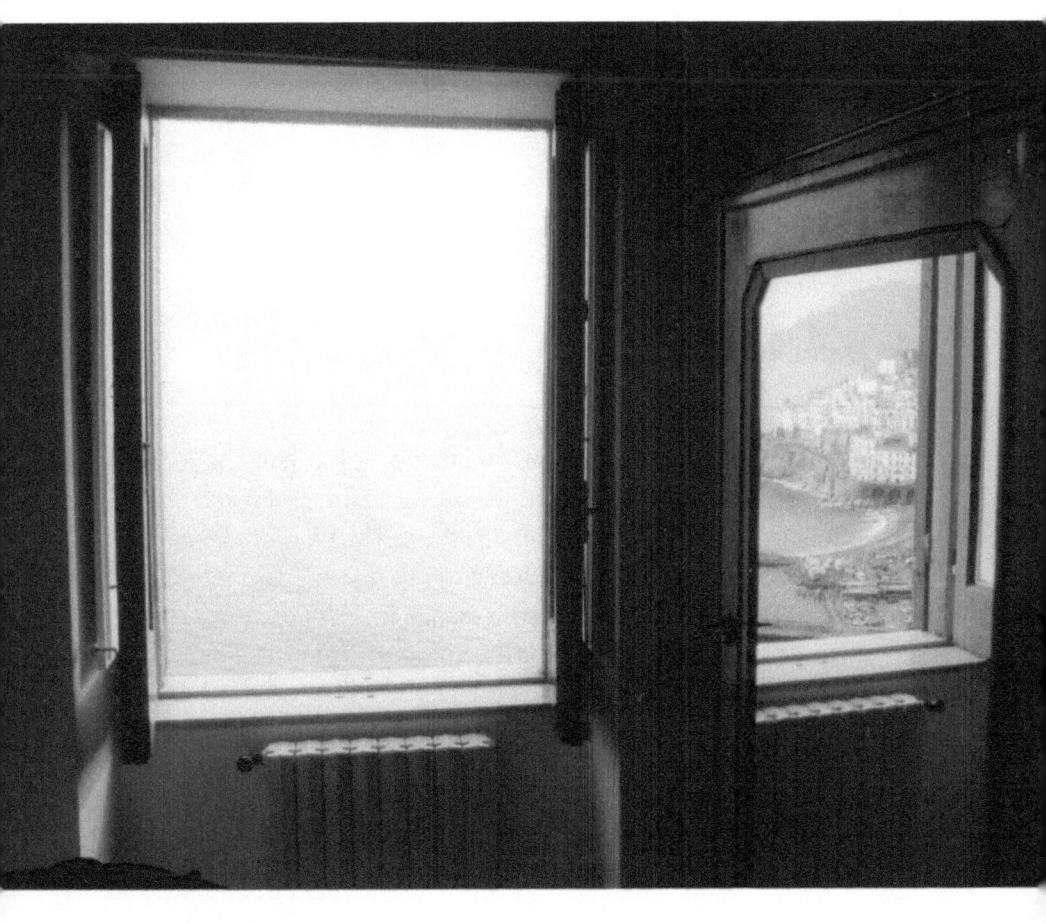

Landscape + Architecture

From the department of Border Lines:
It seemed exhilarating to imagine taking a break at the picnic table that sits at the bottom of Hoover Dam, and reach over the border to Arizona to pick up the salt shaker for the hard-boiled eggs in Nevada. I'm sorry to say that no dam workers were on break when I took this image in 1998 on a field trip with some graduate architecture students from Iowa State University.

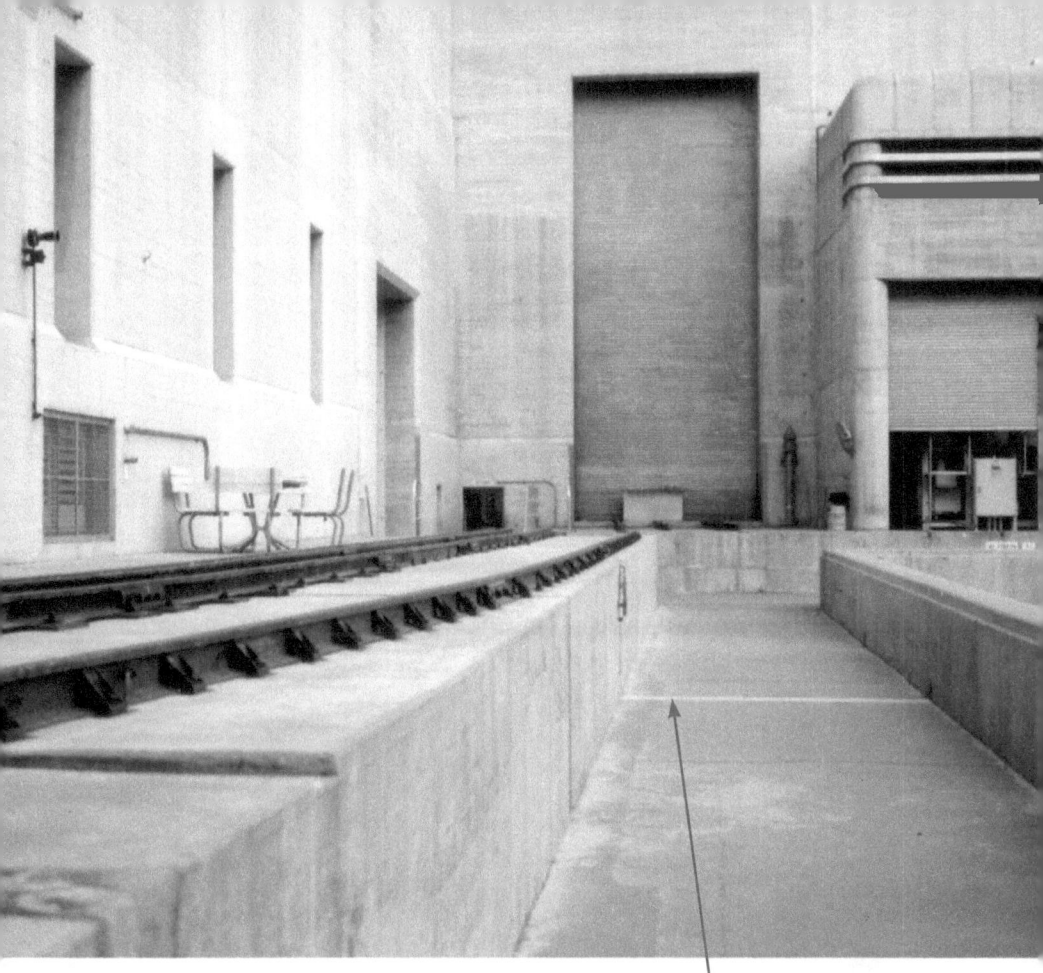

Arizona-Nevada border

In the summer of 1997 I took my Airstream trailer to the Badlands in South Dakota. The lands didn't seem too bad then, but they were beautiful in the late afternoon.

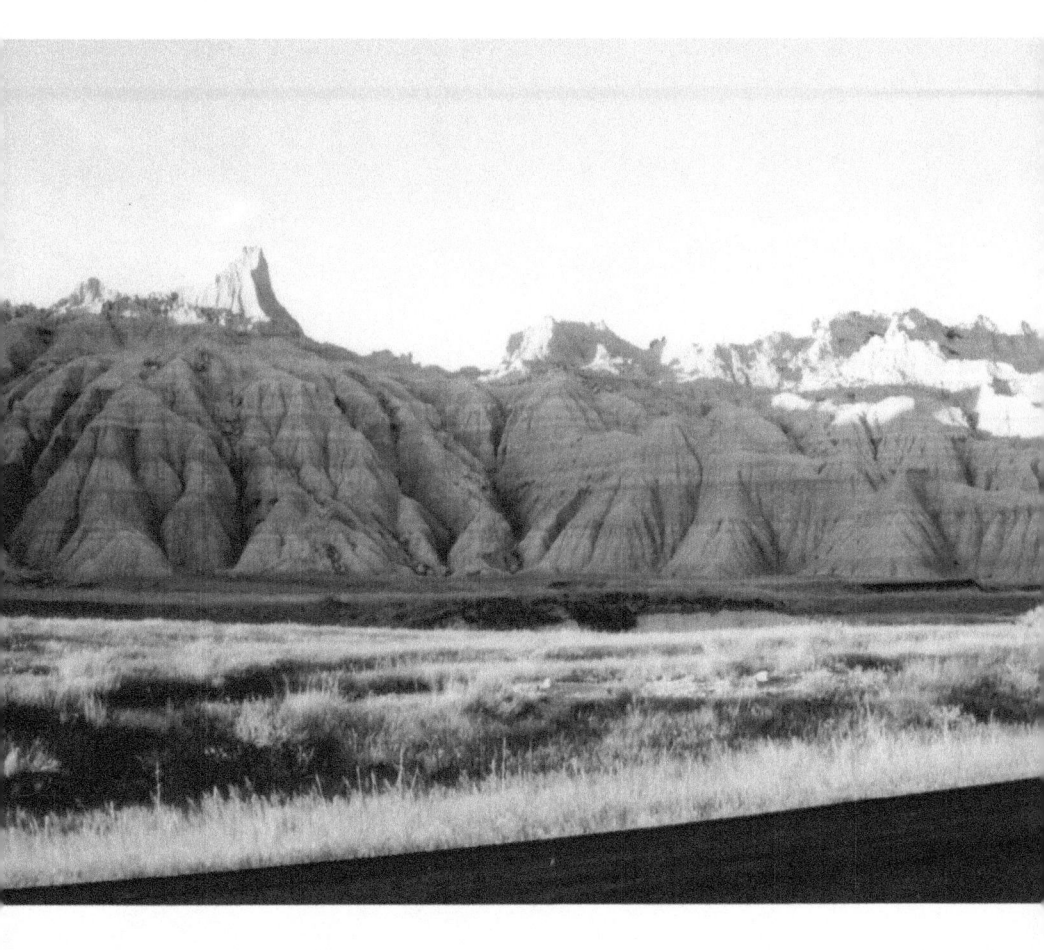

Landscape + Architecture 99

I crossed the Alps somewhere in Switzerland, and saw this old house by the side of the road, with a dry lake bed in the background. The house had been there for a long time but the landscape around it seemed to have been even more patient than the architecture.

I don't know the woman.

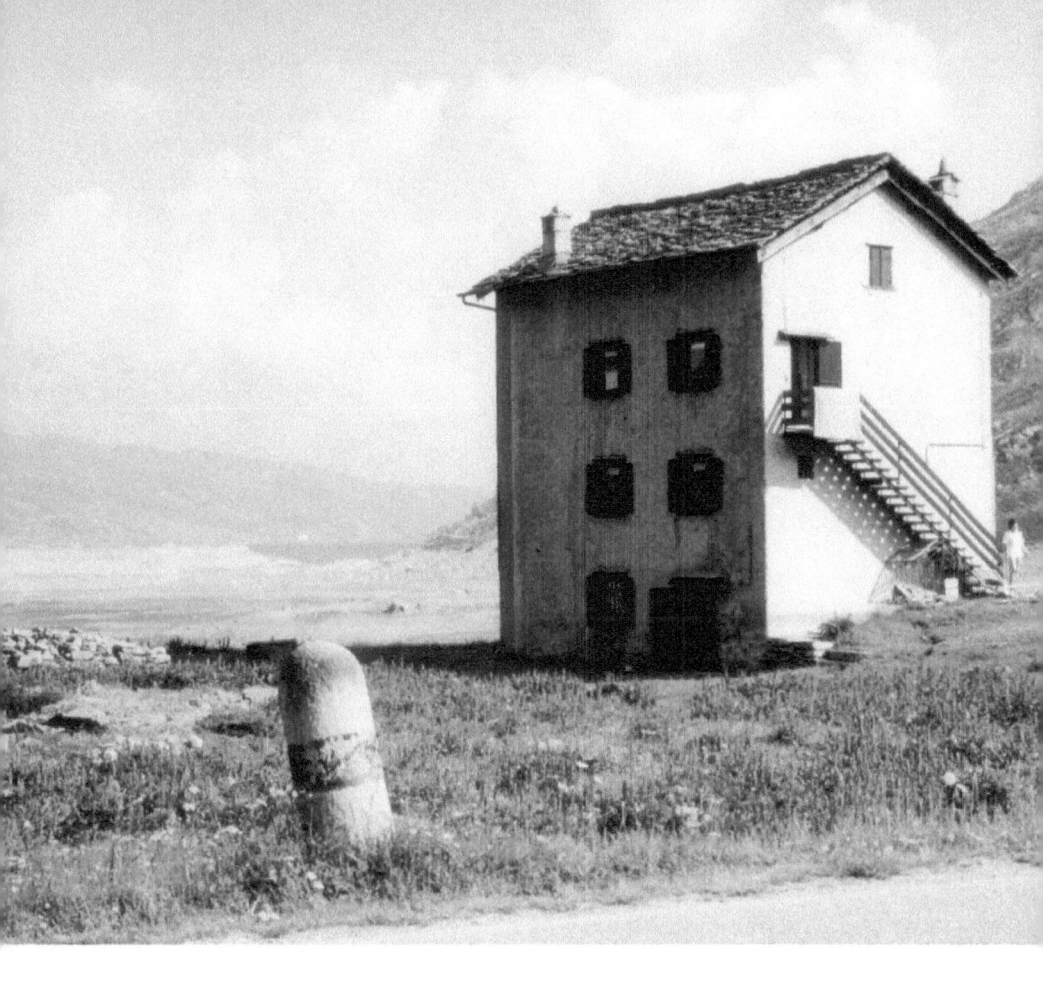

The Renzo-Piano-designed Galerie Beyeler in Riehen near Basel appears to counter the rolling Swiss landscape with its diaphanous termination towards the sky. The small pond in front of the galleries helps, too. It is a tranquil environment.

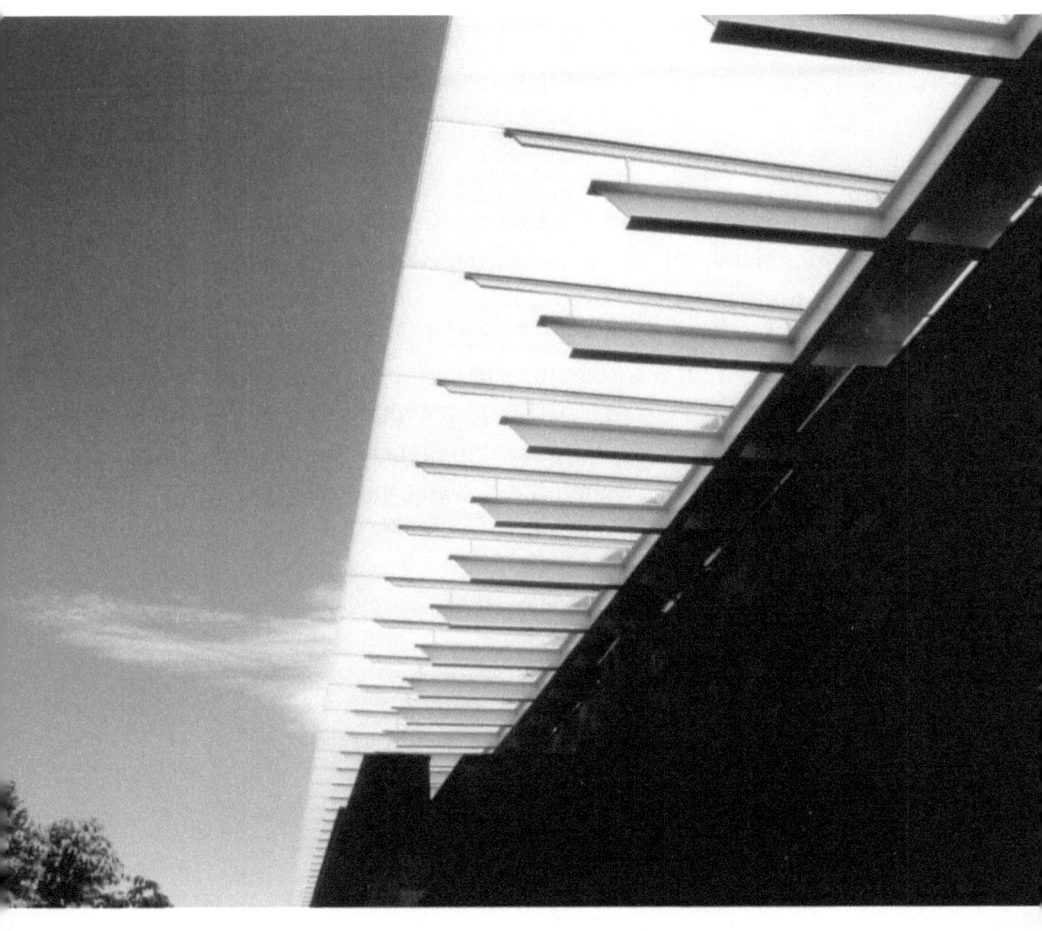

After traveling overnight back to Rome from Vals, Switzerland, Jeff, Ken, and I decided to use the rental car for a quick trip to Palestrina, just south of Rome. It was a beautiful, hazy Sunday, and after driving so many miles the night before it was refreshing to sit on the amphitheatric steps in front of the Palazzo Barberini—which was built on the ruins of the Tempio Fortuna Primigenia—and look out into the far distance, through the two columns that frame the well, toward the Tyrrhenian Sea.

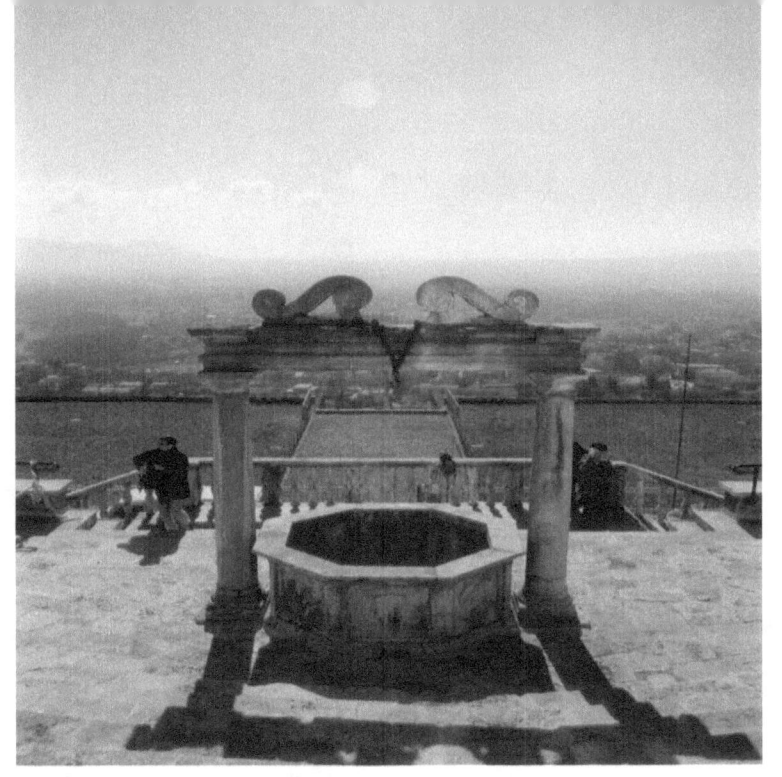

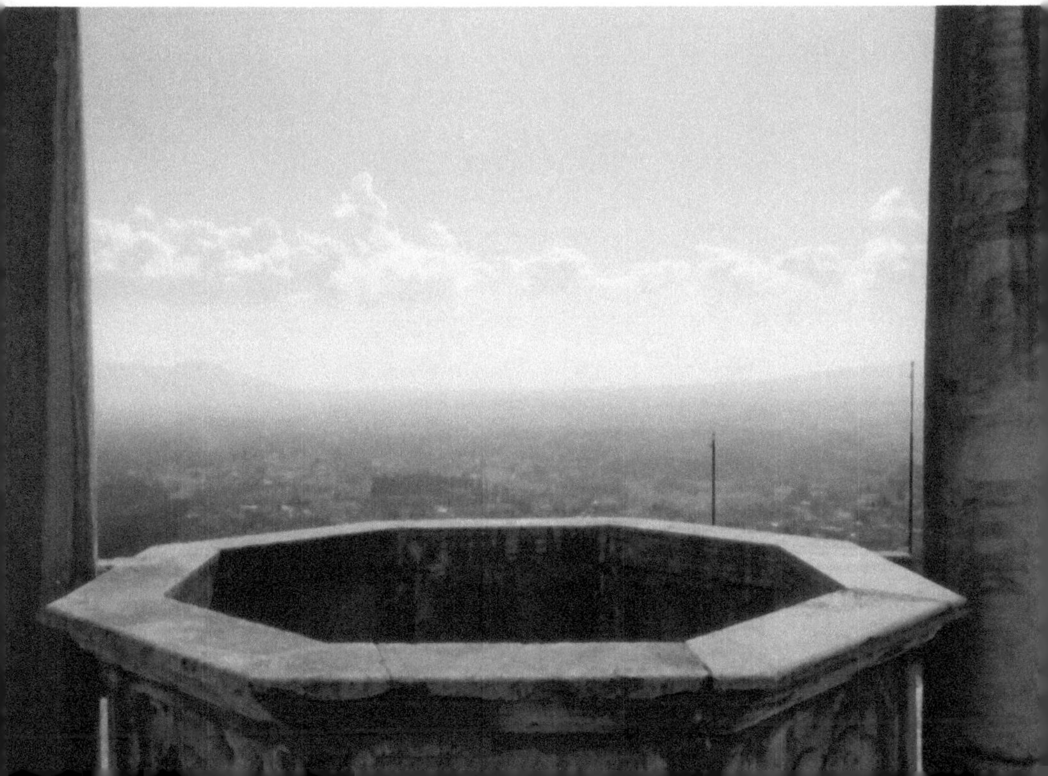

I don't know who that man was, but like so many of us architectural tourists, I'm sure he looked for a good position to capture Corb's Ronchamp chapel near Mulhouse in France.

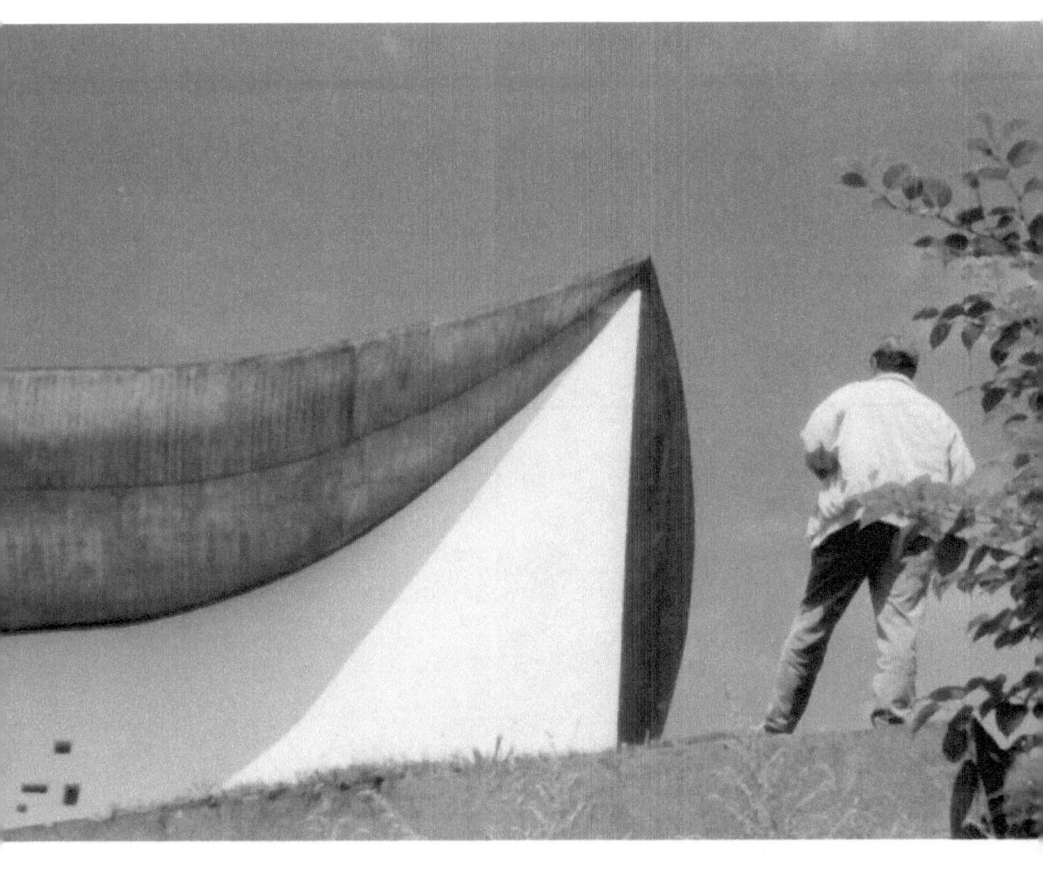

Mobile, Alabama, I think...

...or how to design a beautiful lift bridge by weaving steel, counterweights, and wheels into a dynamically balanced assemblage. The electric poles, lines, and transformers are the icing on the infrastructural cake.

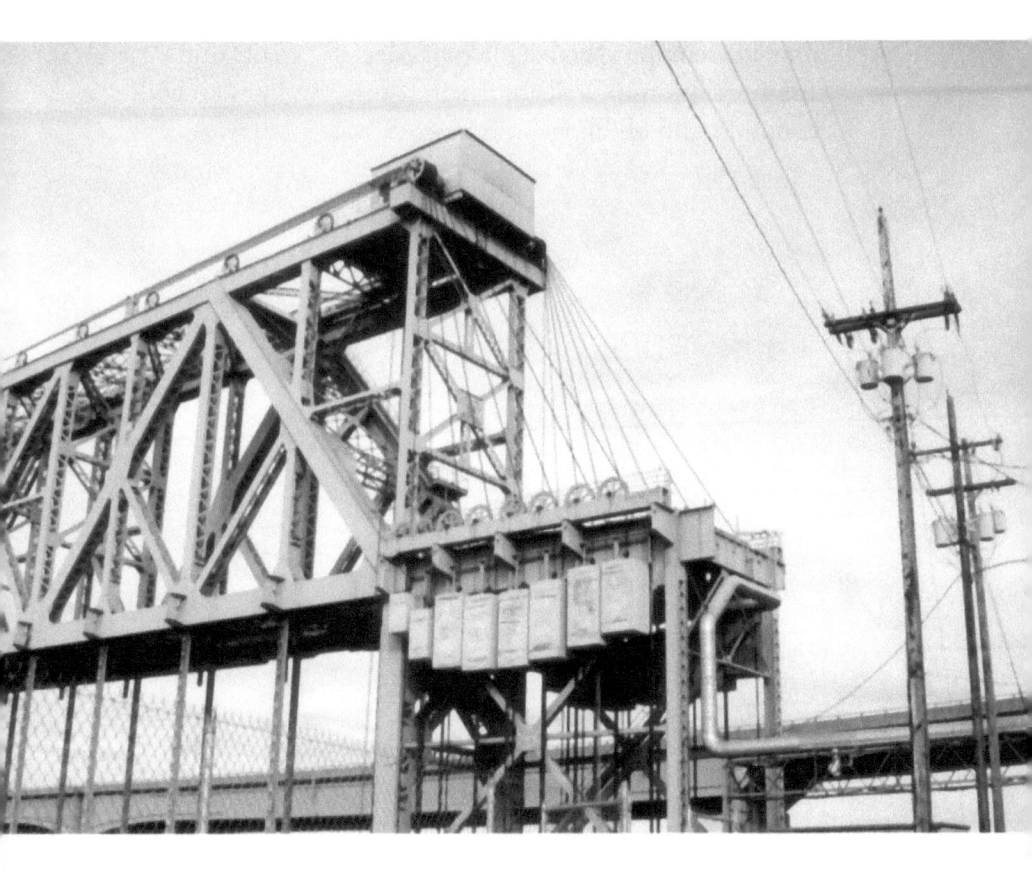

From a certain perspective the roof edge of Zaha Hadid's Vitra fire station in Weil am Rhein, Germany, lines up with the non-Hadid buildings next to it.

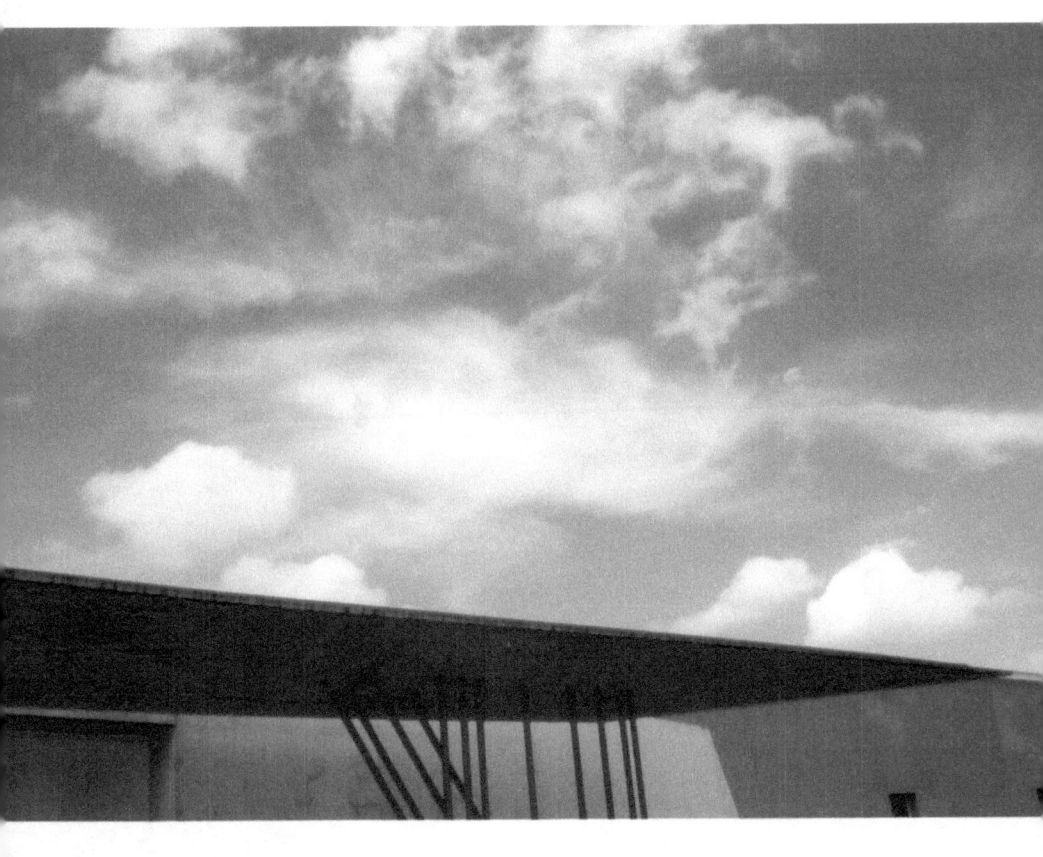

Landscape + Architecture

In the summer, visitors to the *Herkules* monument outside Kassel, Germany, can walk down the hillside toward the town, following the same volume of flowing water passing over artificial steps, a ruined aquaeduct, and gurgling brooks, only to emerge at the end of the path in front of the castle as a tall fountain.

Sometimes—rarely—power and beauty go hand in hand.

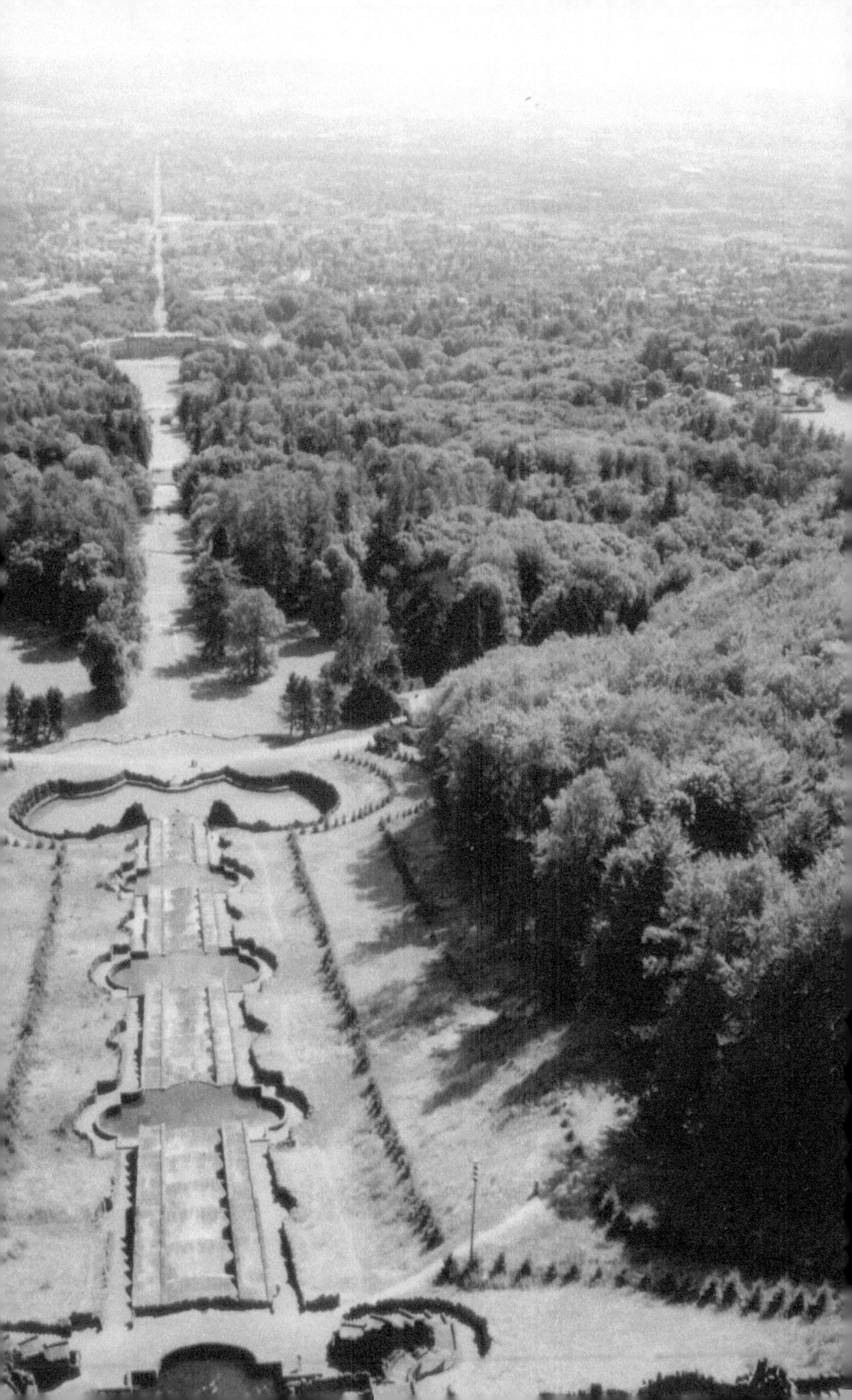

MEMORY

While traveling with my Airstream I would now and then remember sleeping in damp tents, and waking up to the gentle sound of raindrops falling in the morning, only to realize that I would have to pack up a wet tent before movimg on. Traveling like a snail with a silver-bullet hard shell attached to the back of my Jeep is a comparative luxury.

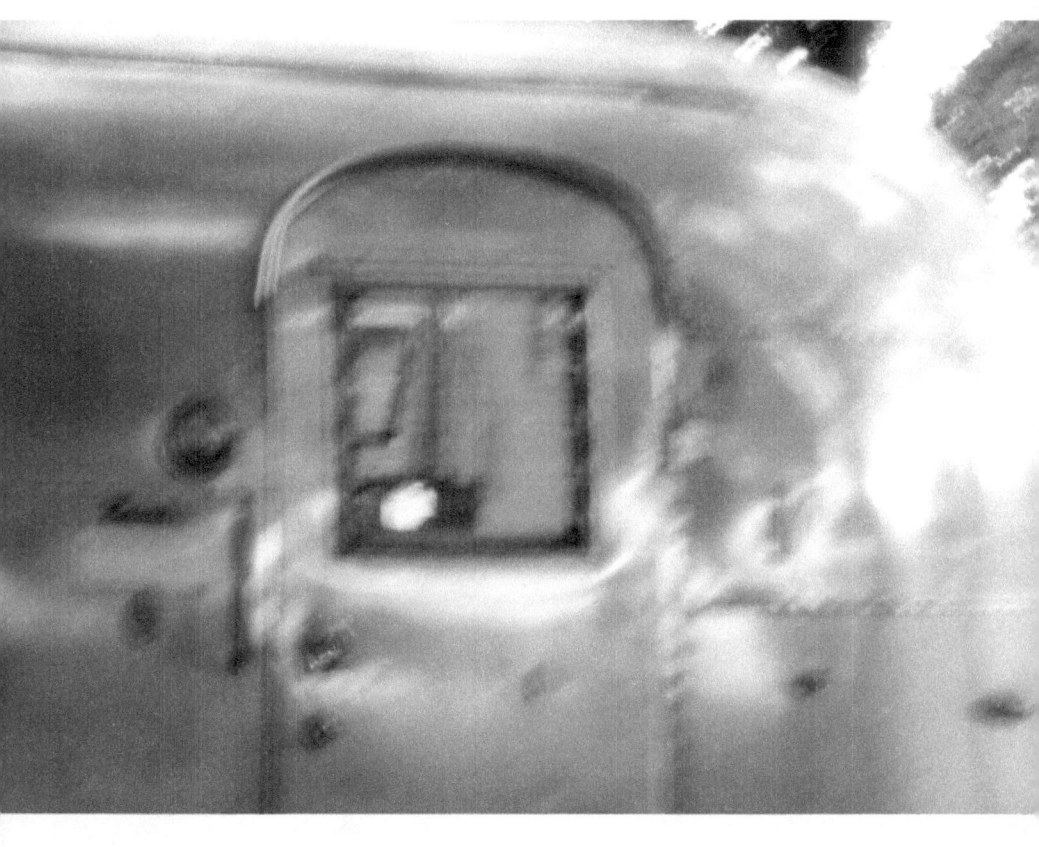

When I went back to Berlin in 1997 some of the buildings in the former east-German part of town still showed the pock marks of WW II (and the by now ubiquitous satellite dish). No one had cared enough to repair the damage, and perhaps this was intentional. Memory enjoys stasis.

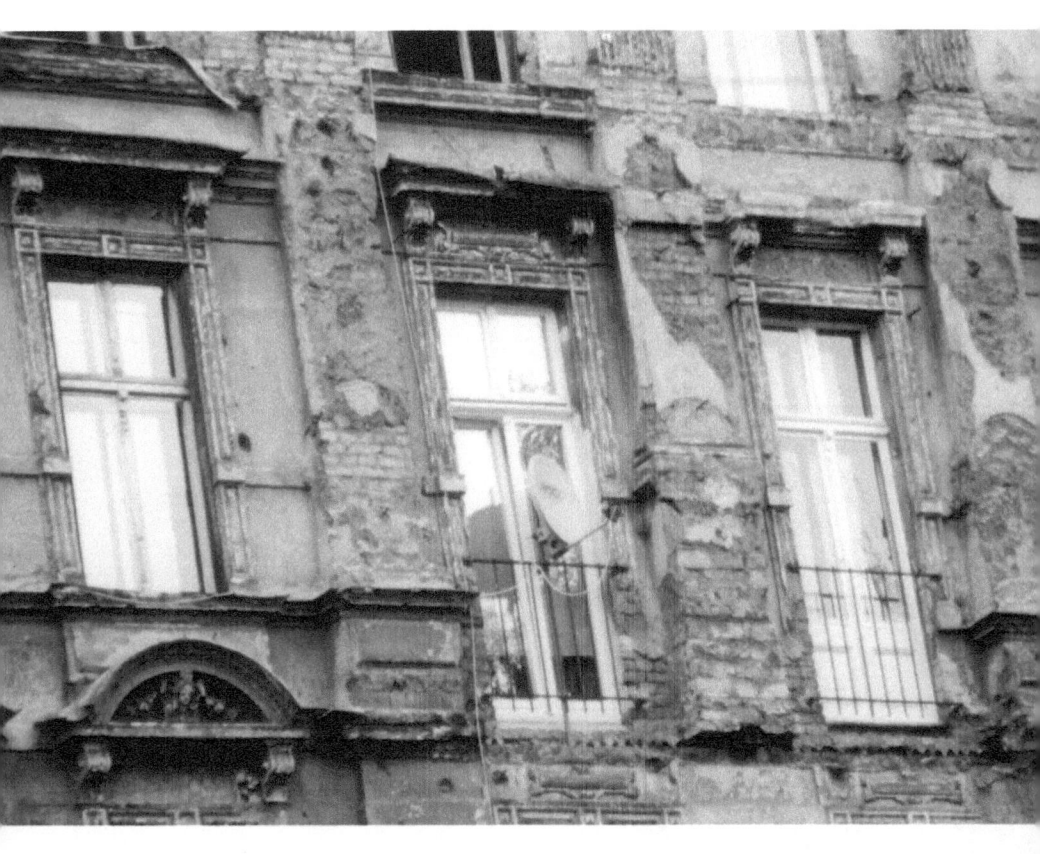

We used to eat lunch in the Brown Pelican Restaurant near the pier in Cedar Key, Florida. The restaurant disappeared, and now we go to Annie's Café.

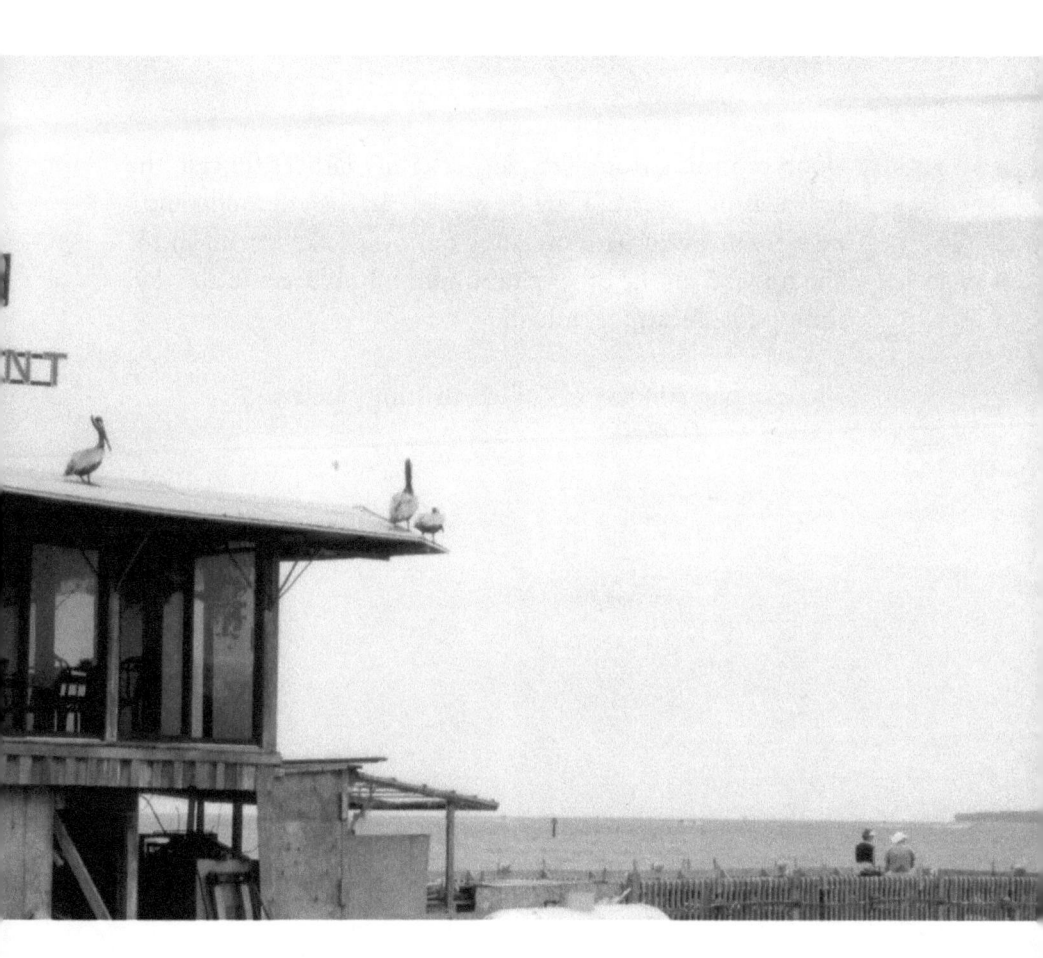

Upon returning from Germany after my father's funeral, the arrival airport was O'Hare. It was late in the afternoon and we were in a wait pattern, going out over Lake Michigan to line up with all the other aluminium bumblebees in the sky aiming for the airport inland.

The lake had still patches of ice, drifting carelessly.

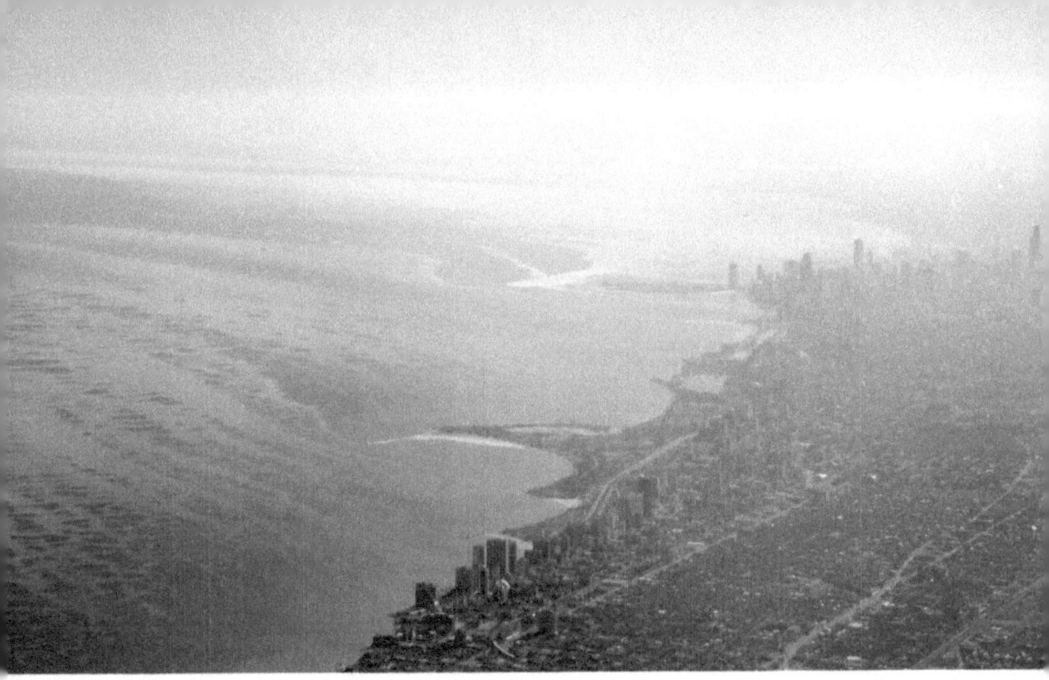

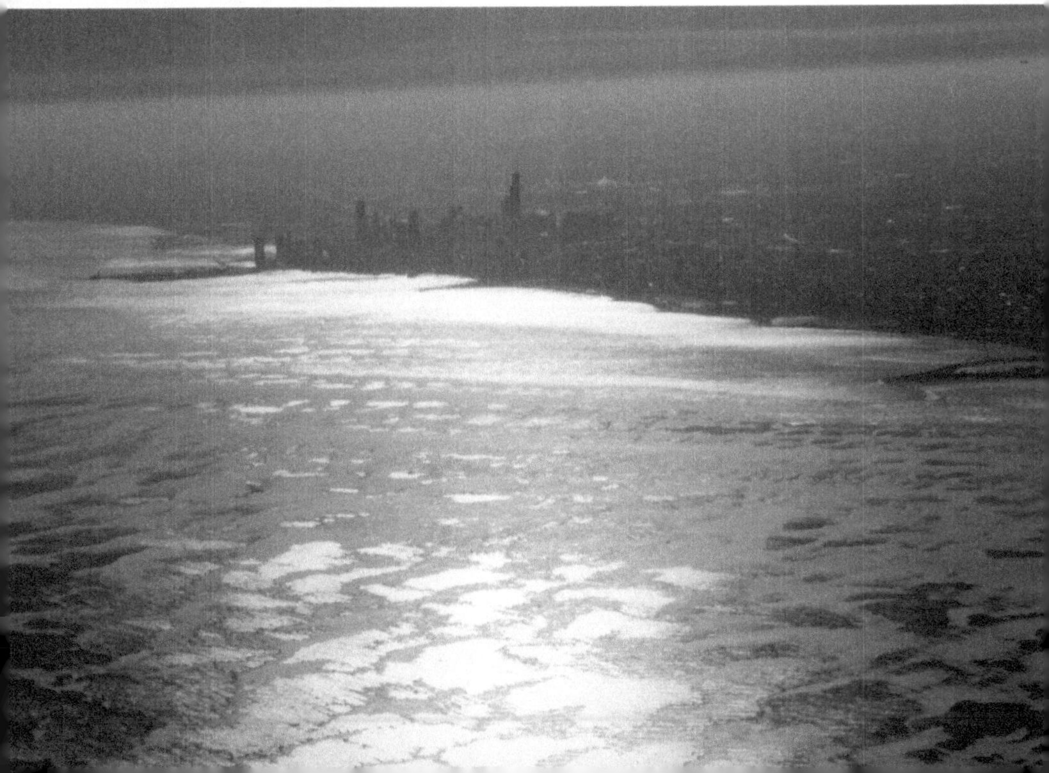

In 1998 I gave a paper at a Romanticism conference in Athens, Georgia. After the lecture I decided to explore the region around the town and drove south on highway #78 where this abandoned house, overgrown with kudzu, sat by the side of the road. It was one of those moments when I thought about what it means to be old.

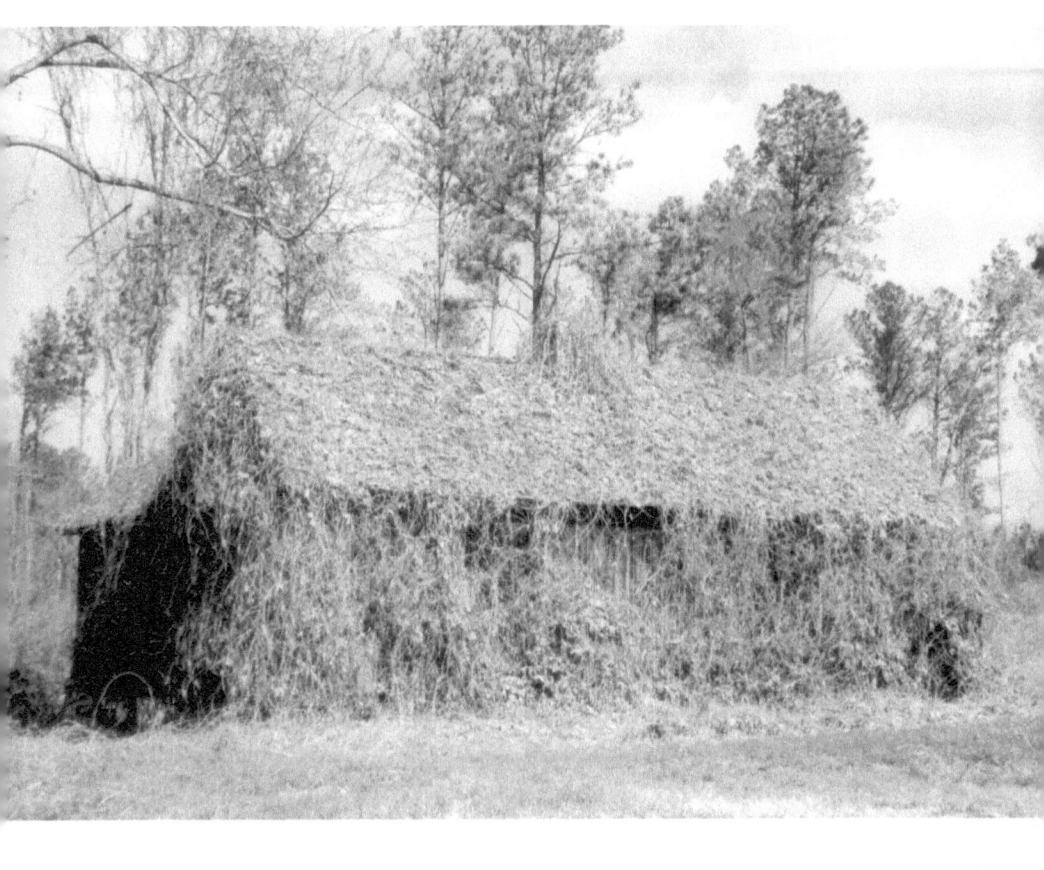

Collecting makes us feel safe, although in most cases it is an illusion that owning things will help us become immortal, but we do it anyway. I never met the person who lined up all those bottles on the window ledge but here is a photograph to immortalize at least the memory of the collection.

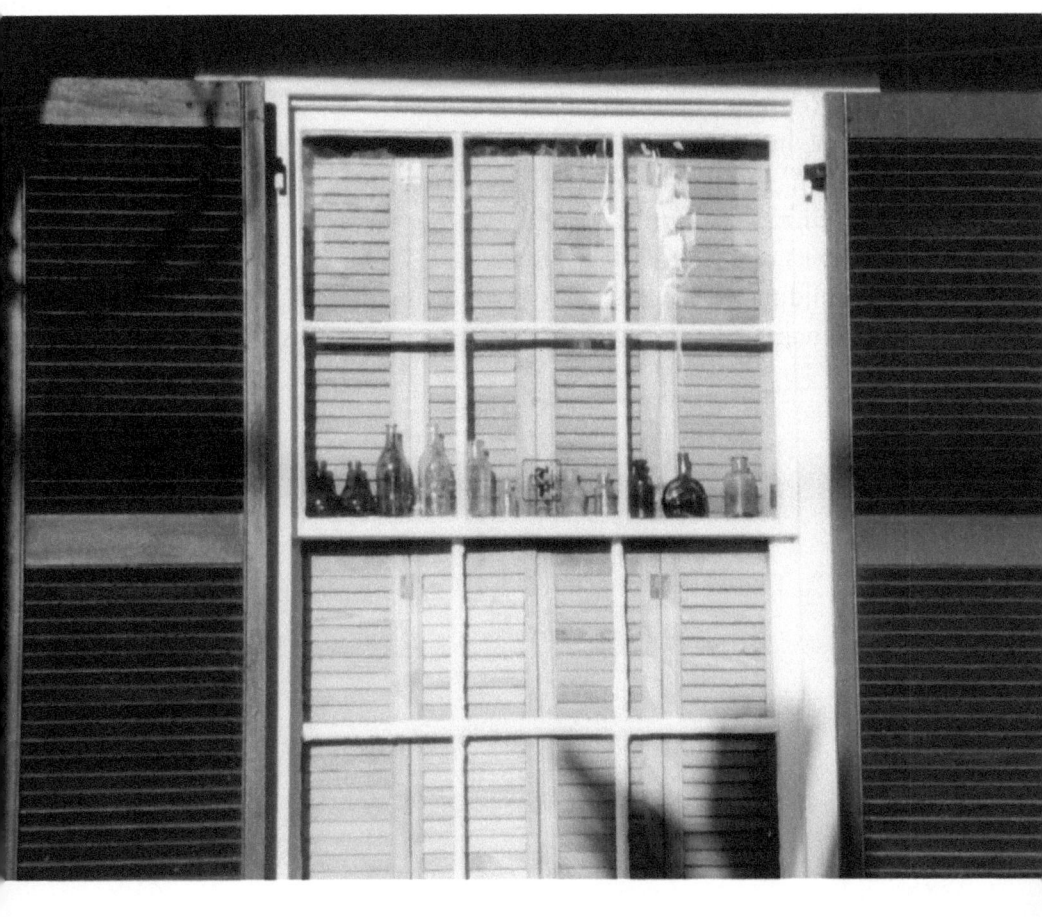

Somewhere along one of the cul-de-sacs that end near the San Diego Bay (E or F Street, I'm not sure) I parked a mint-green 1965 AMC Hornet in the fall of 1978. I left the ignition key on the air filter housing, assuming I would return in the spring of 1979 after exploring Mexico by bus and train. I didn't return until 1997. By then the car was gone, but the layers of infrastructure—trees, water, light, electricity, boats, buildings—and my memory of leaving that car behind, remain.

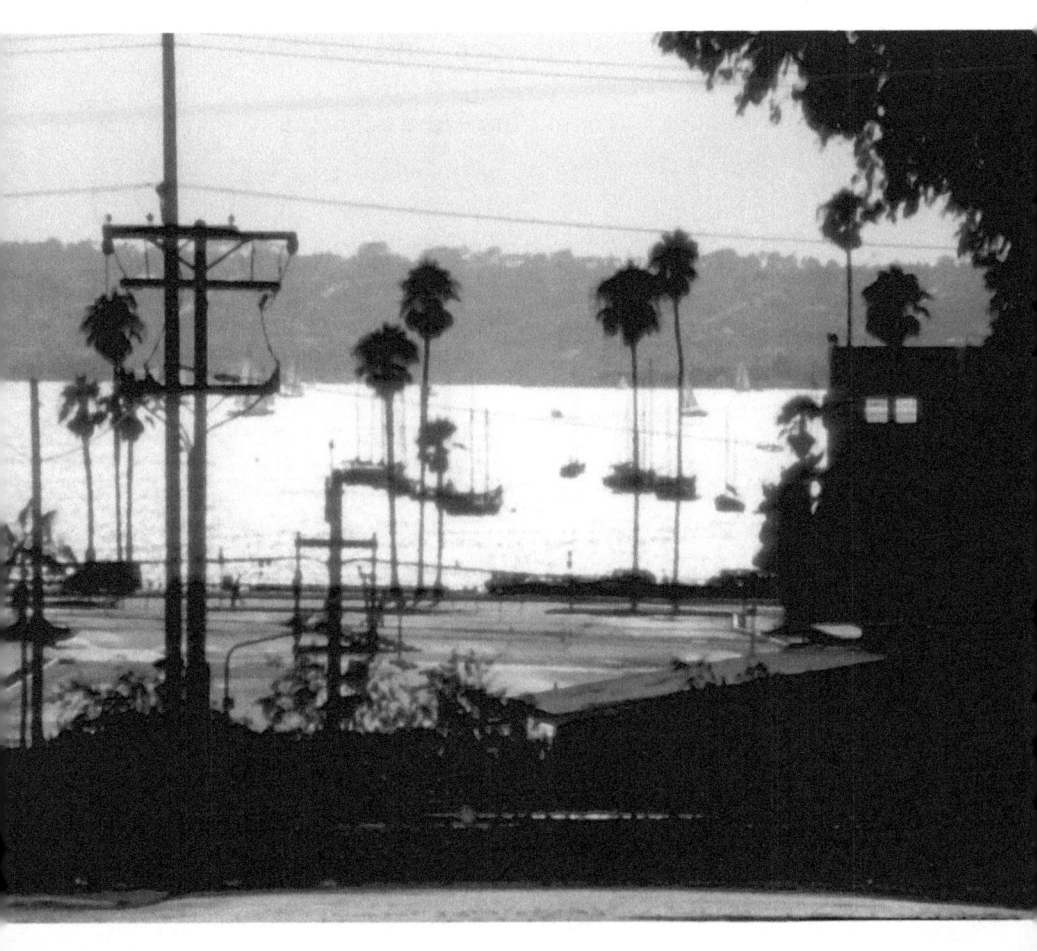

This idyllic scene in a rural region south of Berlin was soon shattered when the owner of the house and my sister disagreed on matters of medium-sized importance.

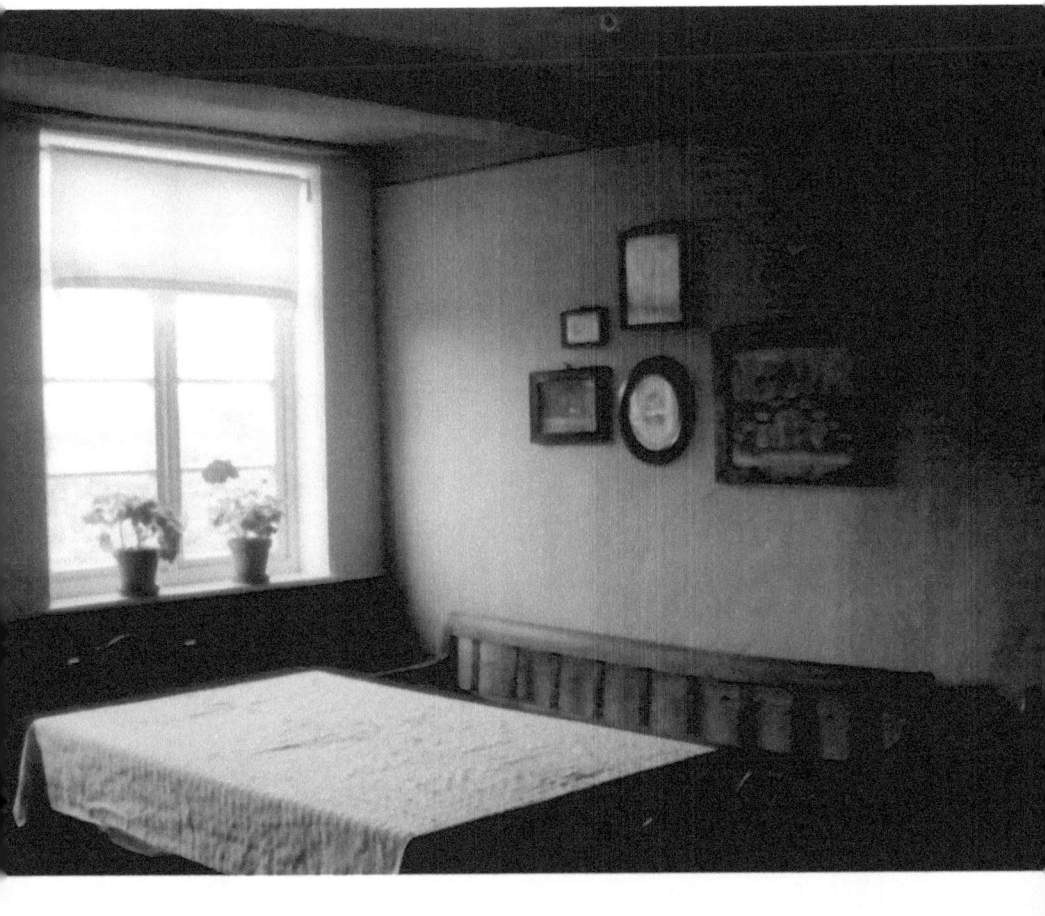

It was a late afternoon on a chilly, humid, and overcast December day. The sun had already set behind the clouds, and the cold was creeping back through my clothes. We stopped by a frozen lake near Pivitsheide, Germany. Seeing all those happy people on that hard white field of ice changed my dreary mood as I recalled the paintings by one of the Brueghel boys.

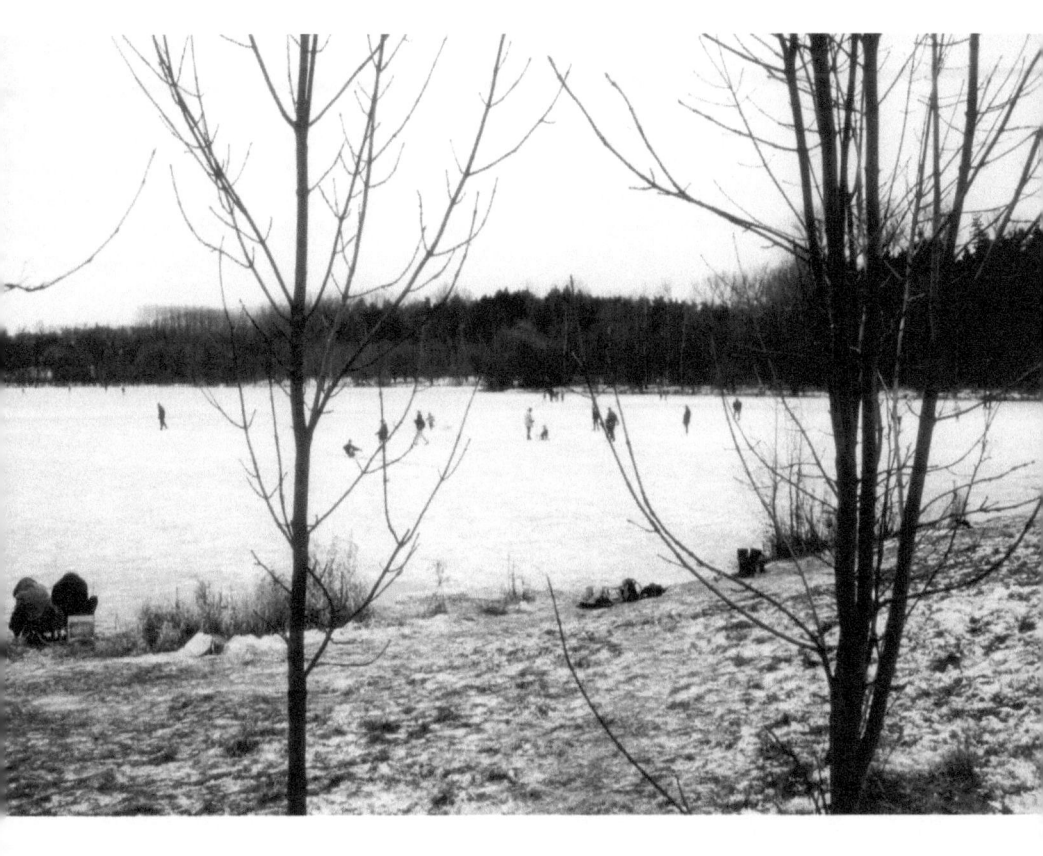

The sun still shines into the *Bauhaus* in Dessau, Germany.

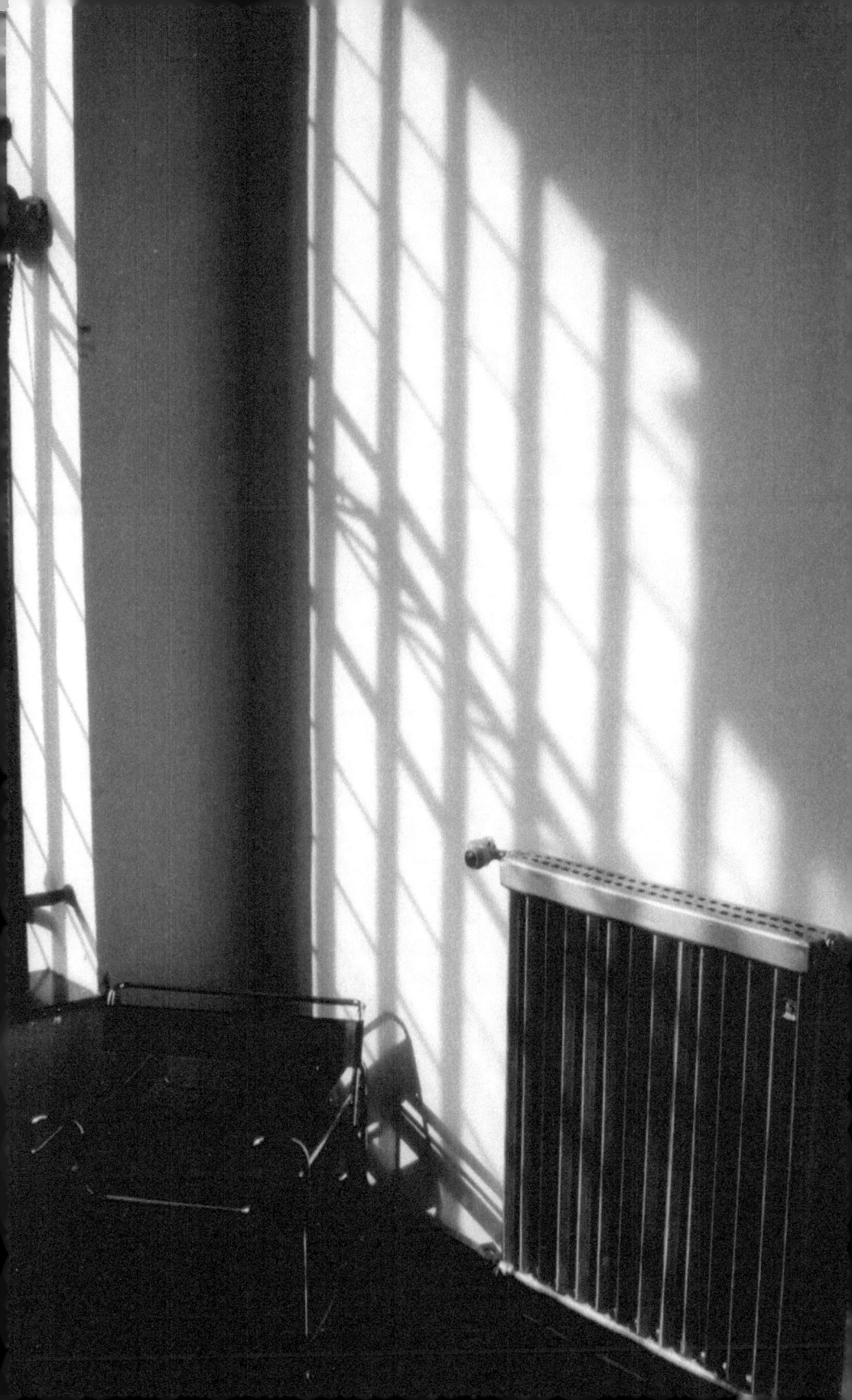

There are some places where we have to go alone. That's my father in the foreground walking on the pier.

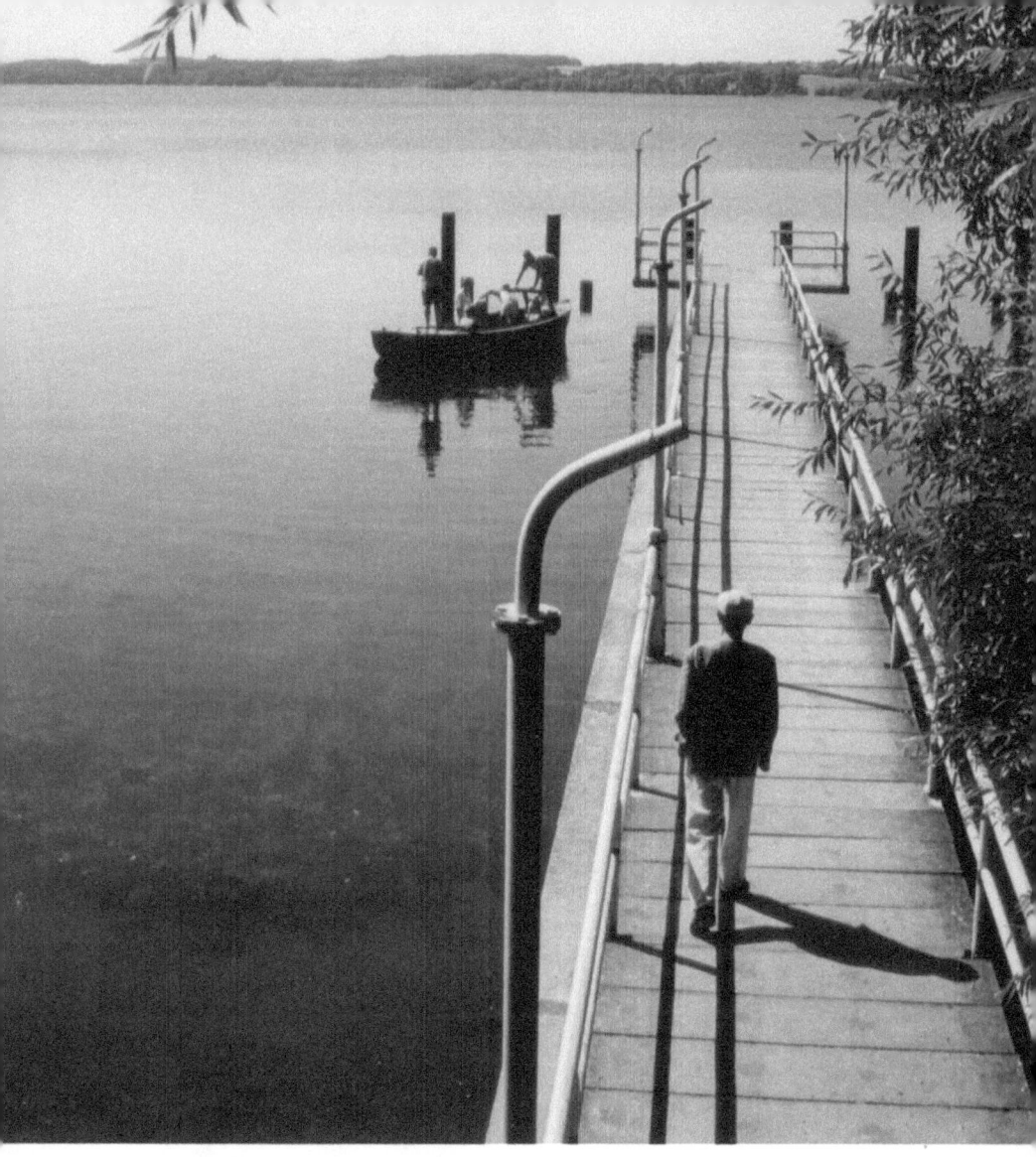

This may look like Germany but it's Milwaukee...

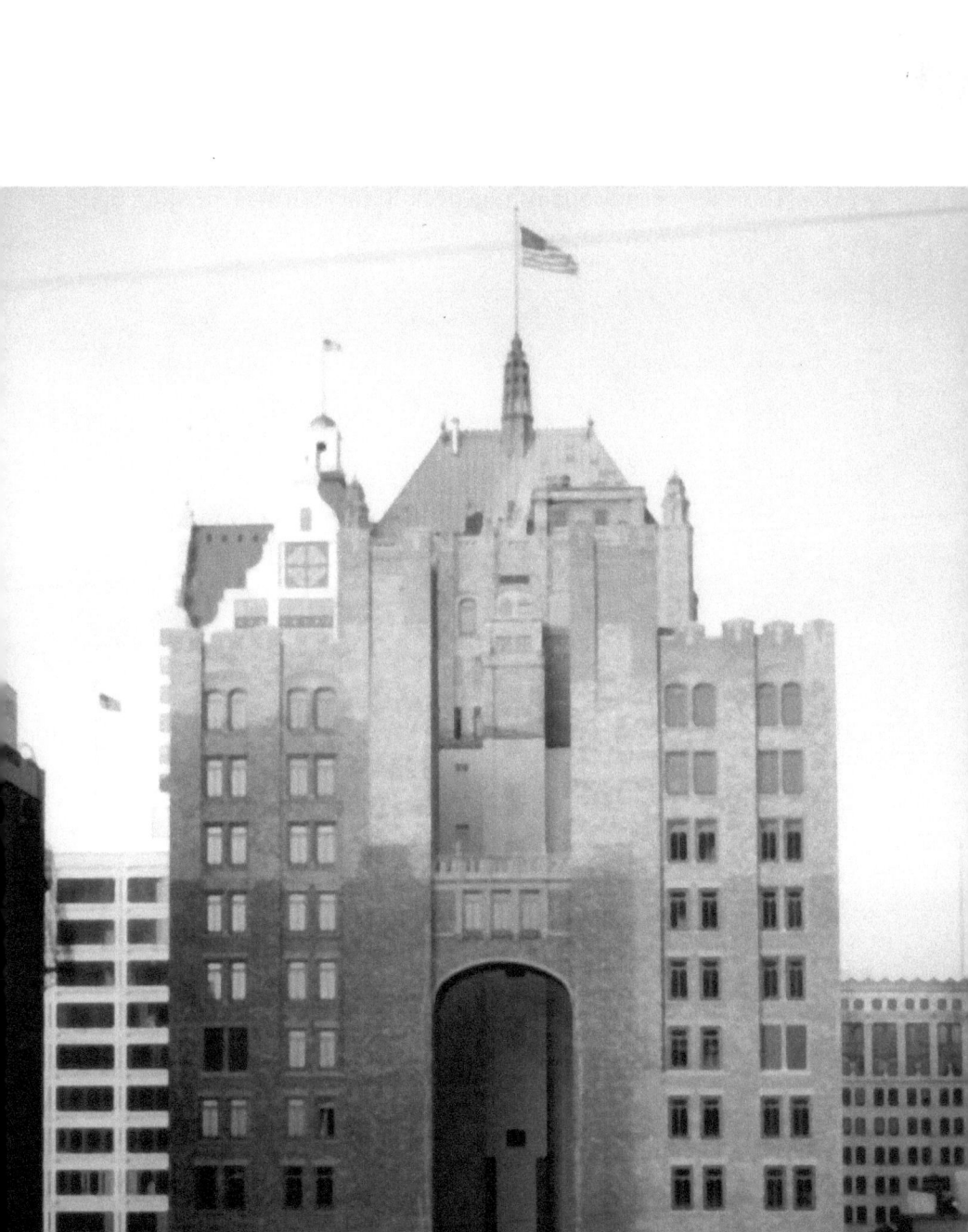

These are not the Spanish Steps in Rome, but stairs leading up to the *Orangerie* in Sans Souci in Potsdam, Germany.

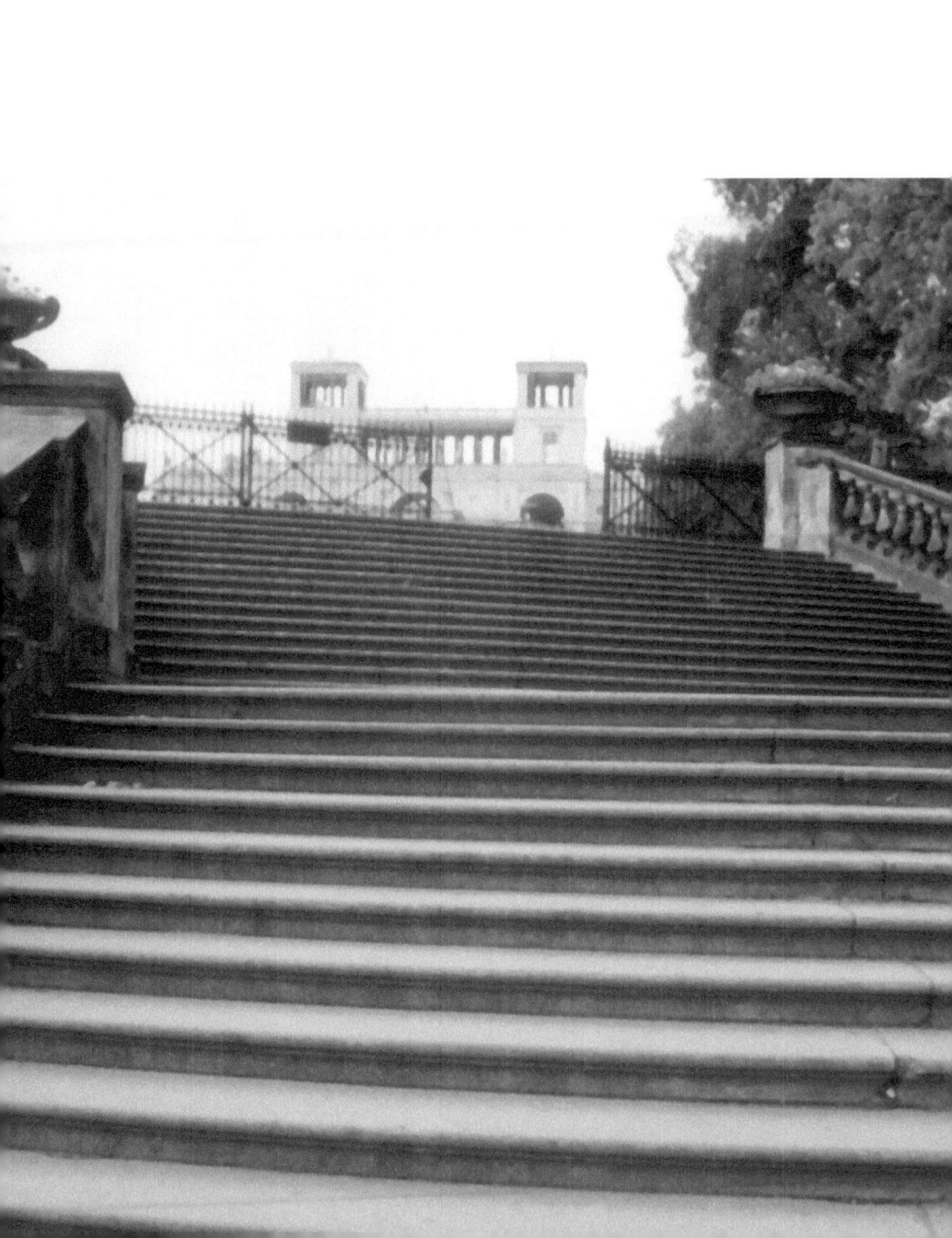

Despite its miniscule appearance this may be one of the oldest cabins in Iowa. It's sitting in the backyard of the Mathias Ham house in Dubuque.

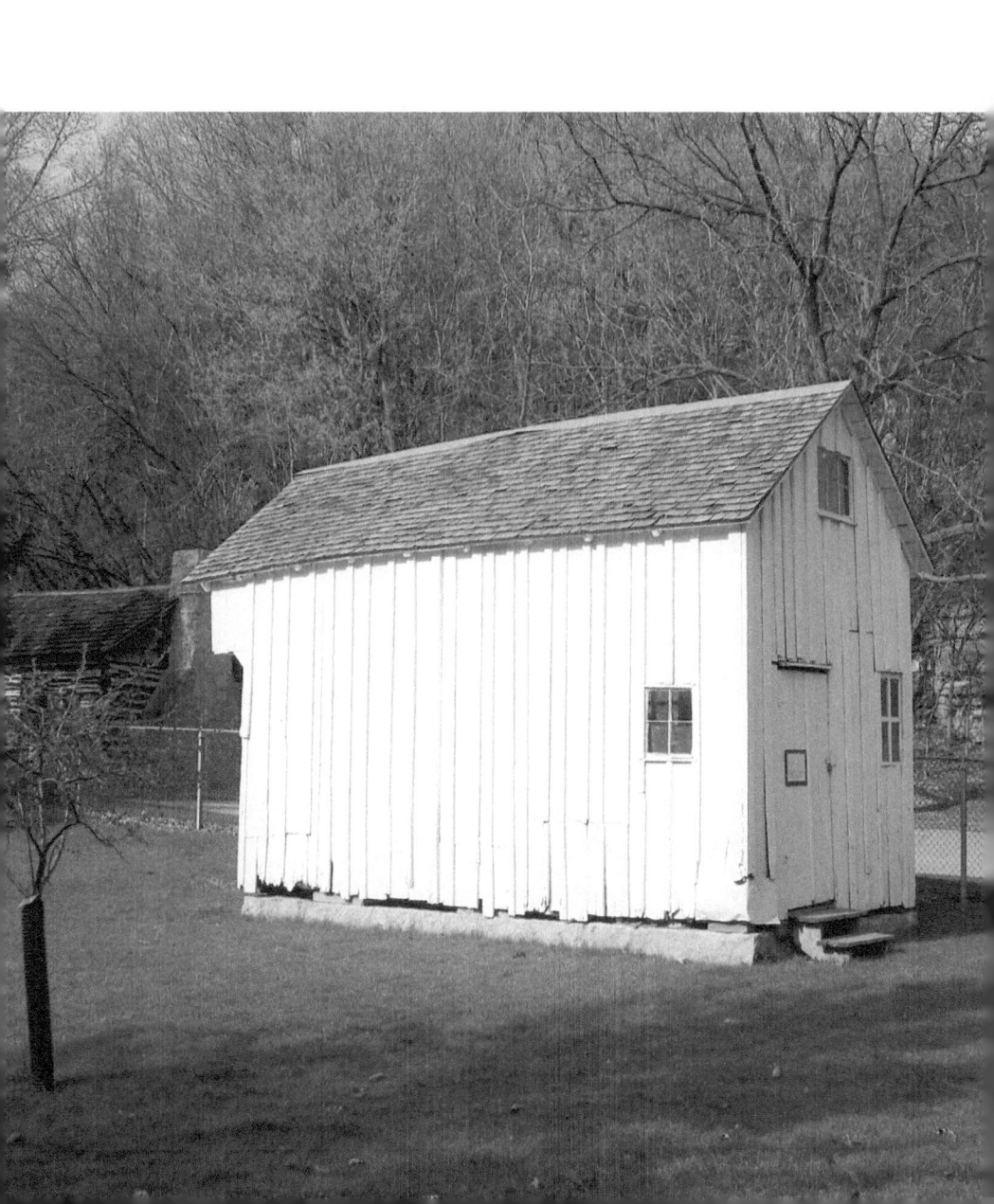

It was a hot summer day and Lambchop lounged on the wood floor while Zsa Zsa just got up to get some water in my house in Ames, Iowa.

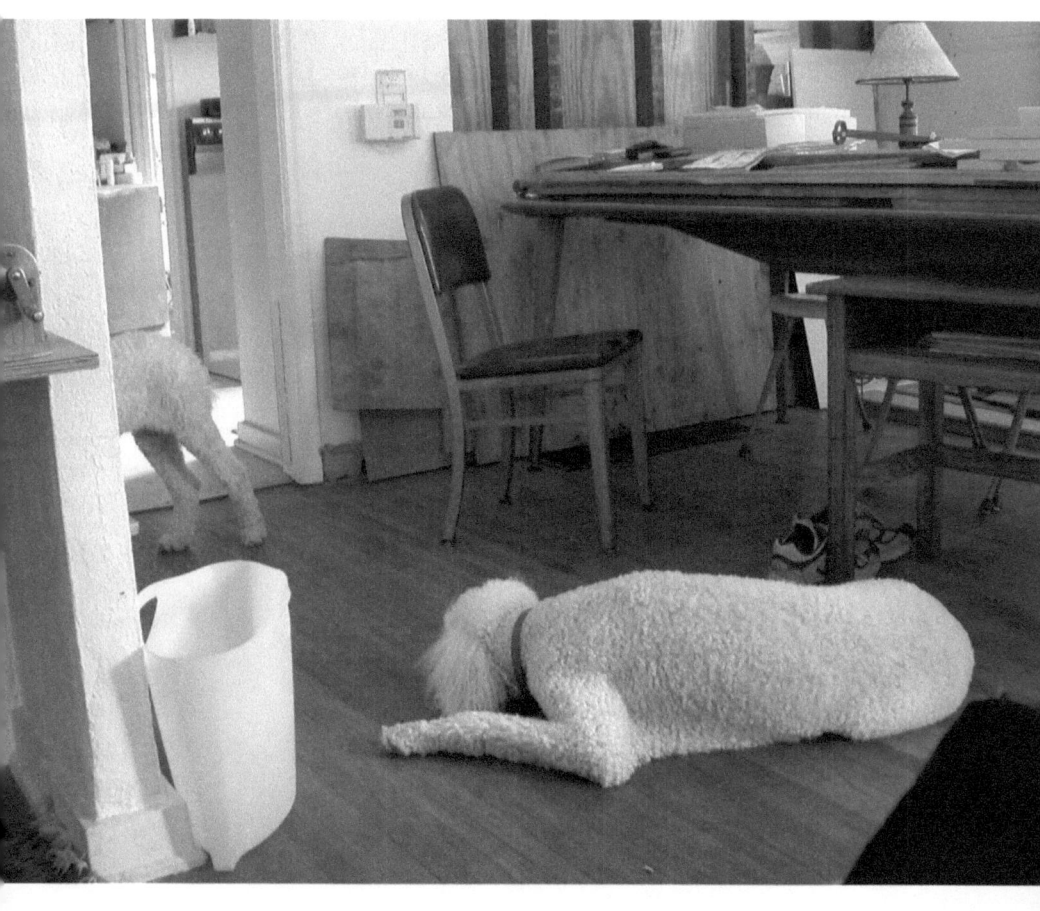

Mother and son on a quiet lake in eastern Germany, wondering where we came from, where we are, and where we will be going (and believe me, we don't know either). Photo by Walter Mücke.

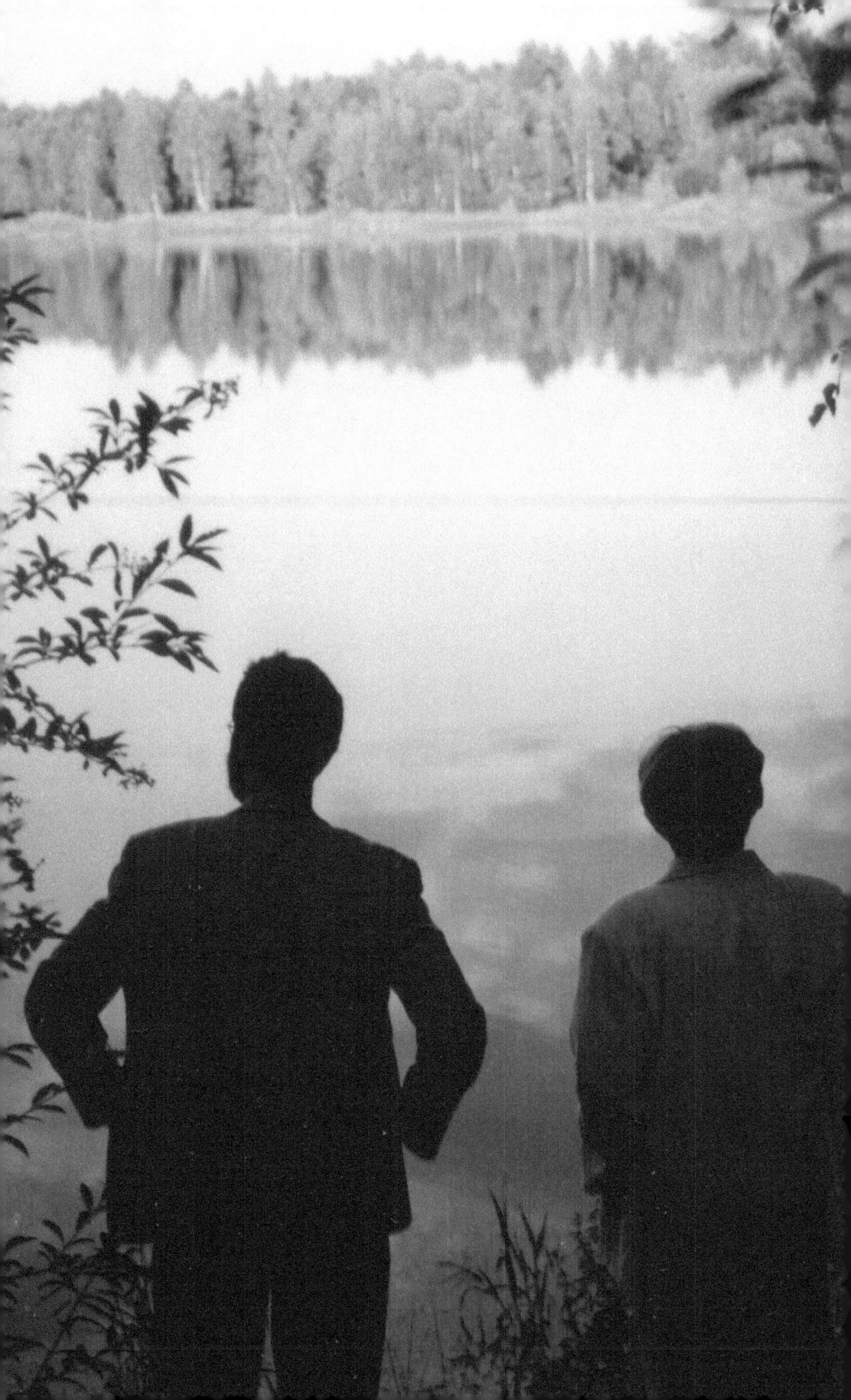

METAMORPHOSIS

It was a bit of magic. Someone unfurled a bermuda-green lightweight chrysalis which quickly billowed up in the wind blowing inland from the Pacific Ocean.

And then a person, hanging from nearly invisible strings, metamorphosed into a bird.

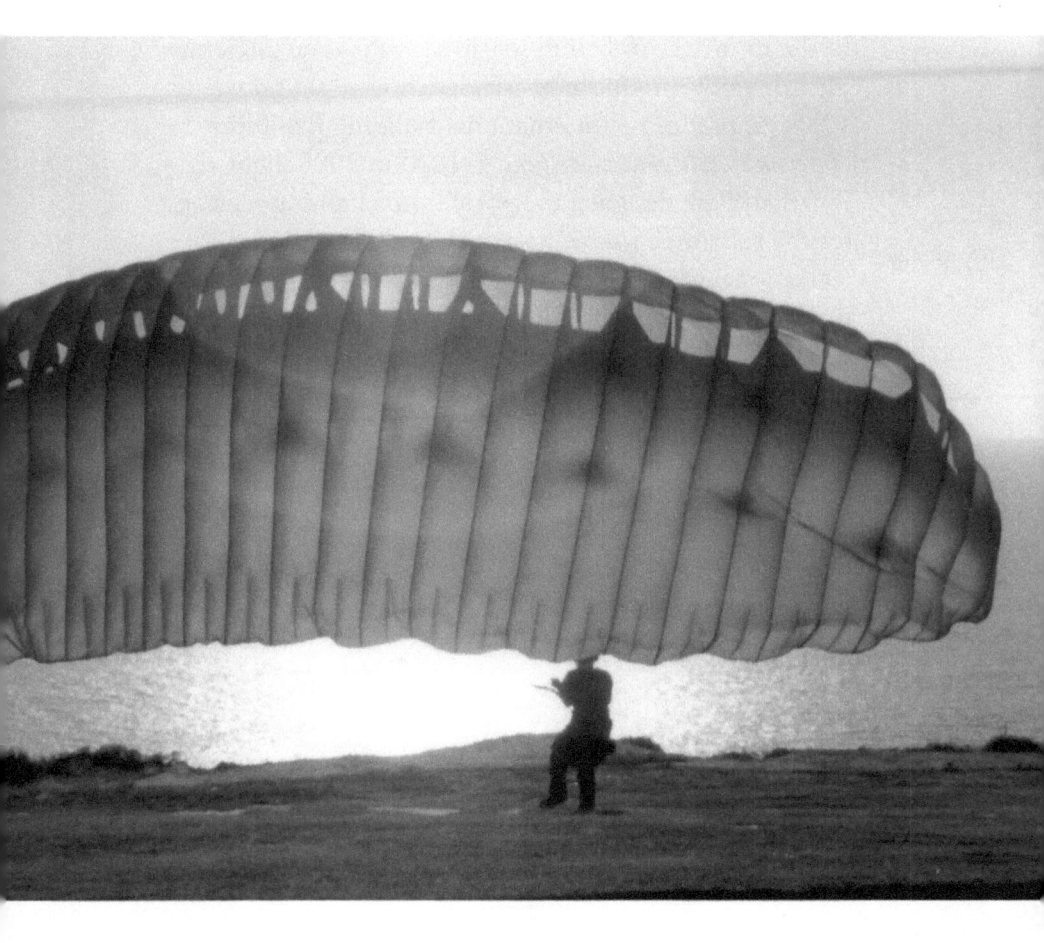

In the former heavyly industrialized Ruhr zone in Germany, the ironworks in Duisburg-Meiderich were shut down in 1985. As part of the International Building Exhibition (*Internationale Bauausstellung* or IBA) in 1996, light artist Jonathan Park designed the polychrome lighting scheme for the reclaimed ironworks which now functions as a recreational space for the surrounding communities. At dusk the computer-controlled lighting bathes the heroic industrial skeletons in quickly changing light, creating a magical space for the eye and mind.

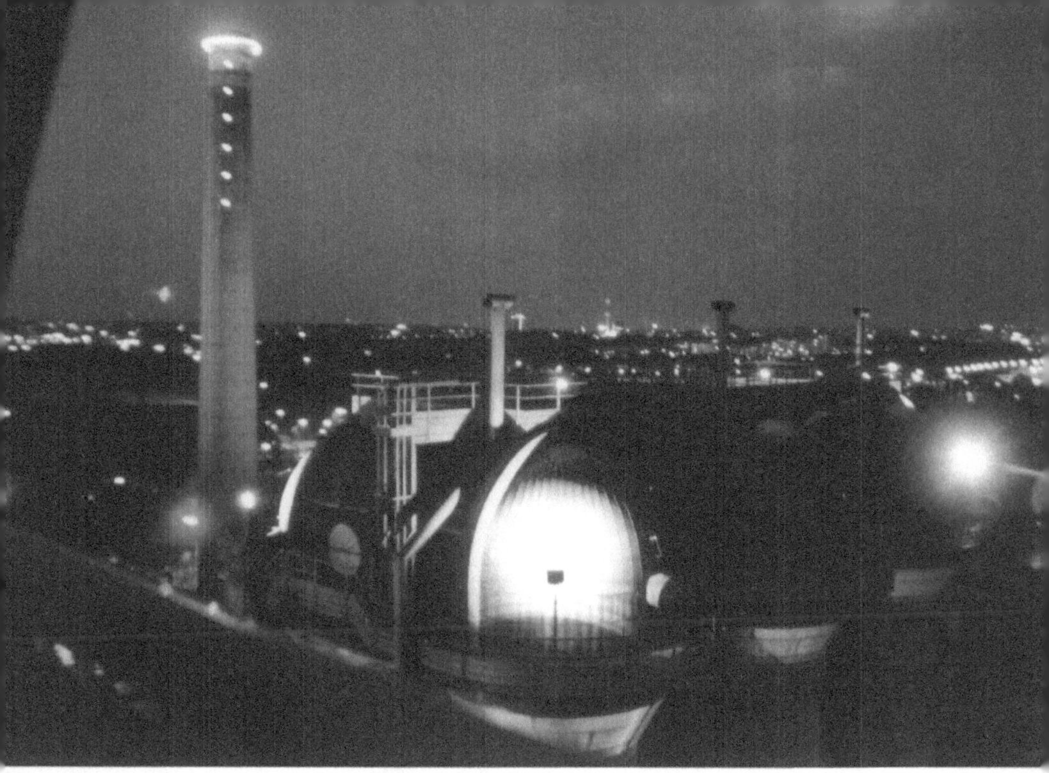

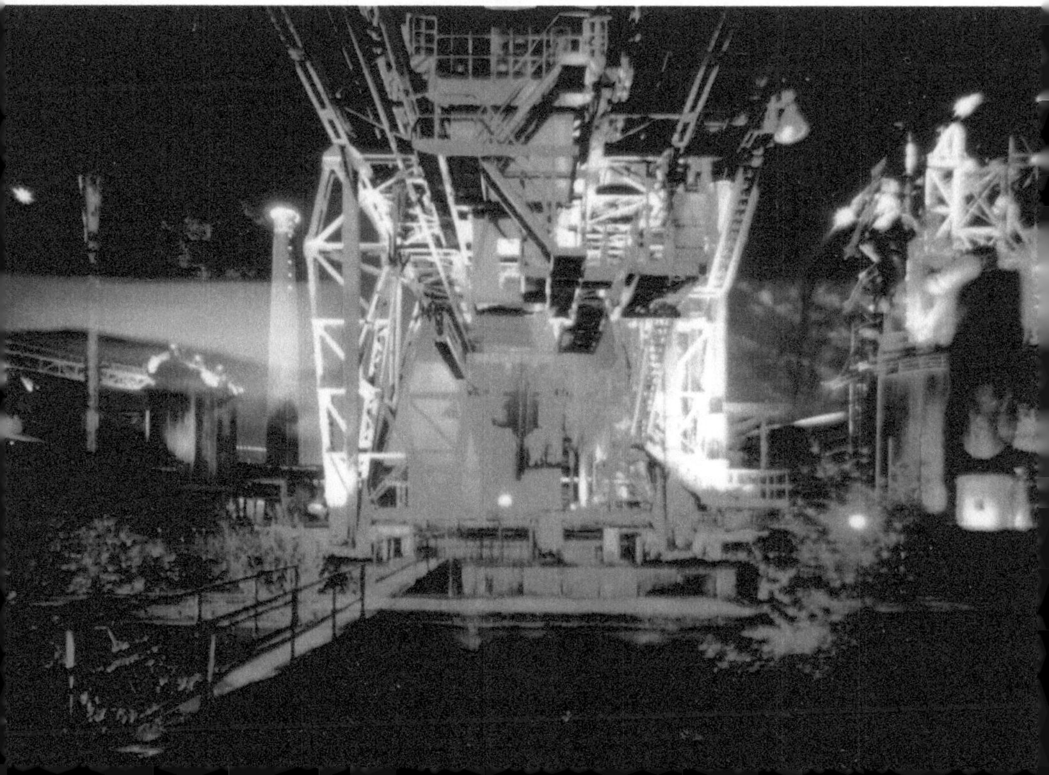

I have often suspected that my late brother might be a cloud.

Metamorphosis 155

Between 1983 and 1985 we lived in a converted circus trailer on the outskirts of a small German village, and on the edge of German society. When we bought the used trailer from a retired circus manager, I drank a lot of coffee, then paid the man with twelve 100 DM bills. The ride back on the tractor was jittery.

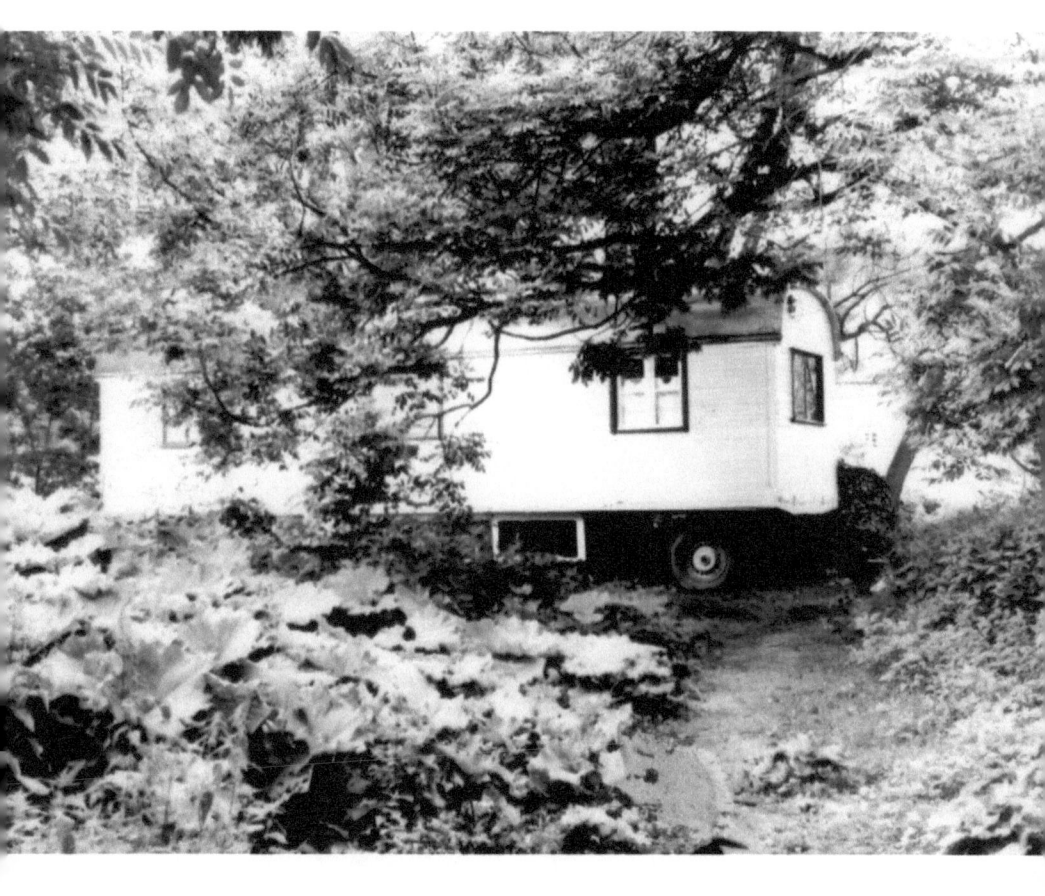

The *Gasometer* (gas tank) in Oberhausen, Germany. A gigantic cylindrical space that used to hold about 25,000 cubic meters of gas before it was converted in the 1990s into one of the most amazing exhibit spaces in Europe. We visited the place when Christo and Jeanne-Claude had just installed *The Wall*, a sculpture consisting of 13,000 stacked 55gallon oil drums. Acoustically the space resonates like a very large bathroom;—)

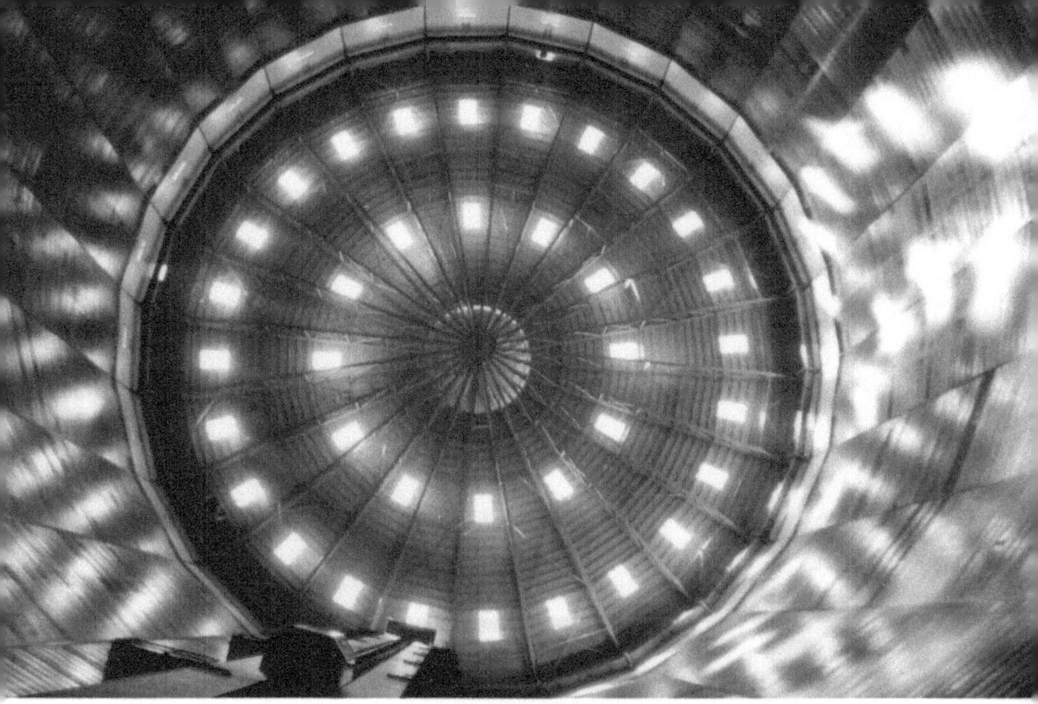

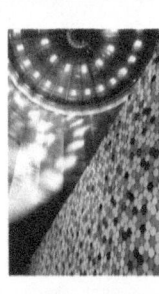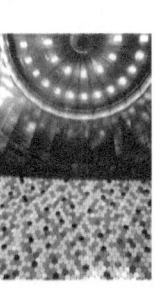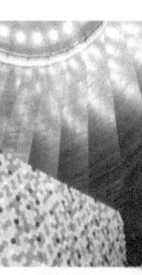

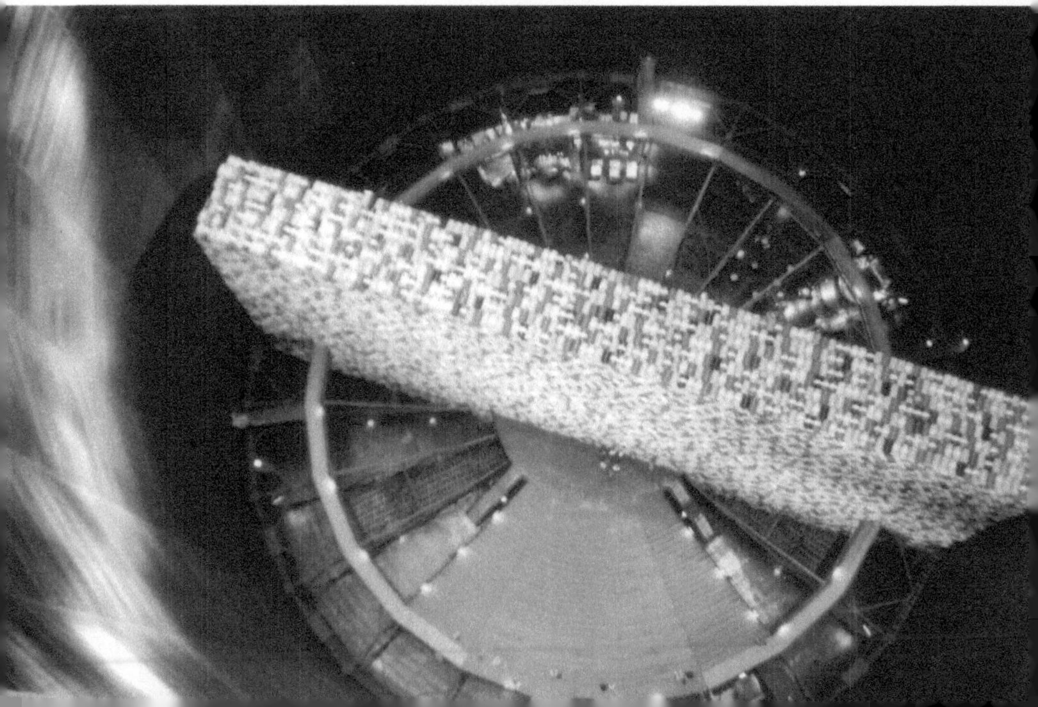

Sometimes the sides of Airstream trailers make crooked faces at you.

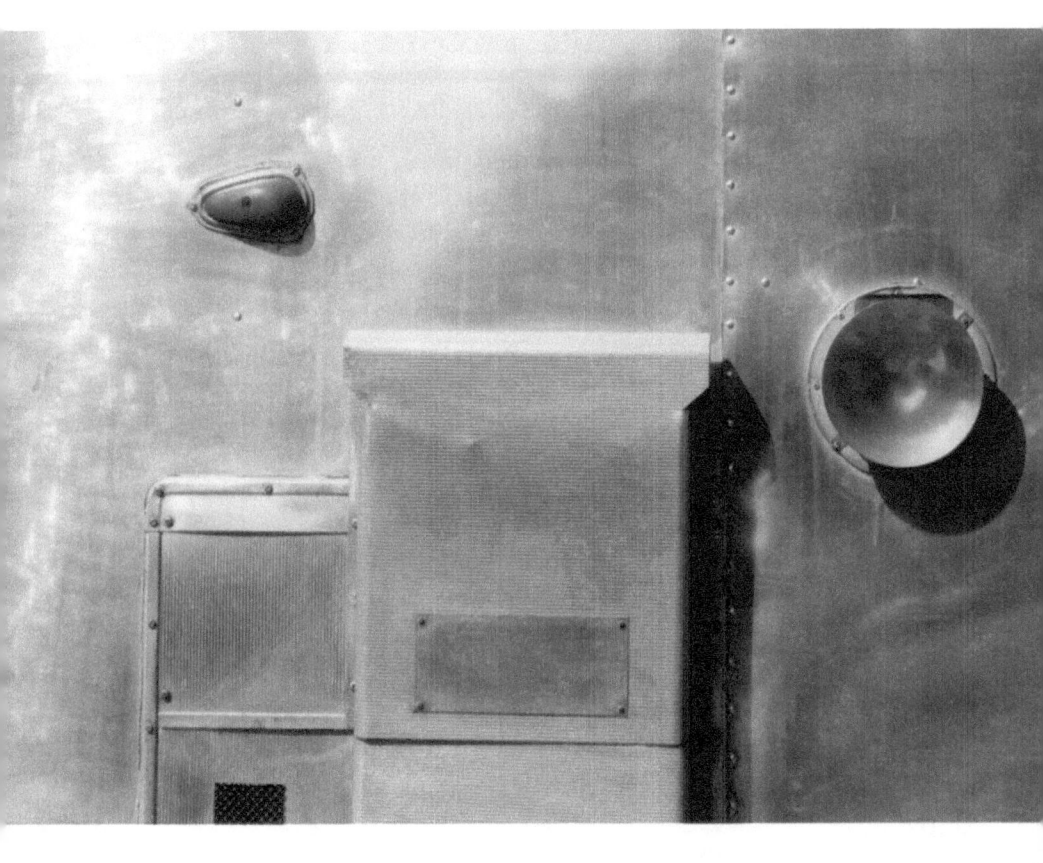

Richard Serra installed this steel slab on an artificial hill made of overburdened rock from the surrounding coal mines in the *Ruhrzone* in Germany. Climbing up the steep hill and arriving at the sculpture seemed preternatural, especially at the moment the sun was breaking through the clouds.

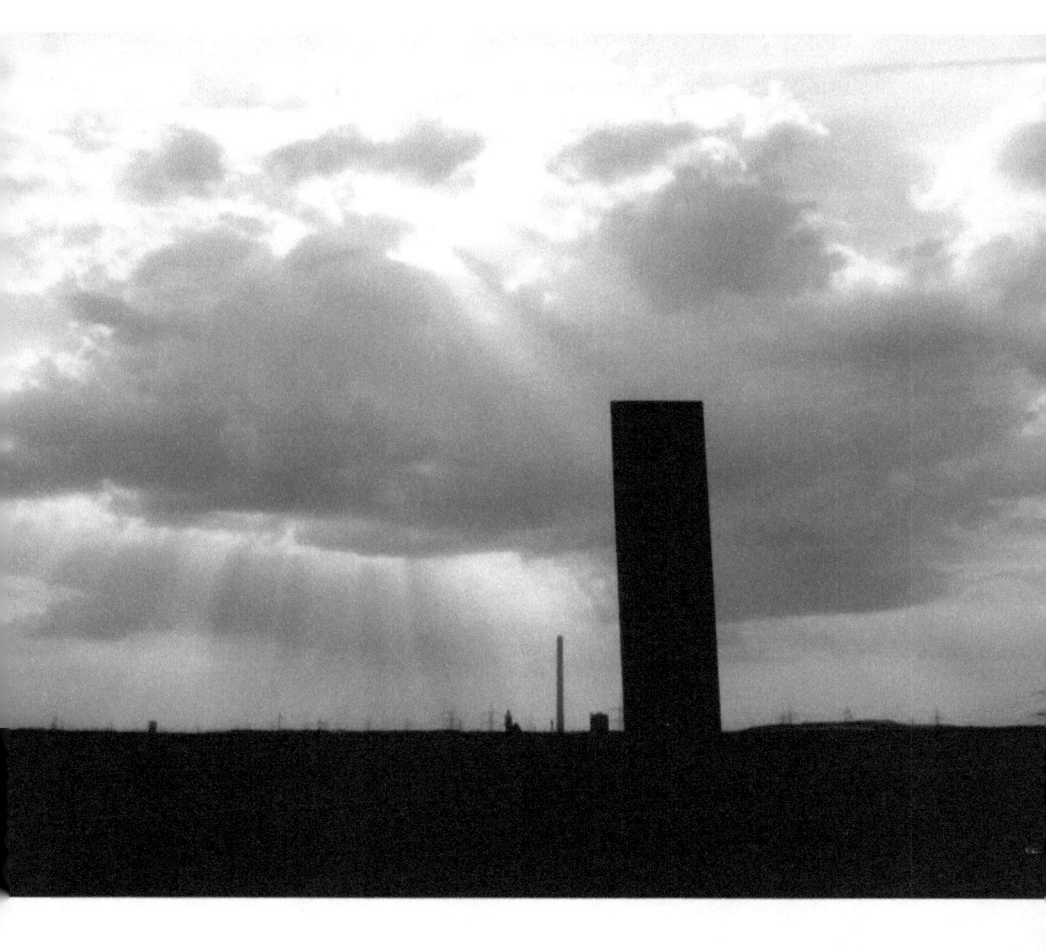

Upon arrival at the Mount Palomar Observatory near San Diego it was already closed for the day, so I never saw the interior. The enormous glistening helmet in the landscape made the trip worthwhile, though.

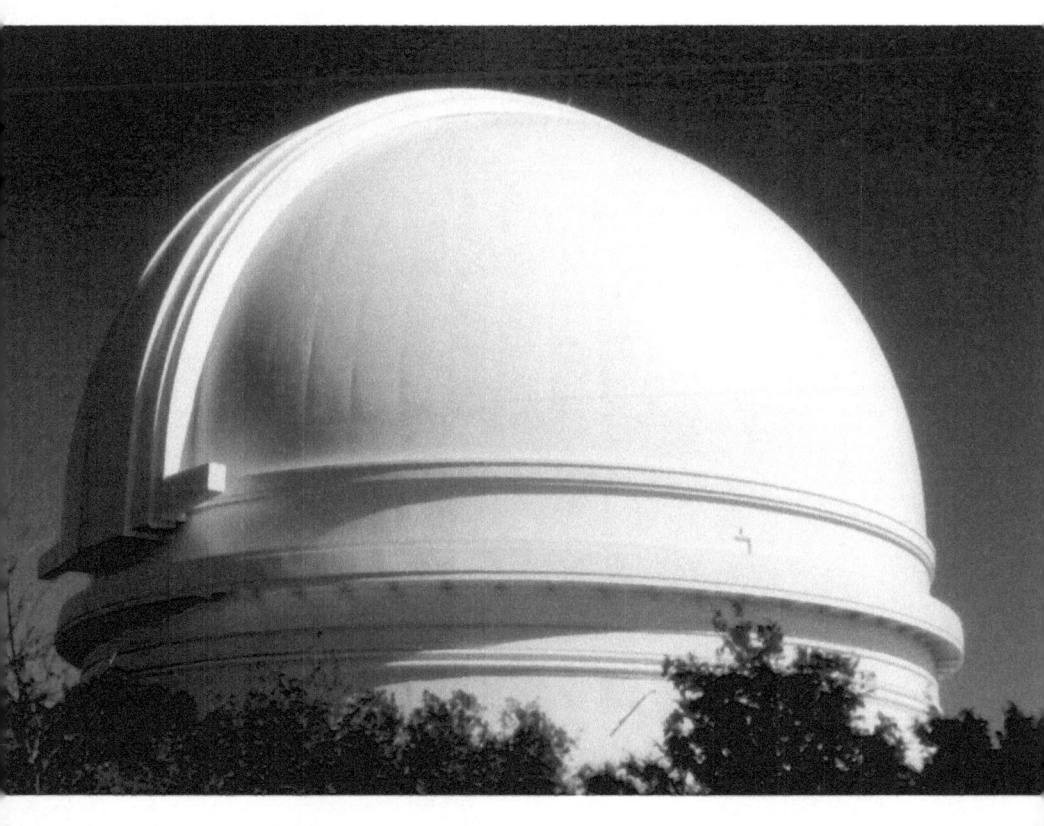

Just outside Alamosa, Colorado, on the road to Taos, stands this steam-locomotive-water-tower-cum-water kettle. It's definitely an architectural duck.

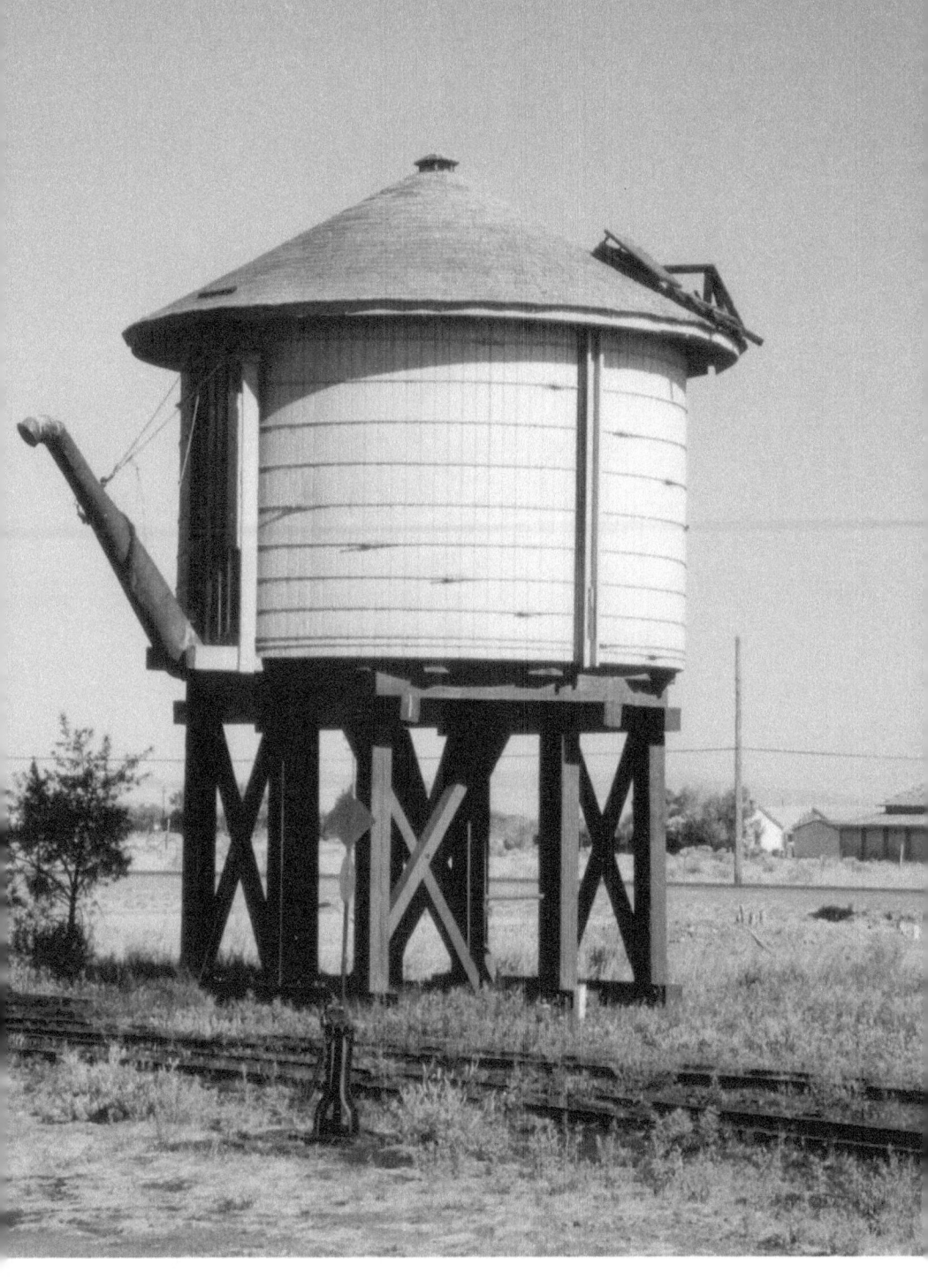

The support structure of the roller dam in Davenport reminds me of ancient Egyptian architecture, or petrified elephants.

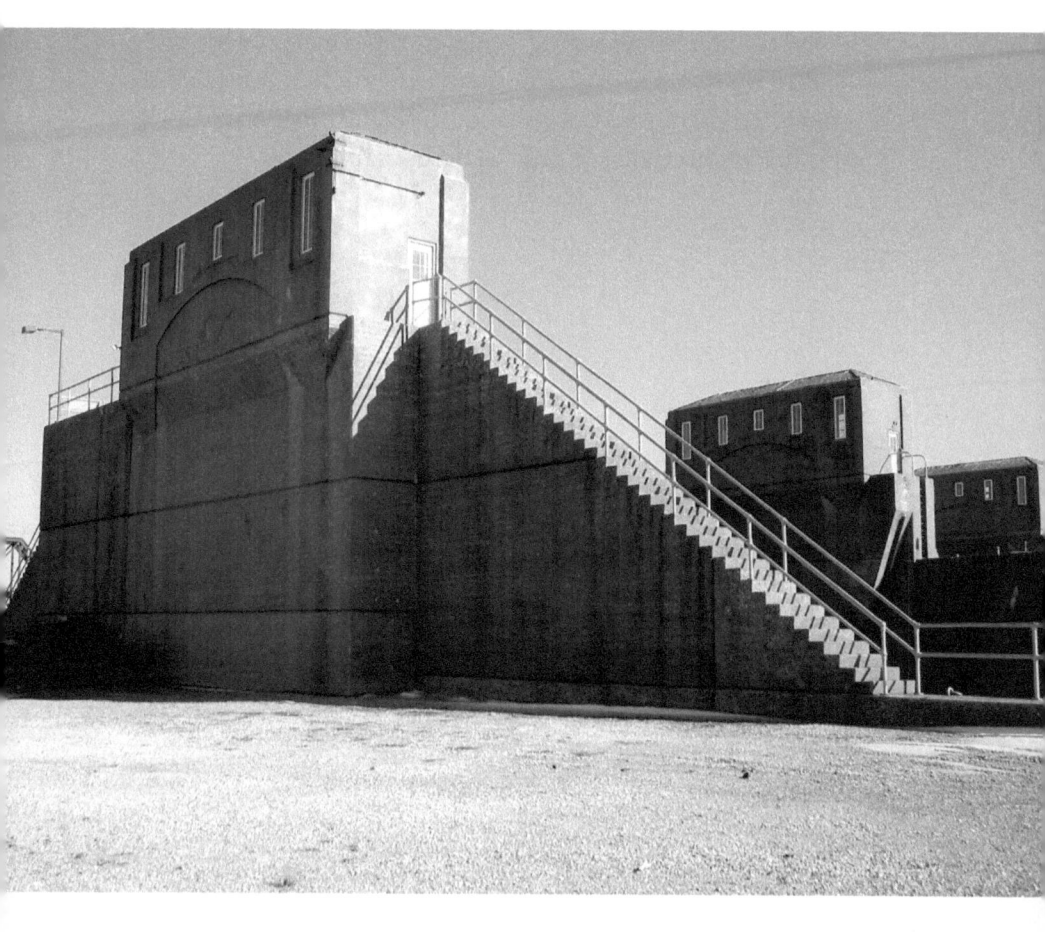

After our commune period in Entrup, Germany in the early 1980s, we bought a series of small construction trailers and converted them into outposts for different functions. This one was my studio trailer (I used to do oil paintings).

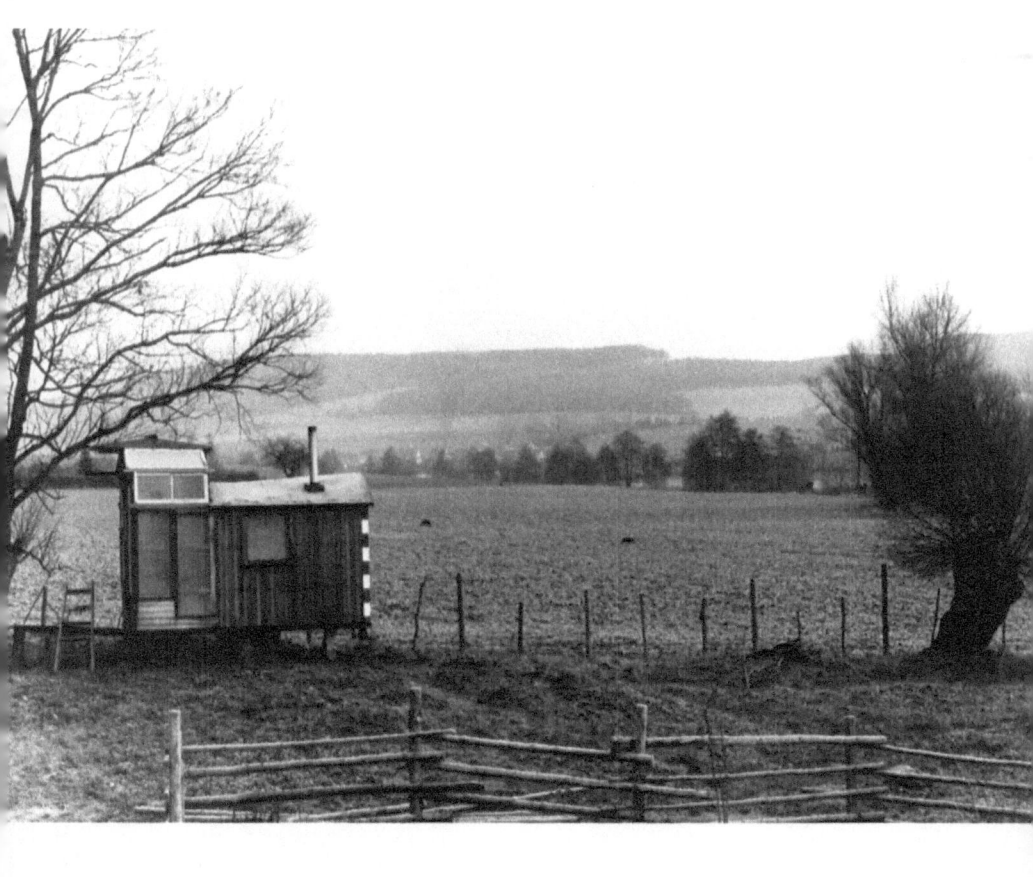

MOBILITY

Cedar Key, Florida. Seeing an inaccessible artificial island in the bay is all that our imagination needs to travel in our heads.

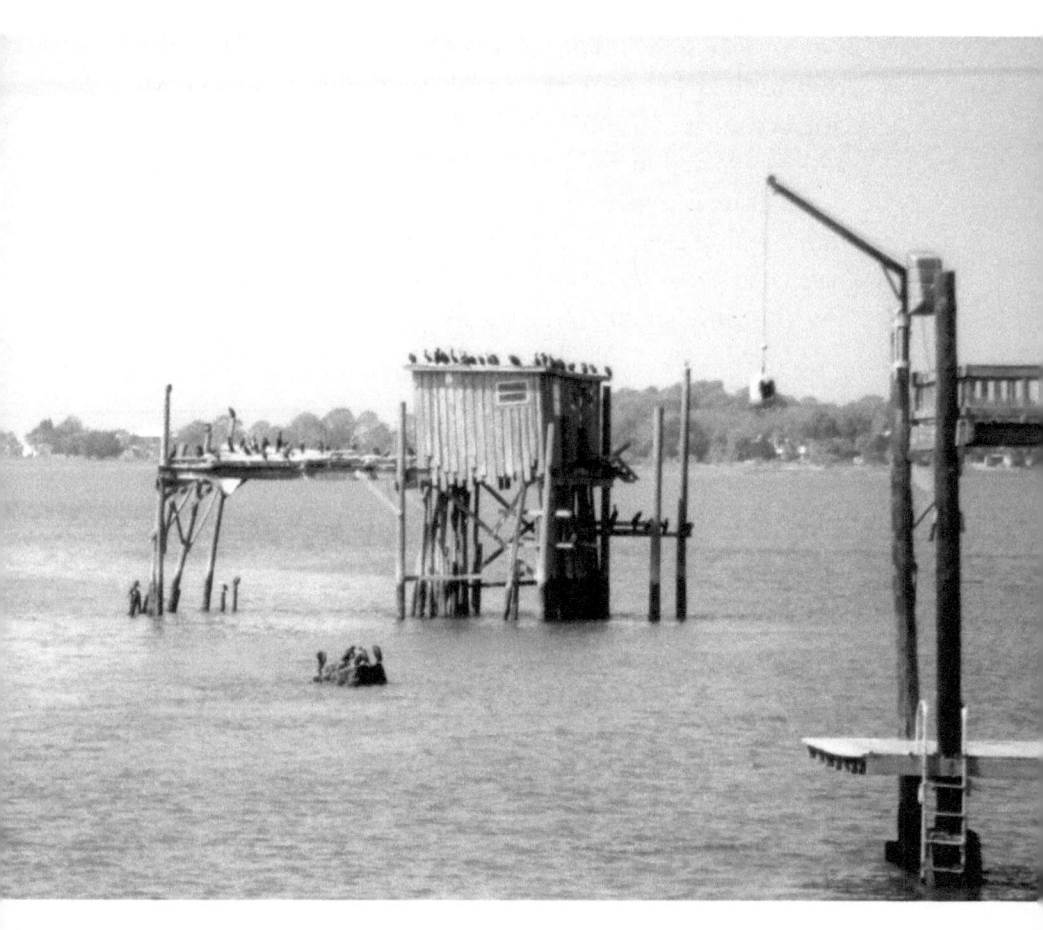

On the way from Rome (Italy) to Vals (Switzerland), the contrast between materials is striking. I made this trip twice. The first time in 2000—with Jeff Balmer, Katleen Wouters, and Ken Wood in a rented Ford KA—when we almost slid down a snow-covered mountain road and died because we didn't realize that even the Swiss need some time after a particularly wet snow shower to clean the secondary roads. But this time, in 2002, the weather gods were smiling.

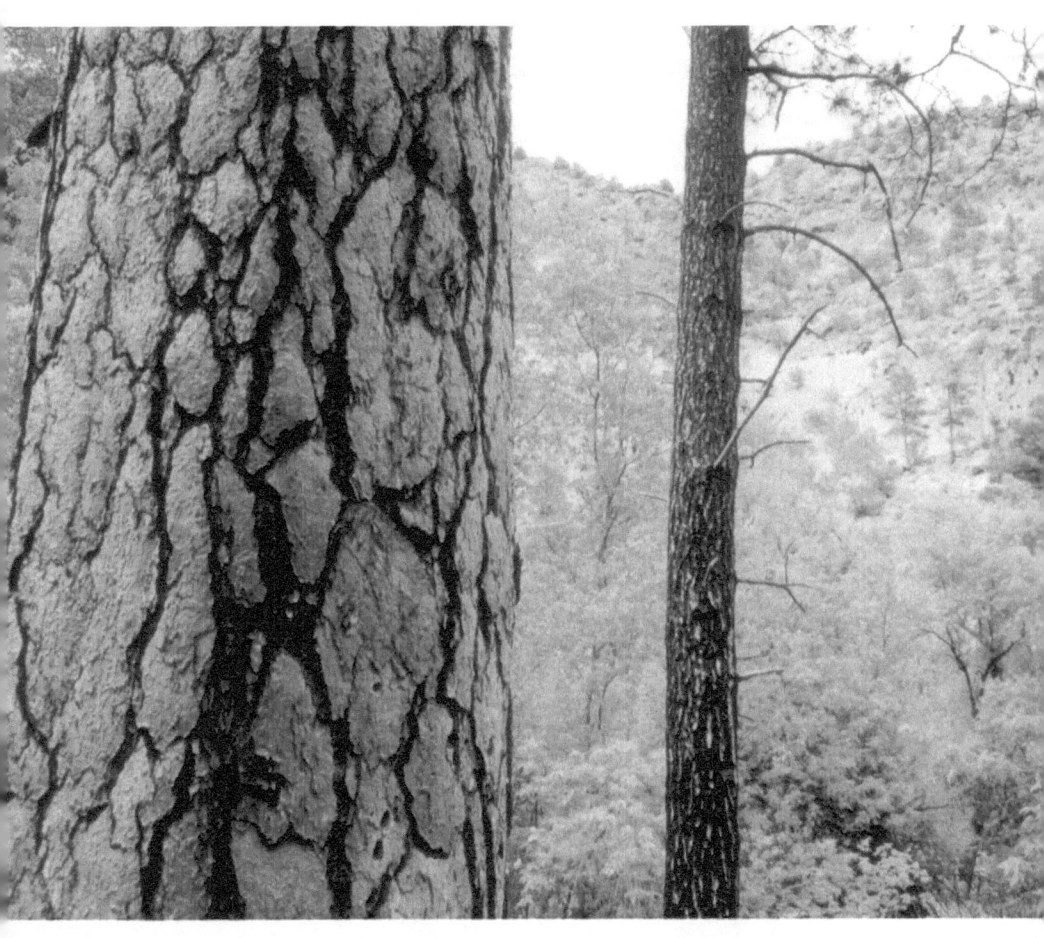

This 1963 Bambi Airstream trailer belonged to a dude who, perhaps, *still* lives in his silver bullet somewhere in southern California.

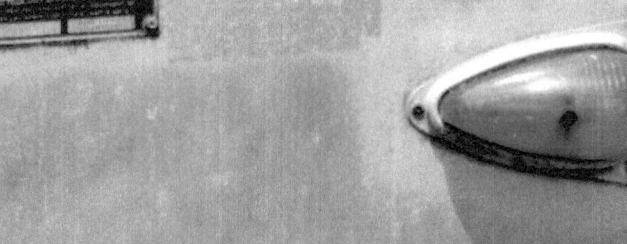

OBSERVATIONS

In Iowa, on cool fall days, when the leaves have already turned, lying on the back in a meadow and looking up into the sky—accompanied by two standard poodles—is divine.

As we drove down the Rhine valley to visit an old friend in Switzerland, we saw an Autobahn exit sign to Baden Baden. My mom had never been, and the next thing I noticed were these angels looking down at the city from the rooftops. We were not in Berlin anymore.

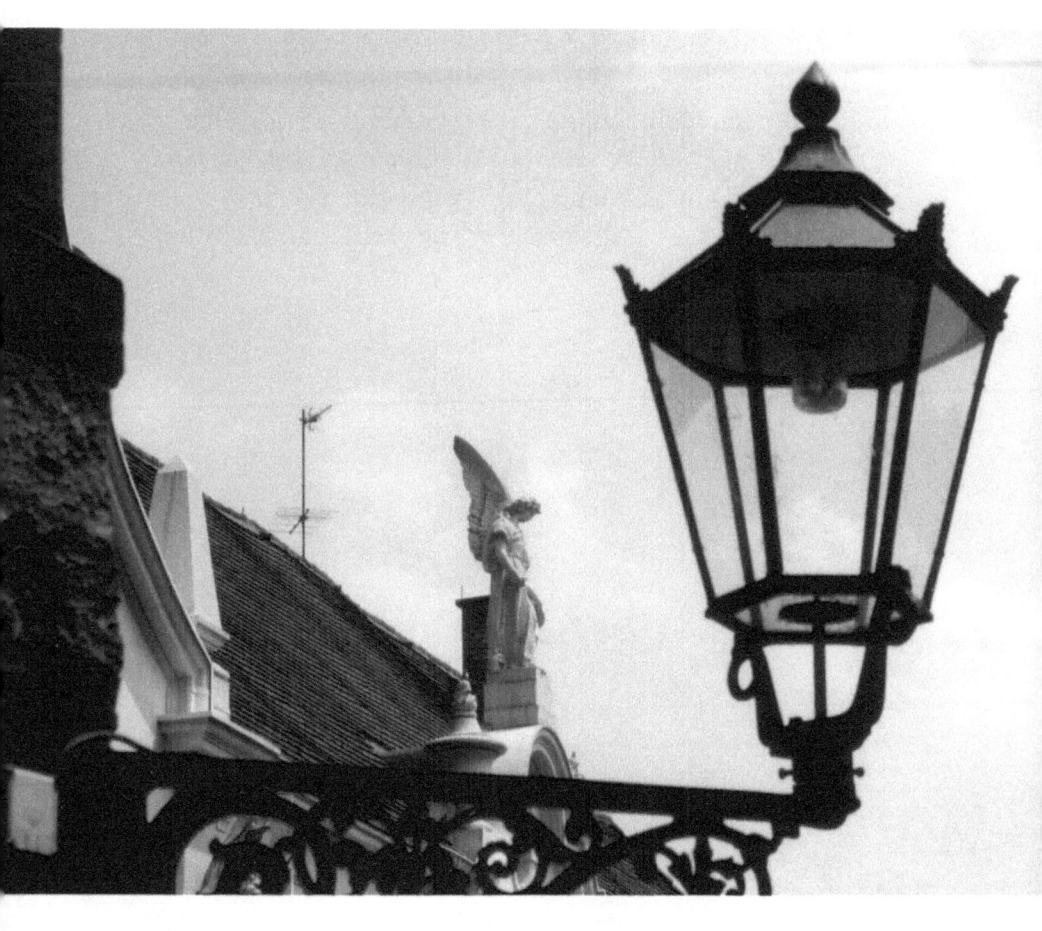

There is much to be learned about how a country responds to its ruins. Here some frugal mind figured out how to temporarily support the crumbling facade of the *Reichsluftfahrtministerium* (one of those long German words that actually means something; in this case it is the German Aviation Ministry), designed by Ernst Sagel in the 1930s in Berlin.

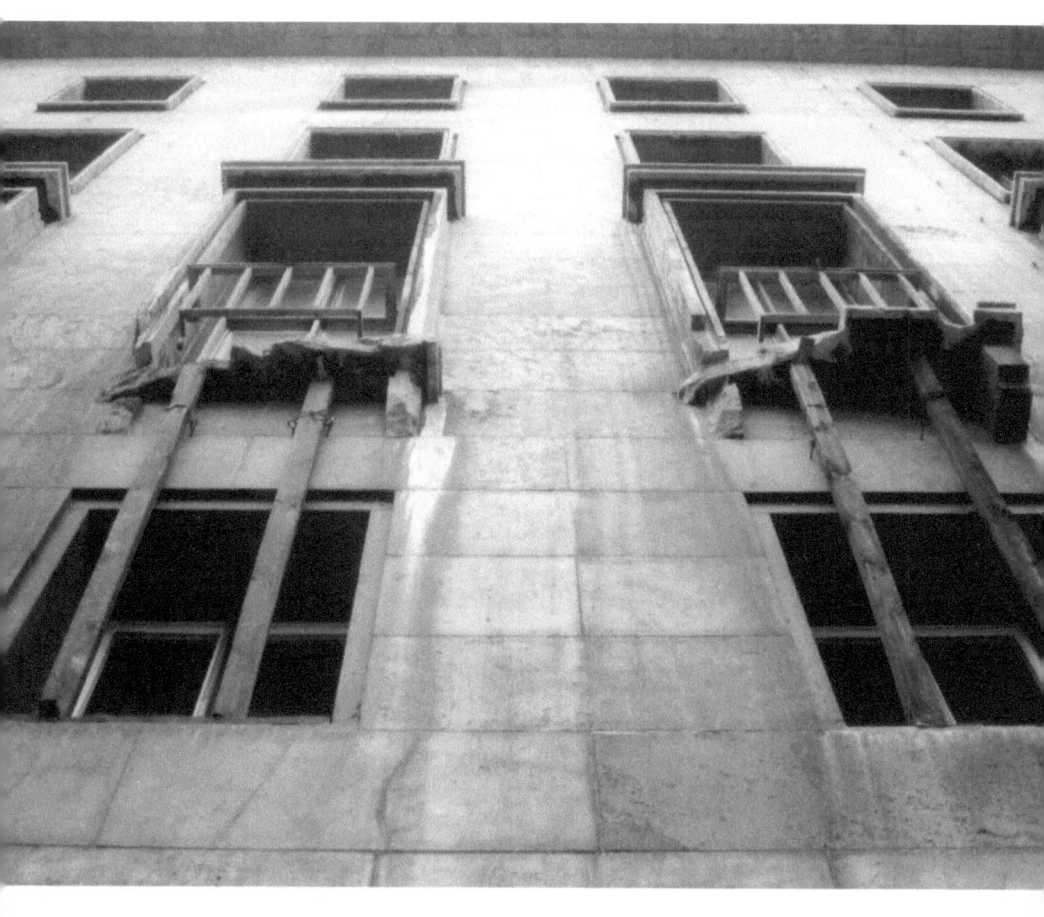

That the citizens of Hollywood live in fear is advertized at the curb of their homes.

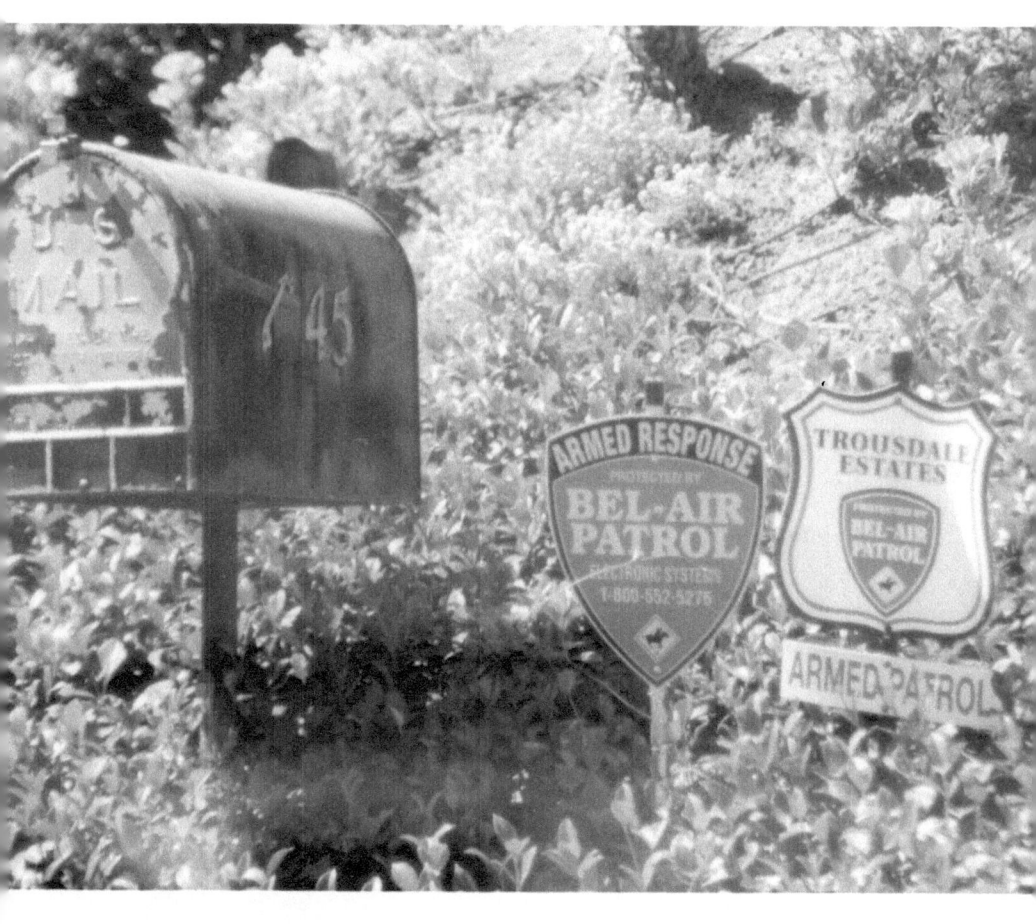

The Chicago 'L' system dates back to 1892. As architects we are quite fascinated by raw structures. The jumble of lines that hold up the space-making surfaces around us seem to reassure us with their repetitiveness.

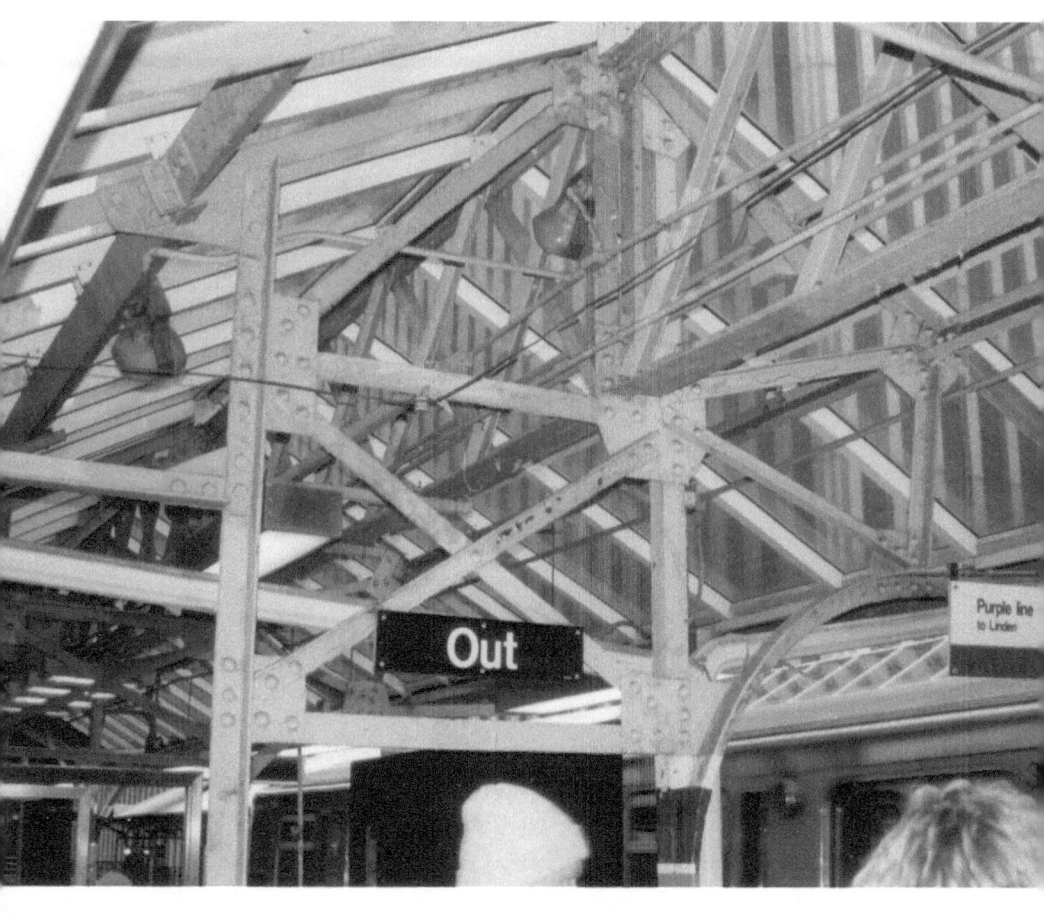

Observations 191

To the ancient Greeks the word *kosmos* meant world order and ornament. It was odd to see the English version, *COSMOS*, inscribed on the side of a vintage WWII fighter plane at the Strategic Air Command Museum in Omaha.

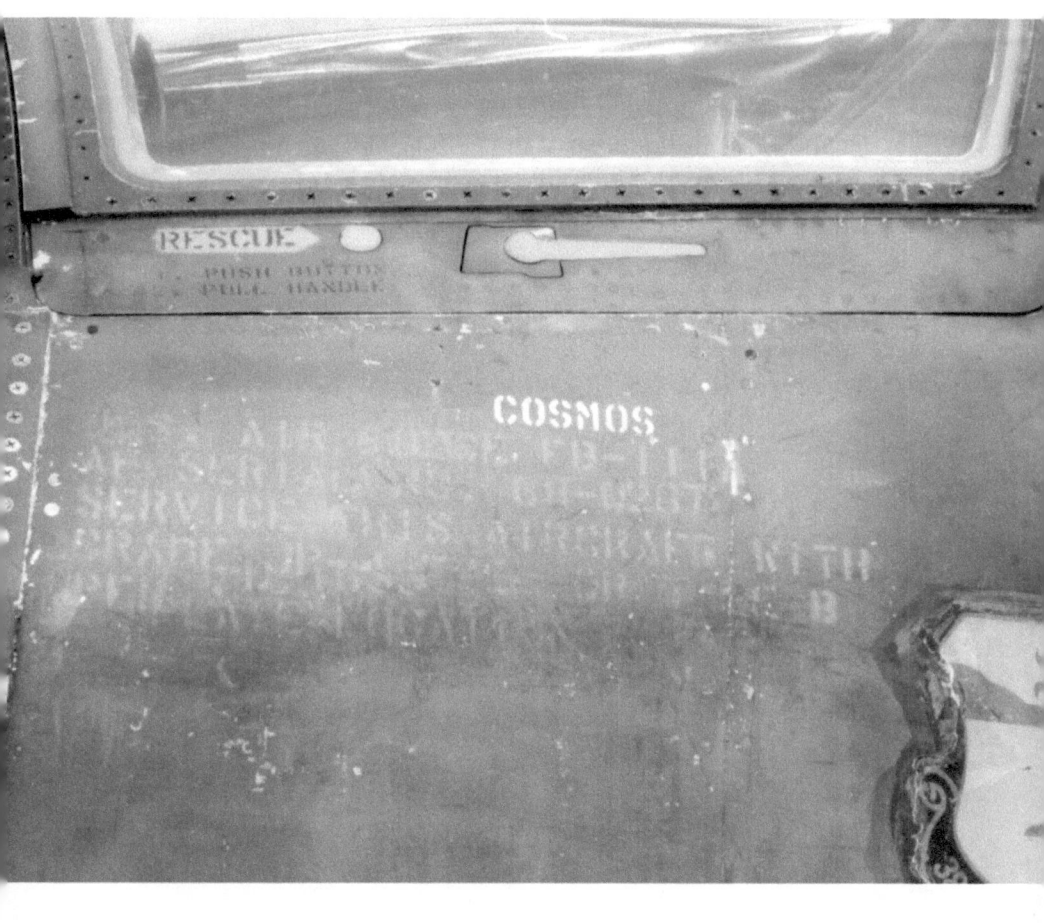

The University of Florida maintains a Marine Biology Research Laboratory on Seahorse Key, a small island off of Cedar Key in the Gulf of Mexico. The students live in an old lighthouse on the ridge of the island. We visited on a lazy Saturday in February, and the place seemed to ask us to stay for a while.

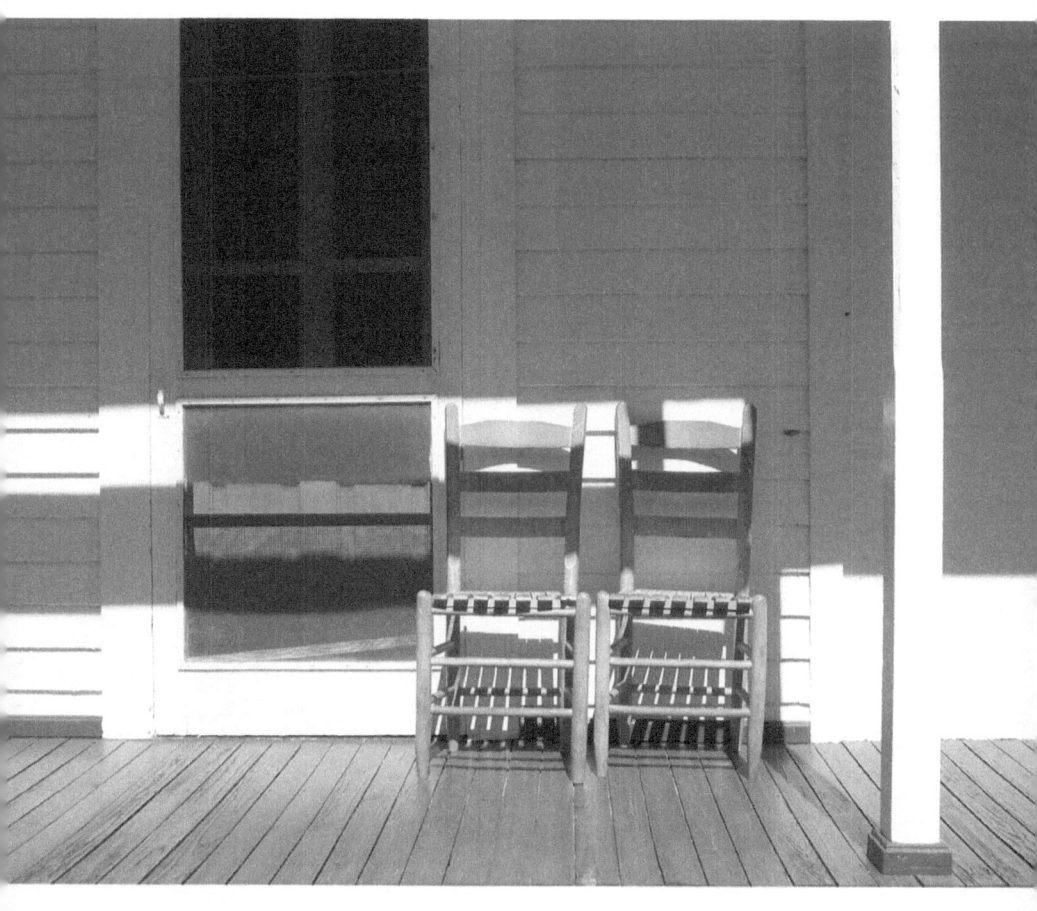

Observations 195

It never ceases to amaze me how some designs of objects that have no functional or historical precedent end up with anthropomorphic references that mirror some aspect of ourselves. It is as if, in the absence of familiarity, we have to return to what is familiar, even if it looks slightly strange. This little morsel with a helmet and an appropriate name, the Goblin XF-85, was parked on the tarmac outside the old Strategic Air Command Museum in Omaha, Nebraska.

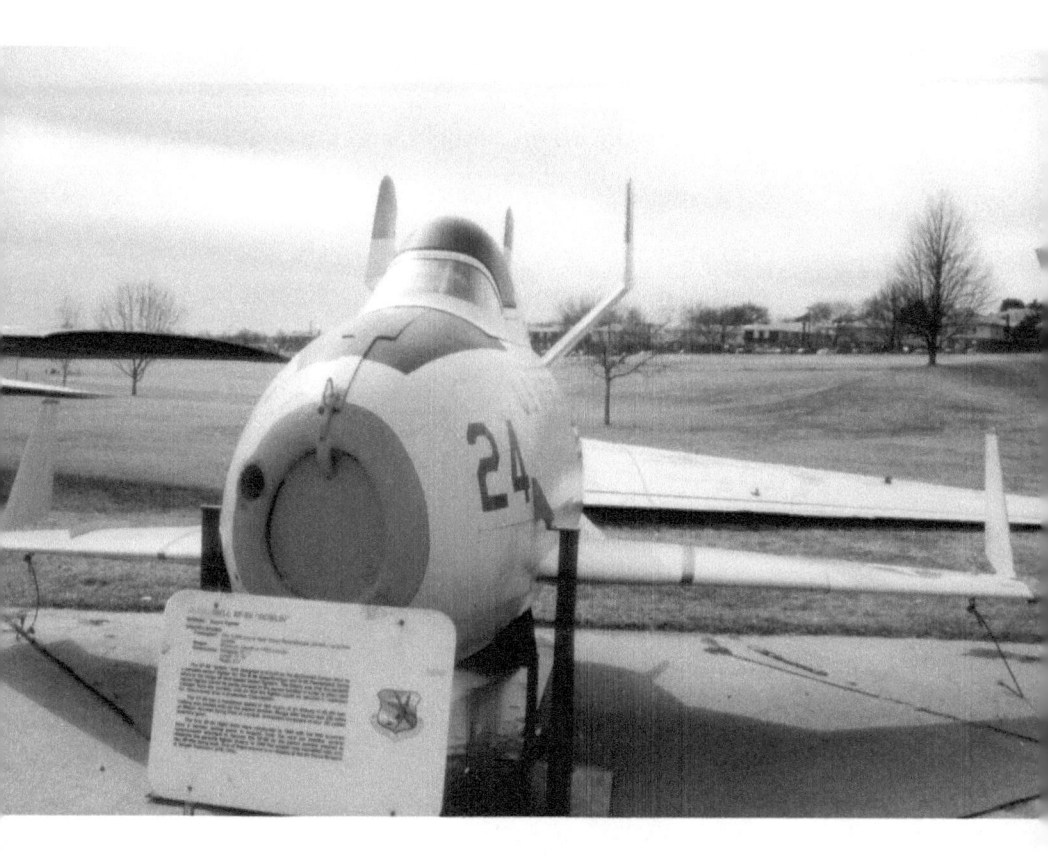

Observations 197

On those rare occasions when the air is full of humidity on a crisp winter morning, the smallest limbs high up in the trees begin to glisten in the bright sunlight, and the branch tips turn into brilliant light reflectors.

According to our research no men will be flipping matresses in your motel room today.

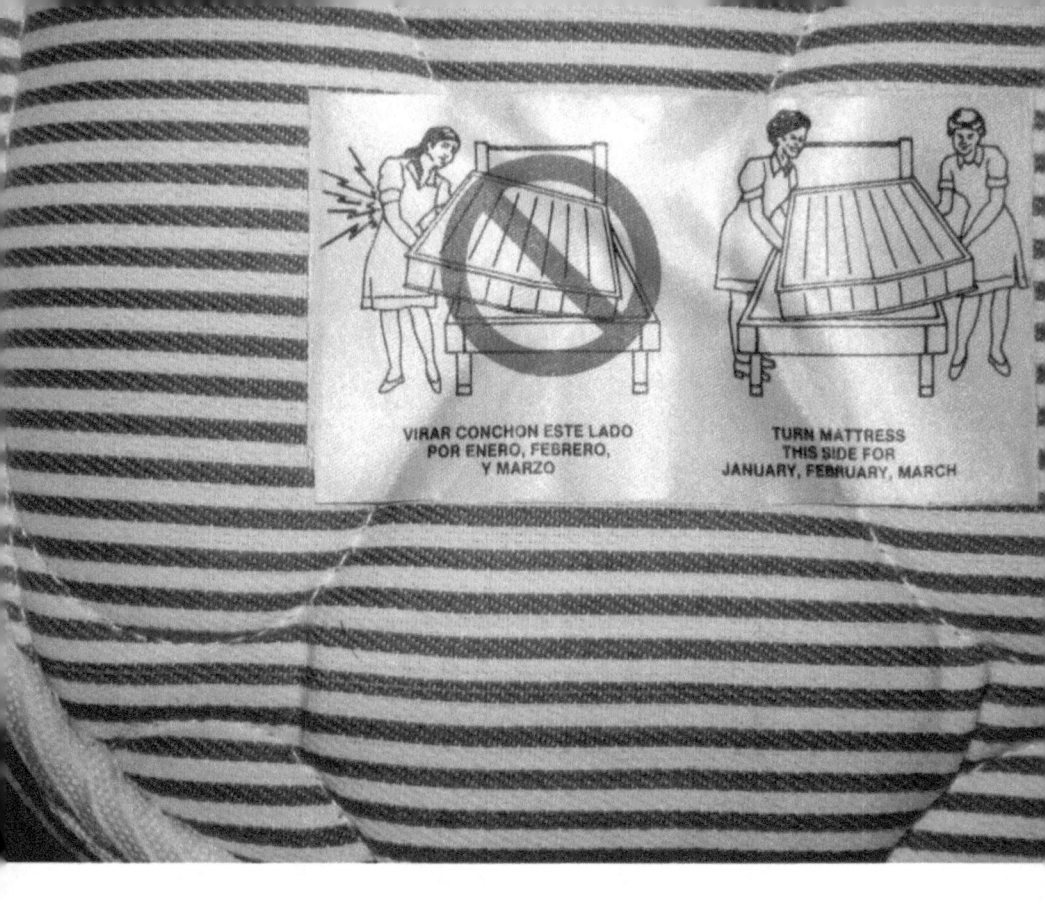

It was a late summer day and we drove from Stein, Aargau (Switzerland) to Rheinfelden (Germany) for dinner. The sun was low on the horizon, bouncing off some dense cumulus clouds, creating one of those rare moments when the light makes everything glow, including a contemporary Catholic church clad in stainless steel.

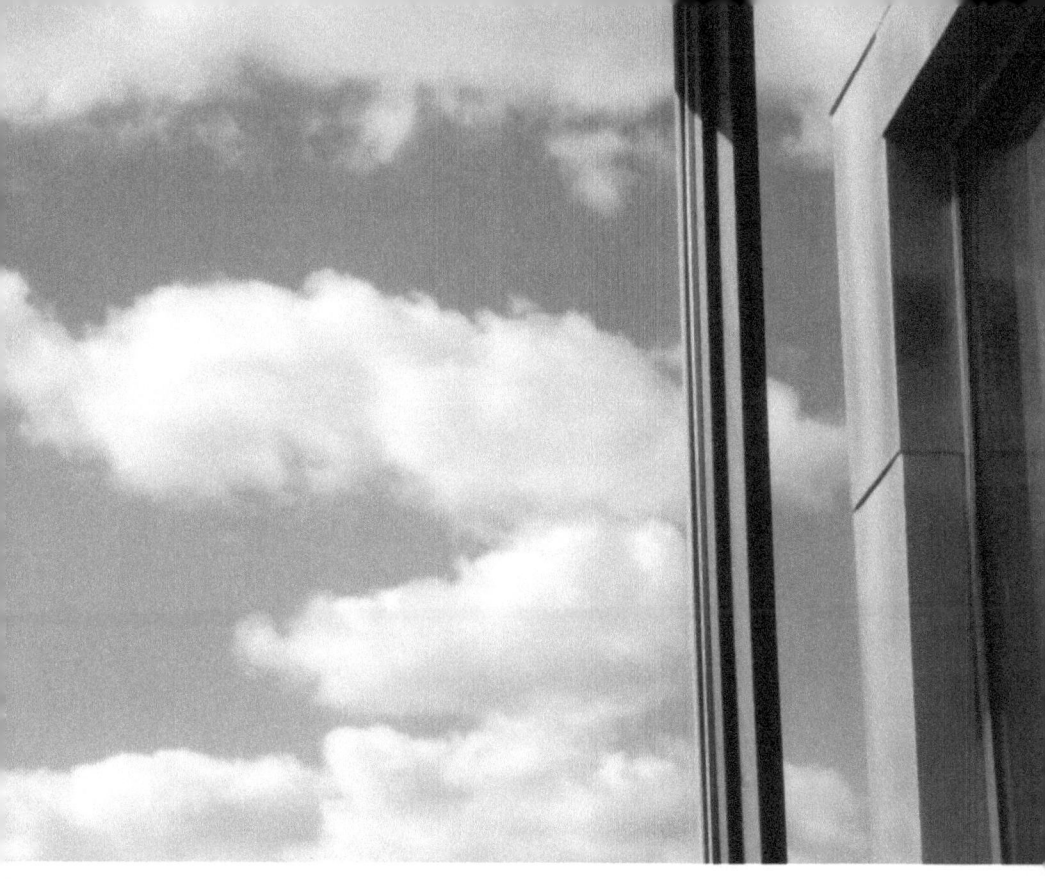

The palm tree didn't seem to pay attention (neither did the finial on the tower) as the moon ascended over Balboa Park in San Diego.

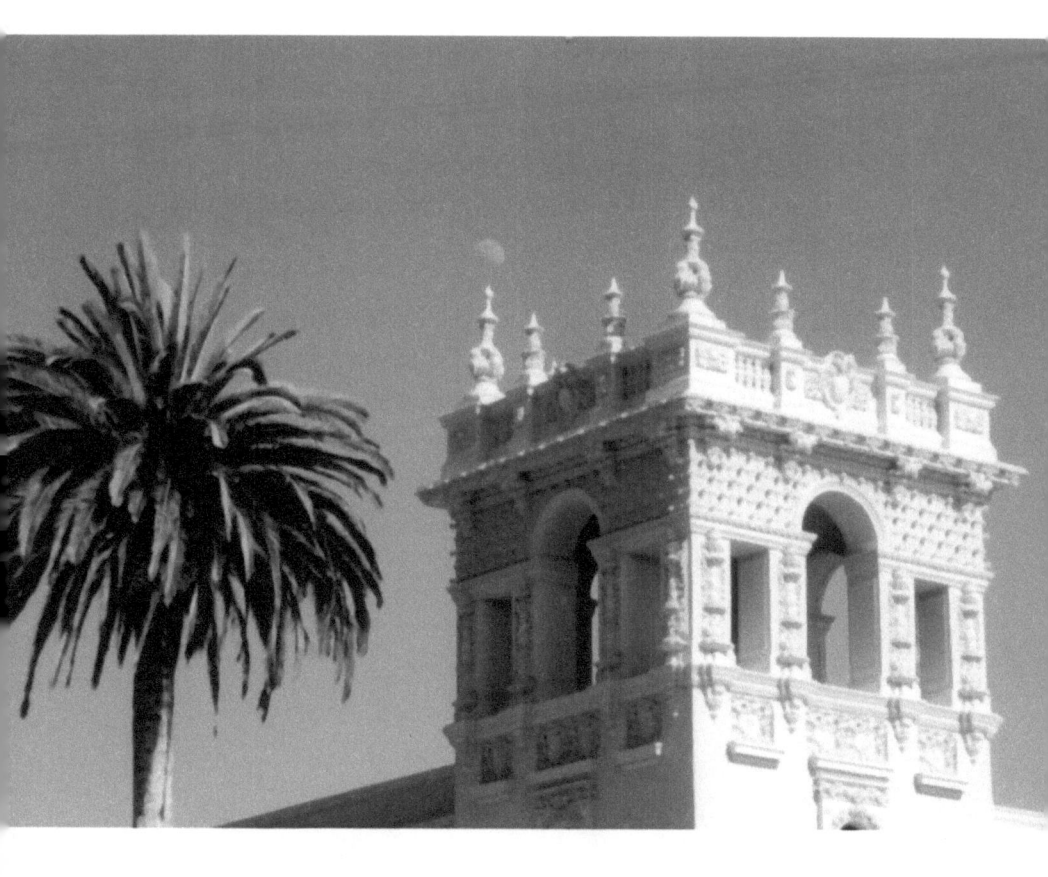

I'm still not sure why there is a full-scale replica of the undestroyed Parthenon in Nashville, Tennessee. When I finally stopped to take a look in the late 1990s, the building was being renovated and chicken wire covered the pediment sculptures which did not seem be happy being caged like common fowl.

2015 Update: I now know that the building was constructed in 1897 as part of the Tennessee Centennial Exhibition, and it played an important role at the end of Robert Altman's 1975 epic movie 'Nashville'.

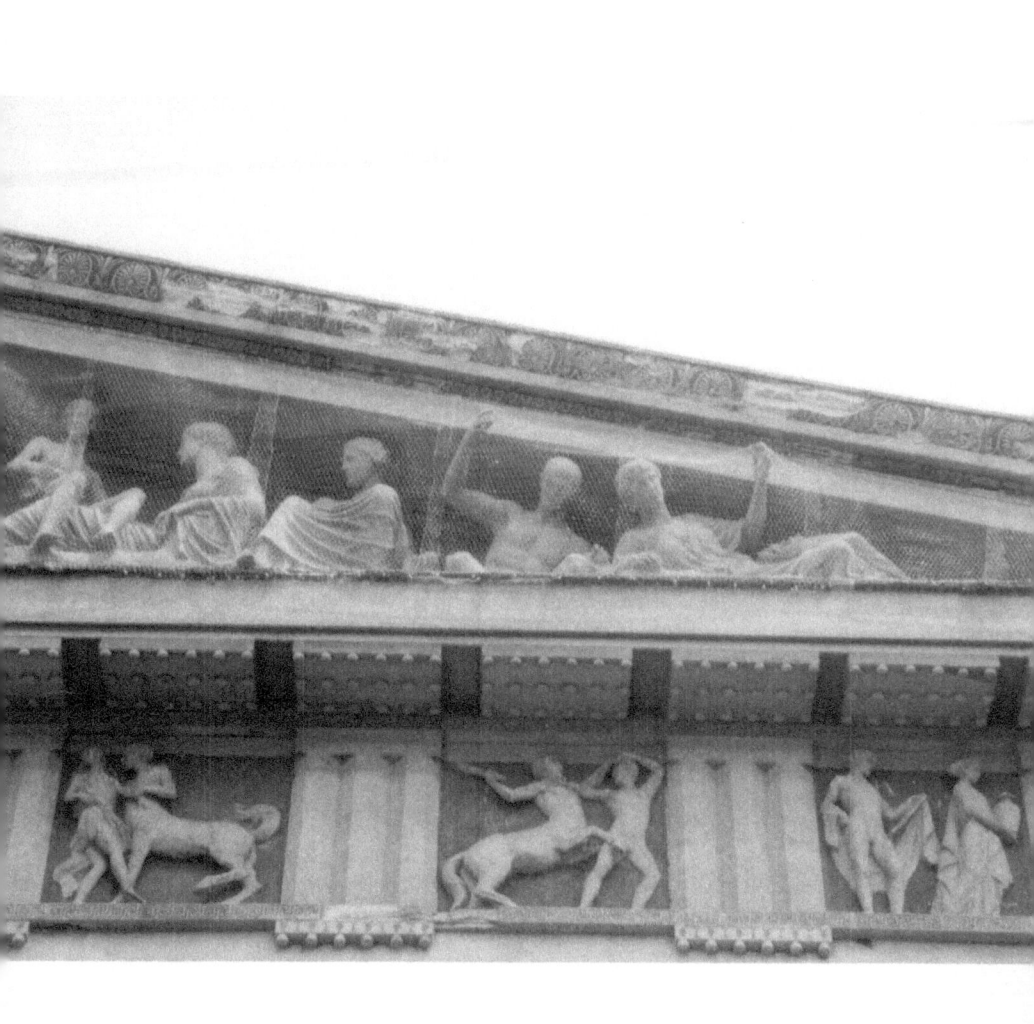

"Hey, Athena, look at this dance step! Care to tango?" said the golden boy on the right, in Sans Souci near Potsdam, Germany, but alas, Athena was not interested.

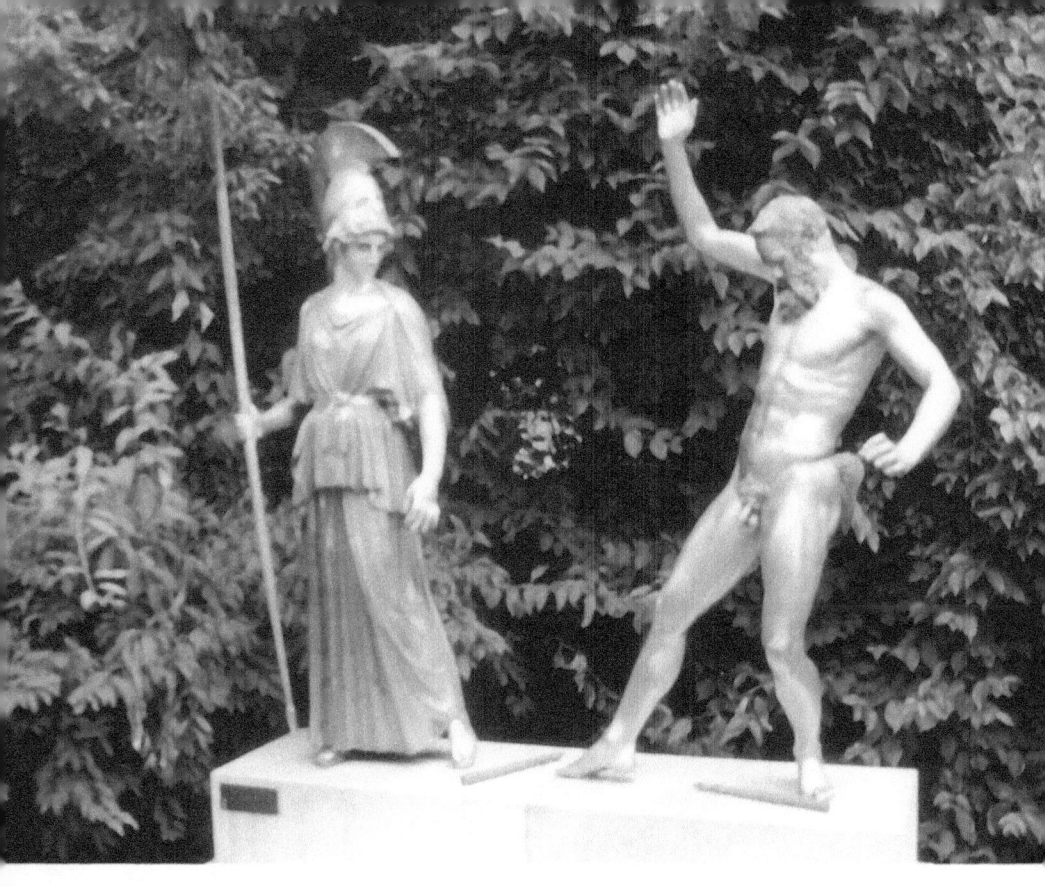

How it works: captured snow on a shallow stone-slab roof in the winter insulates the spaces below.

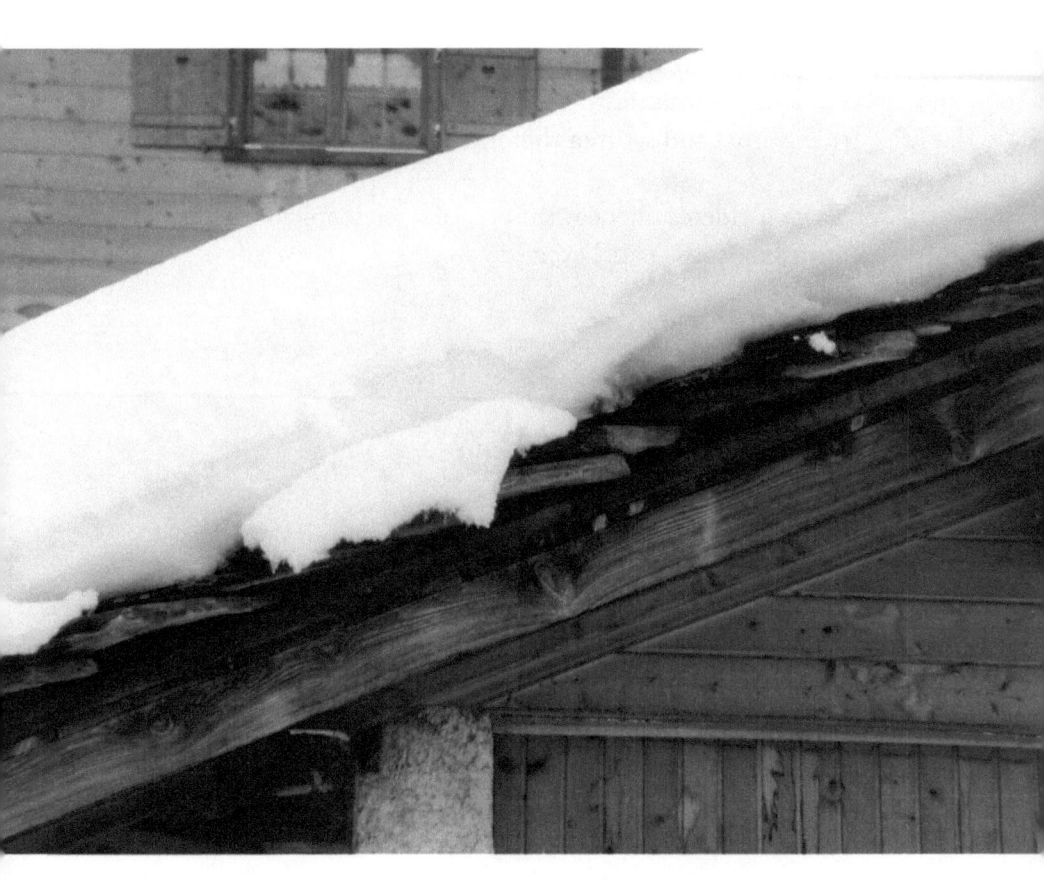

In the past few decades the Vatican has learned to utilize modern communications technology quite effectively. Until then verbal and written rhetoric had to suffice; and it did.

That's a video camera at the end of a telescopic boom recording some papal event.

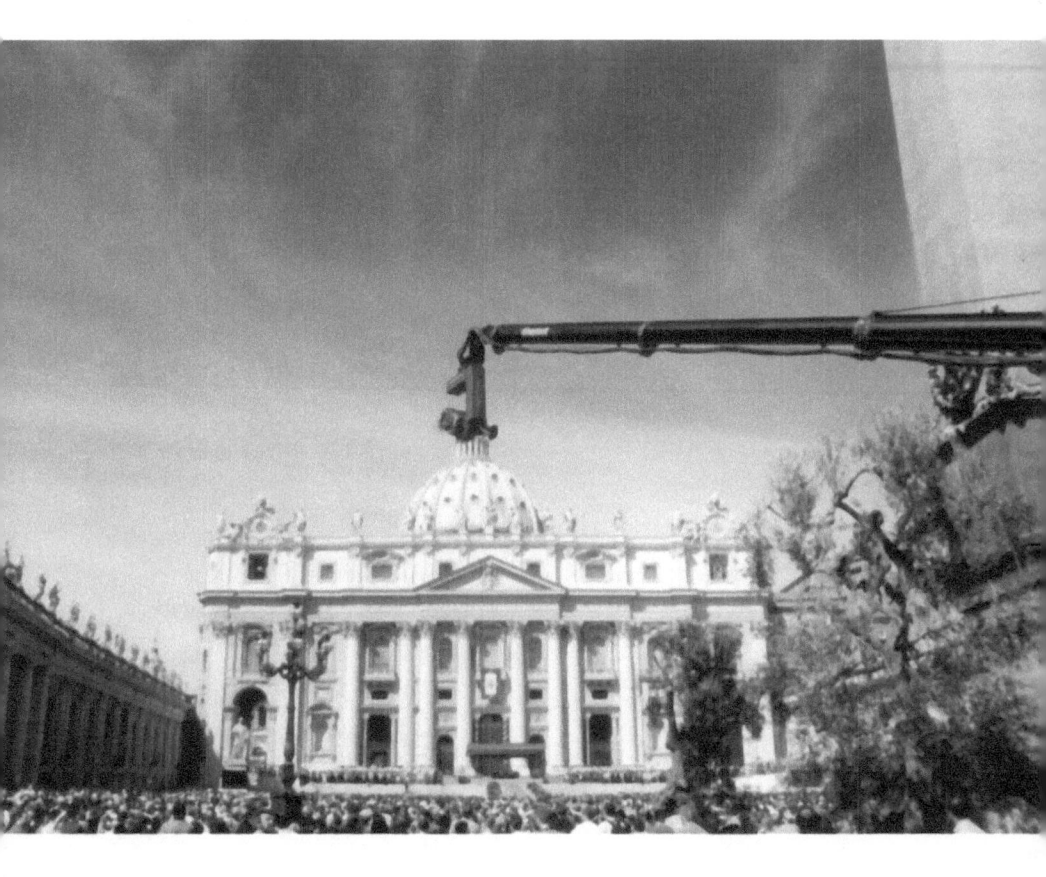

The firemen's bathroom mirror in Zaha Hadid's design for the Vitra fire station in Weil am Rhein, Germany, works only for humans of average height like myself. If you're below 6'-2" or above 7'-0" be prepared not to see yourself when cleaning up before or after a fire.

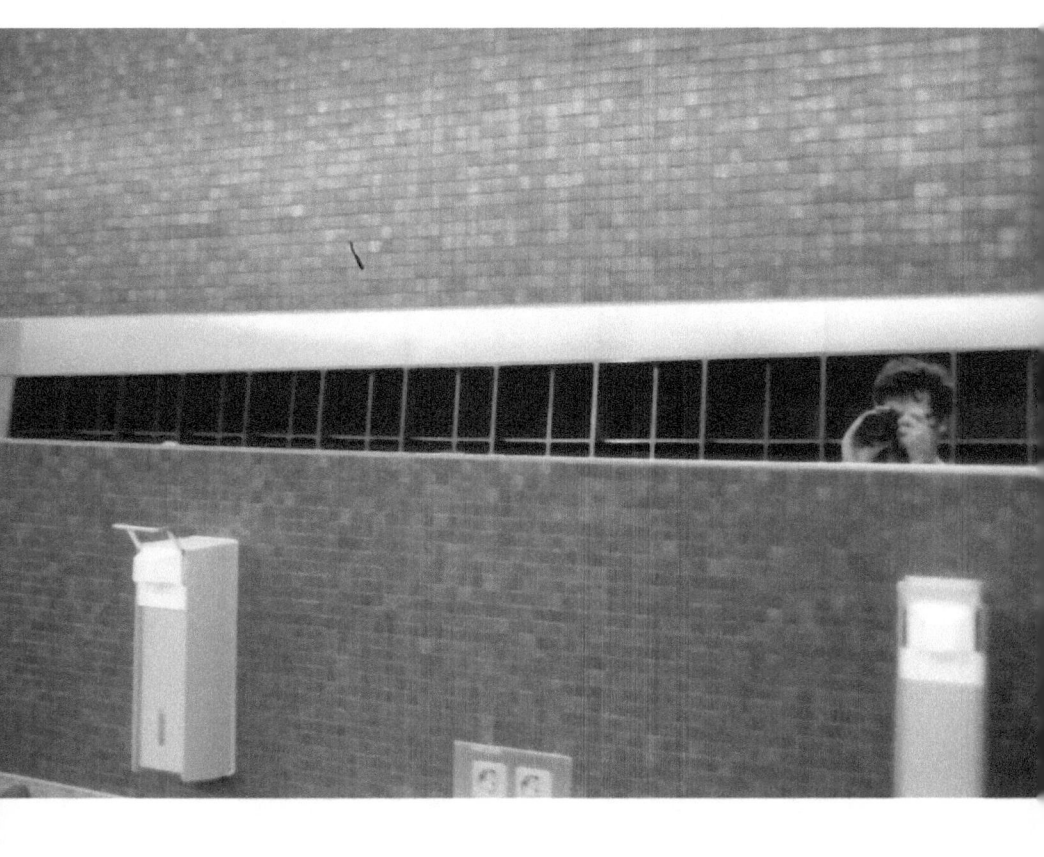

There are people who enjoy living on the edge, even when they are on vacation, especially if they're visiting the Danish island of Bornholm.

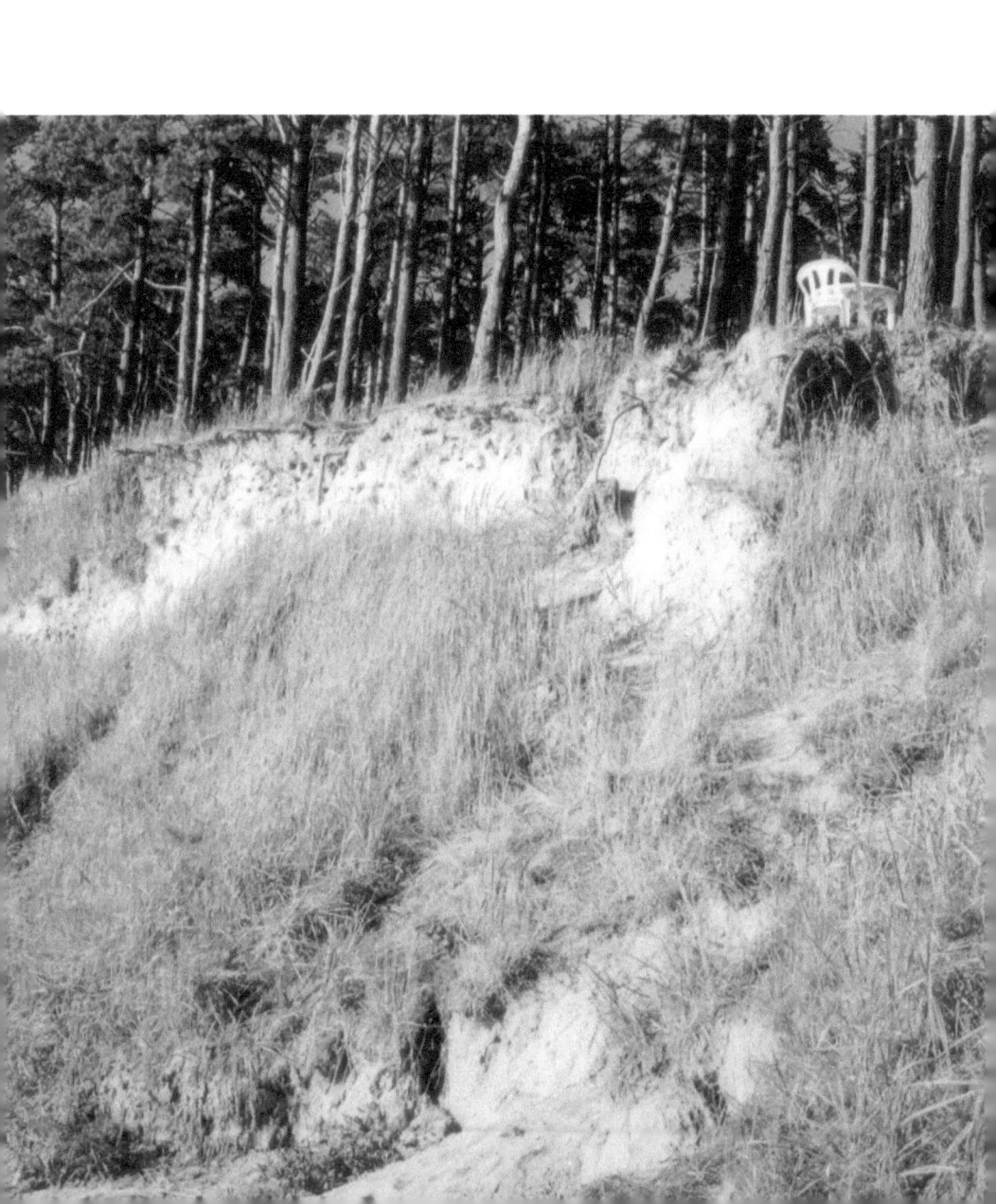

Some critics think that the Exeter Library by Louis Kahn seems burdened by too much spatial rigidity. This condition, if true, hardly distracts from the building's beauty and usability.

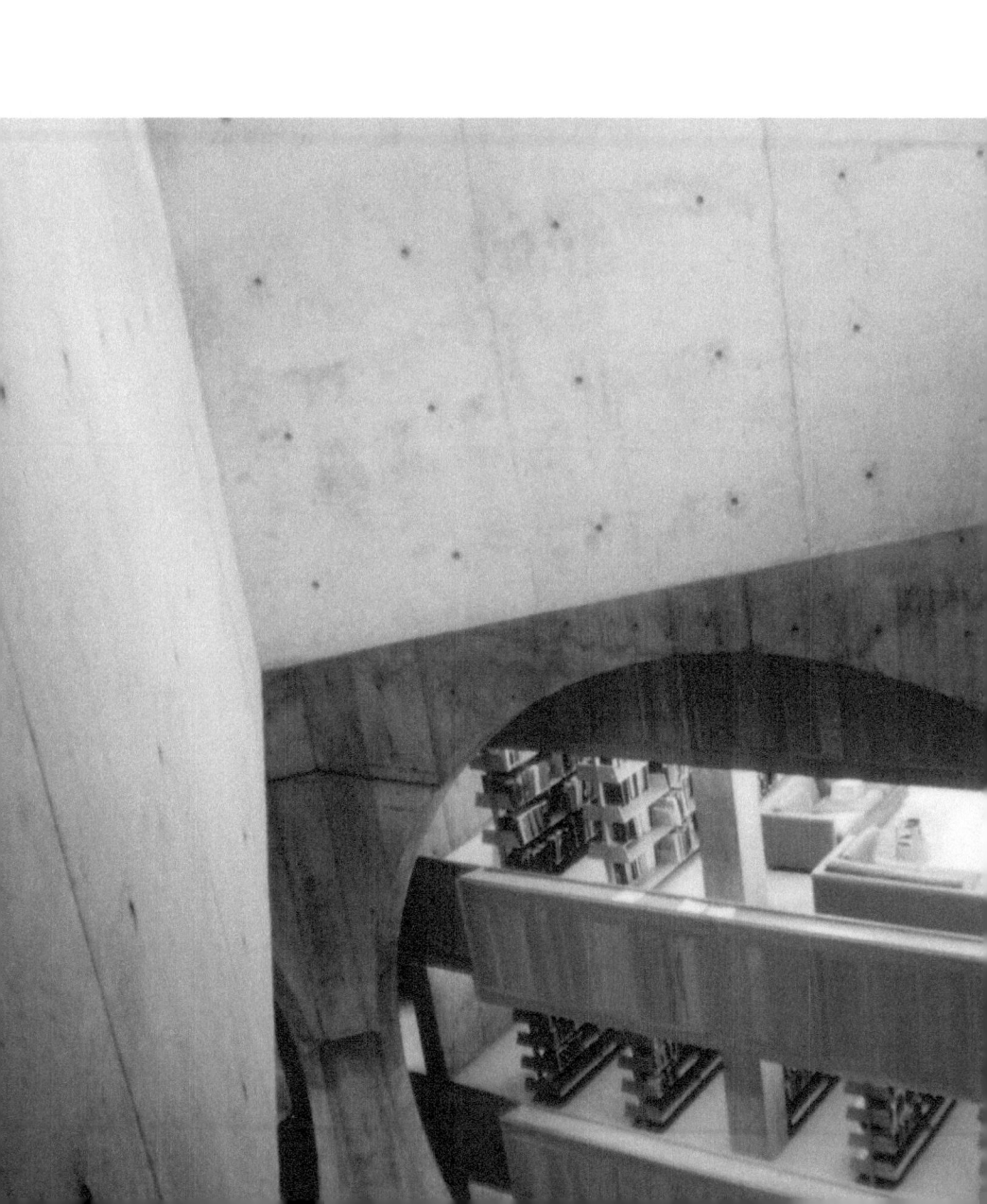

Bertram Goldberg knows how to make cars happy, as here in the Marina City Towers in Chicago.

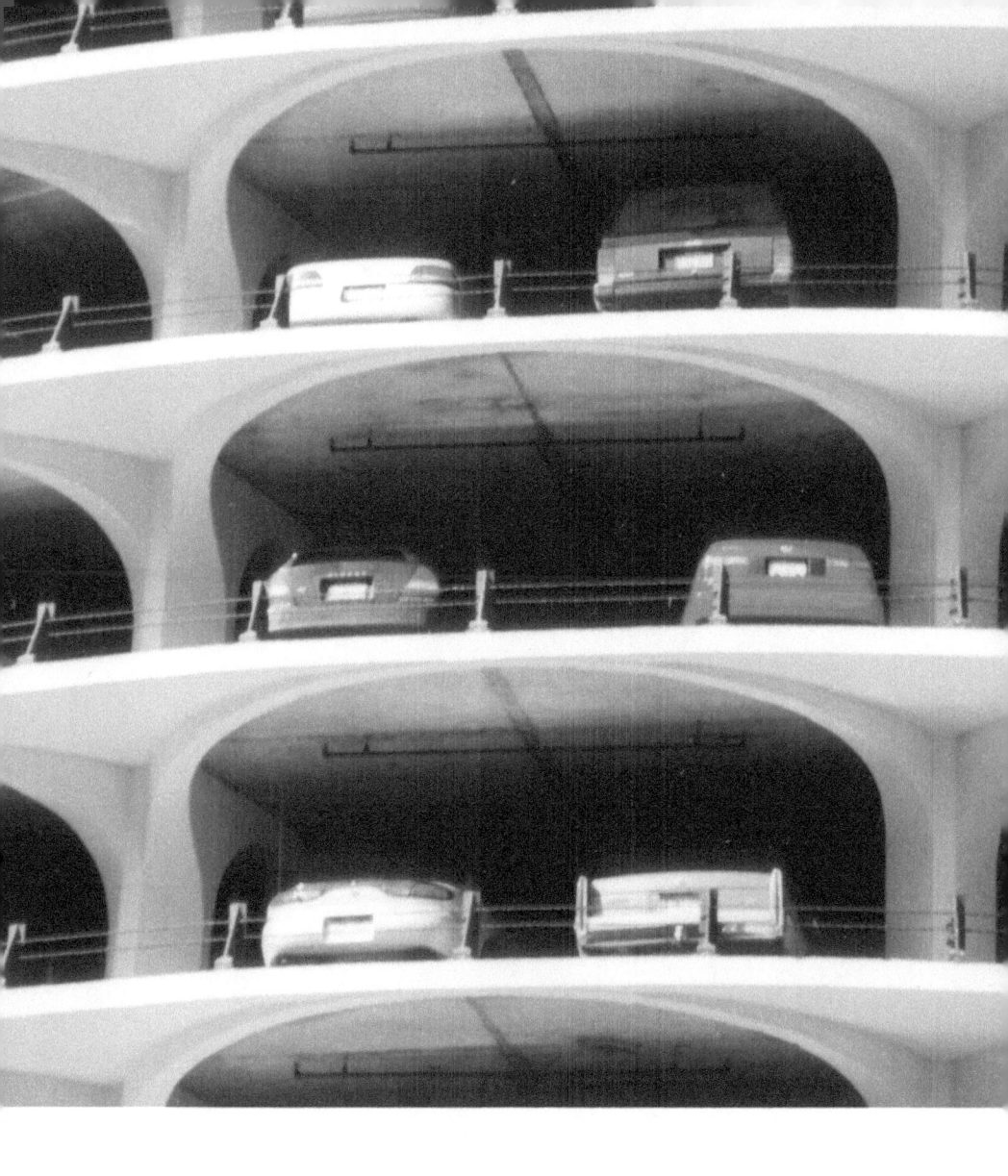

In 1995 we made a pilgrimage to the Gottfried Semper monument in Dresden, Germany. Gottfried needed cleaning then.

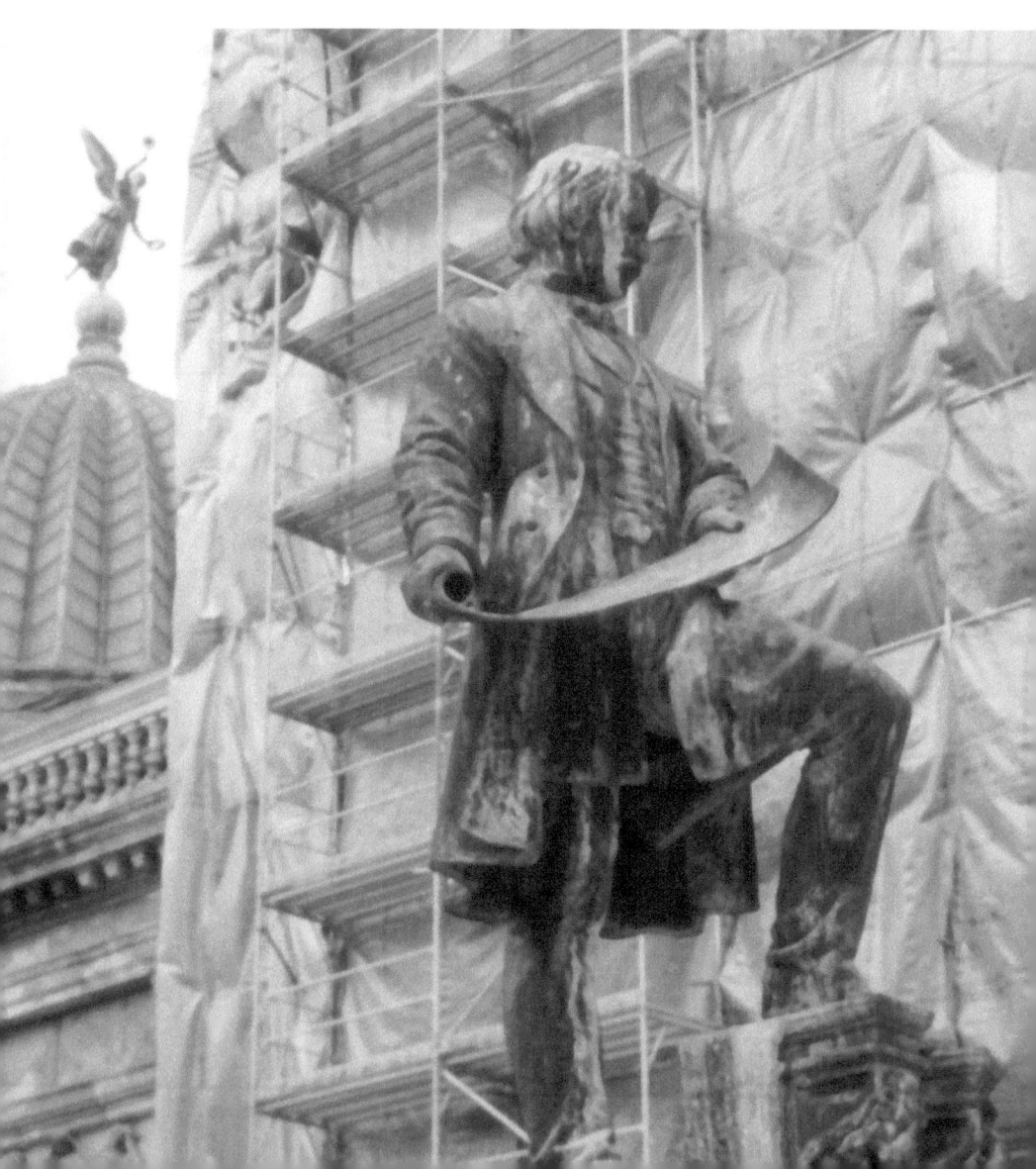

The interaction of clear water and light makes life worthwhile, especially on a hot spring day in a mountain village in the Alps.

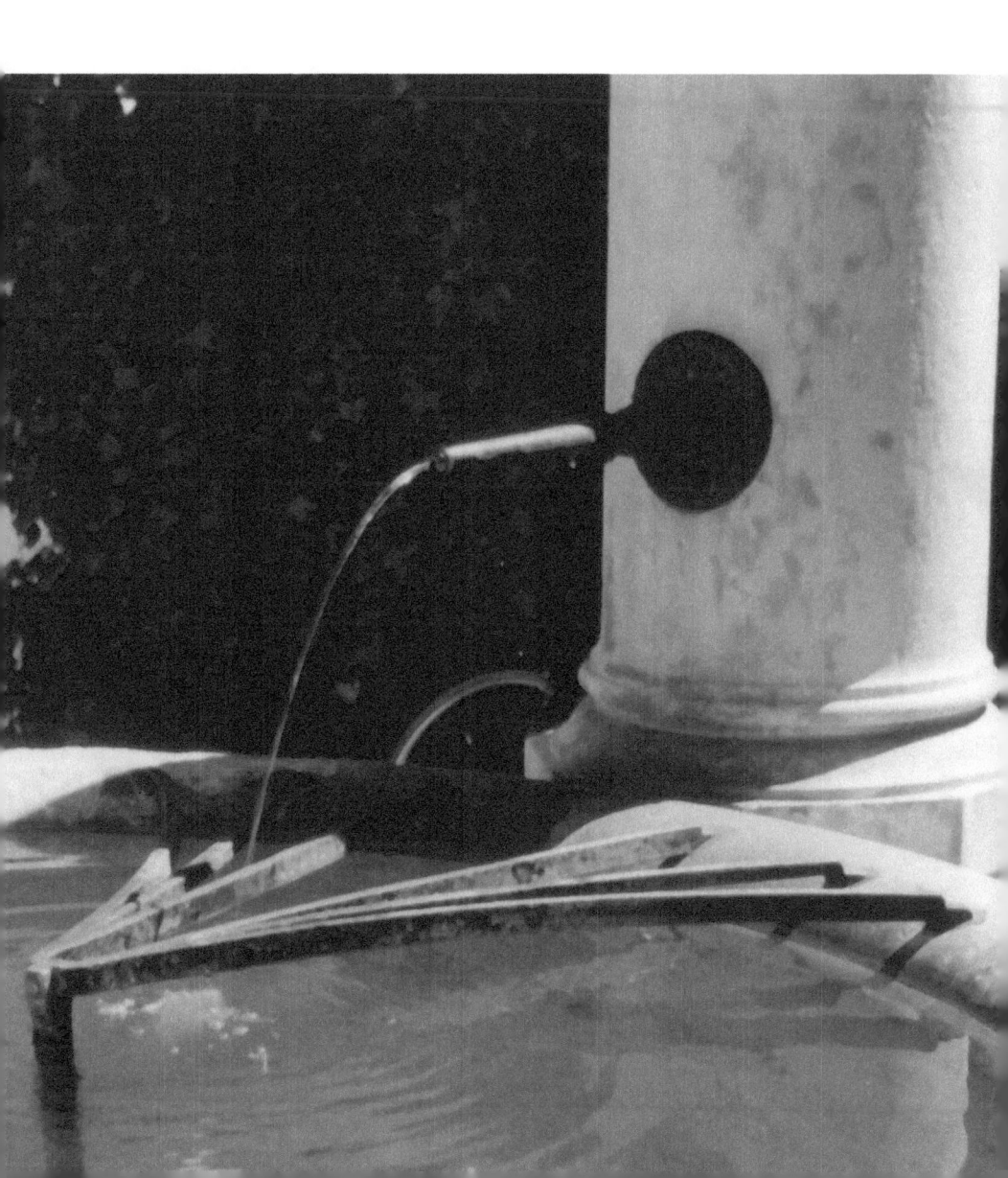

Sometimes all it takes is iron, wood, steel, and a piece of rope to hold up the 'L' platform in Chicago's loop.

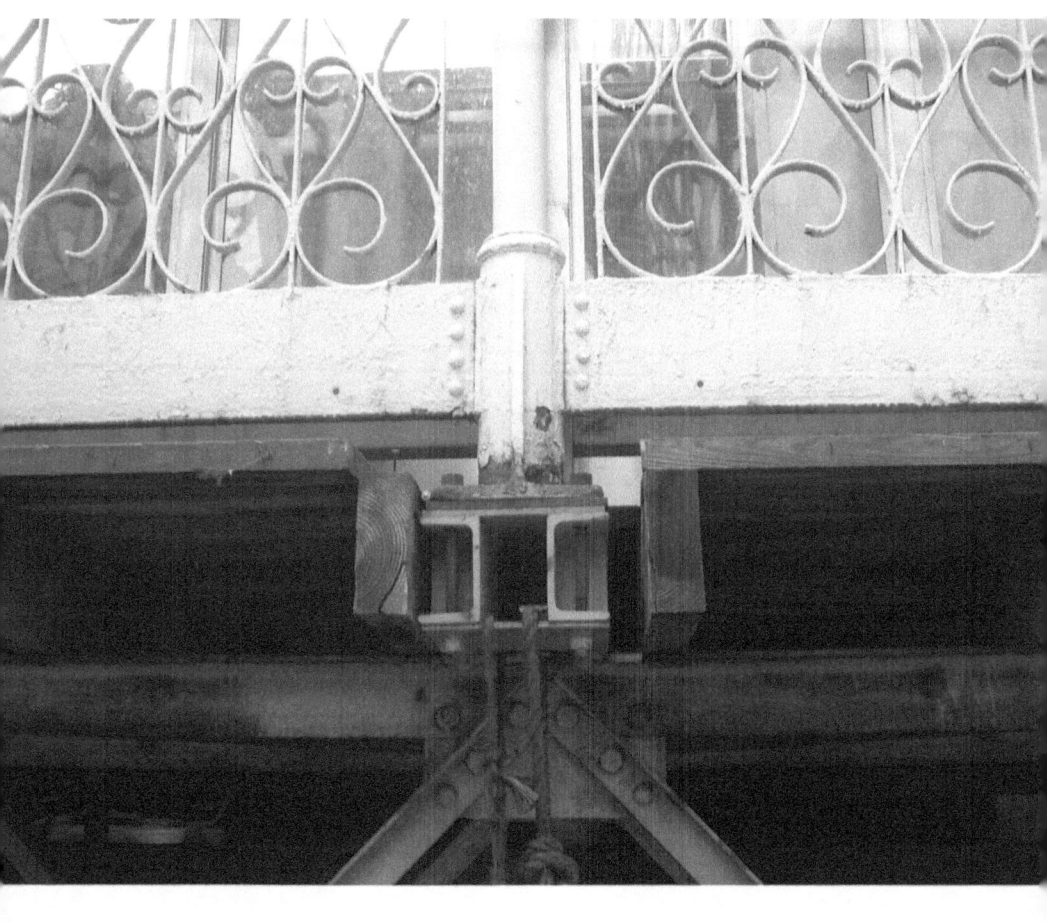

There are bald eagles and overweight men in boats fighting for fish south of the roller dam in Davenport, Iowa.

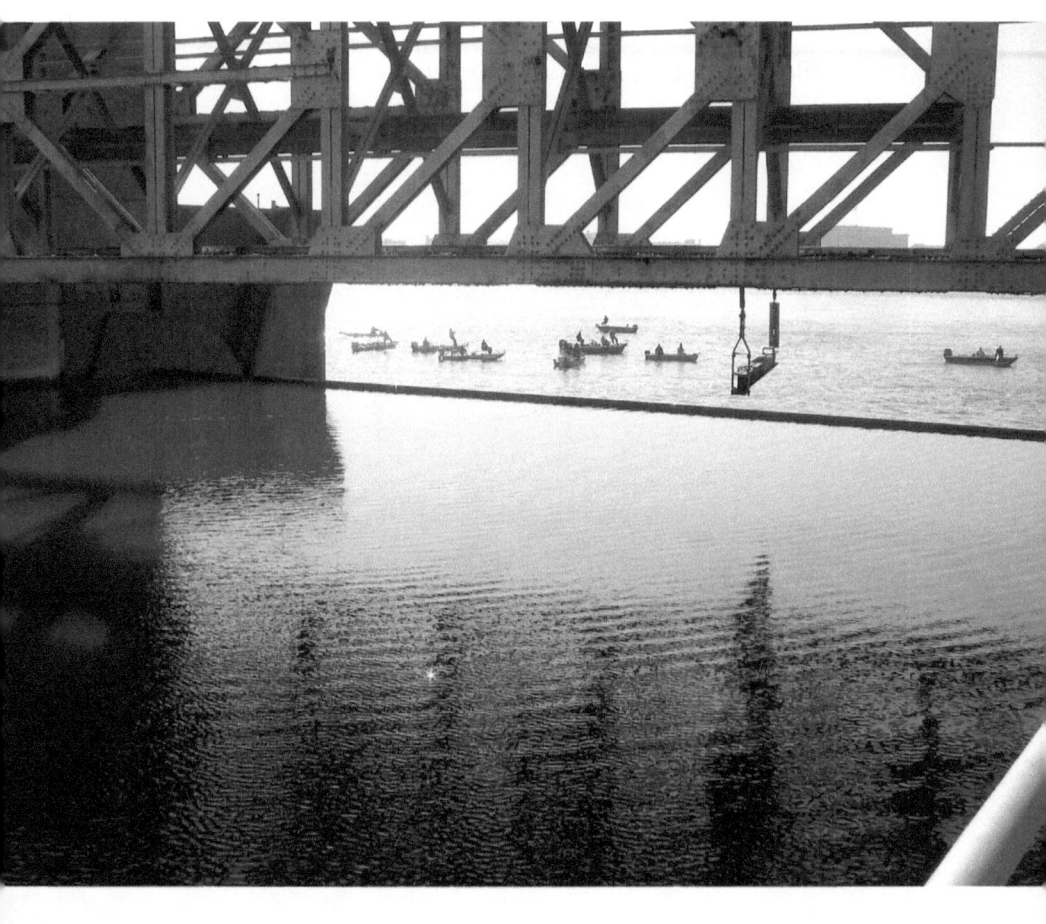

A few weeks after 9-11 we filled up our car in the red state of Florida, and I noticed this request to God crawl across the information screen at the local Gate gas station.

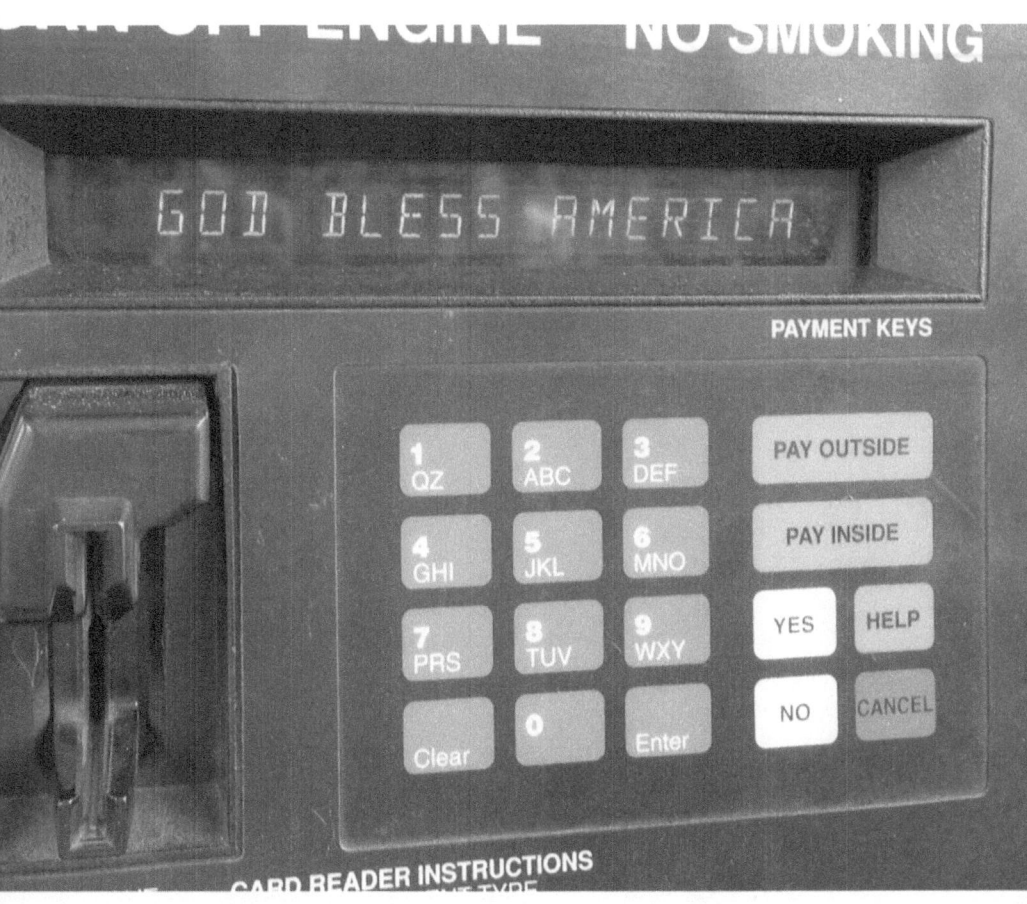

When we went for lunch to the Columbia Restaurant in St. Augustine, Florida, I saw this wall outlet with the Muzak knob next to the reception desk. Only then did I realize that the Muzak volume could in fact be adjusted, although it still didn't explain where the *muzik* came from....

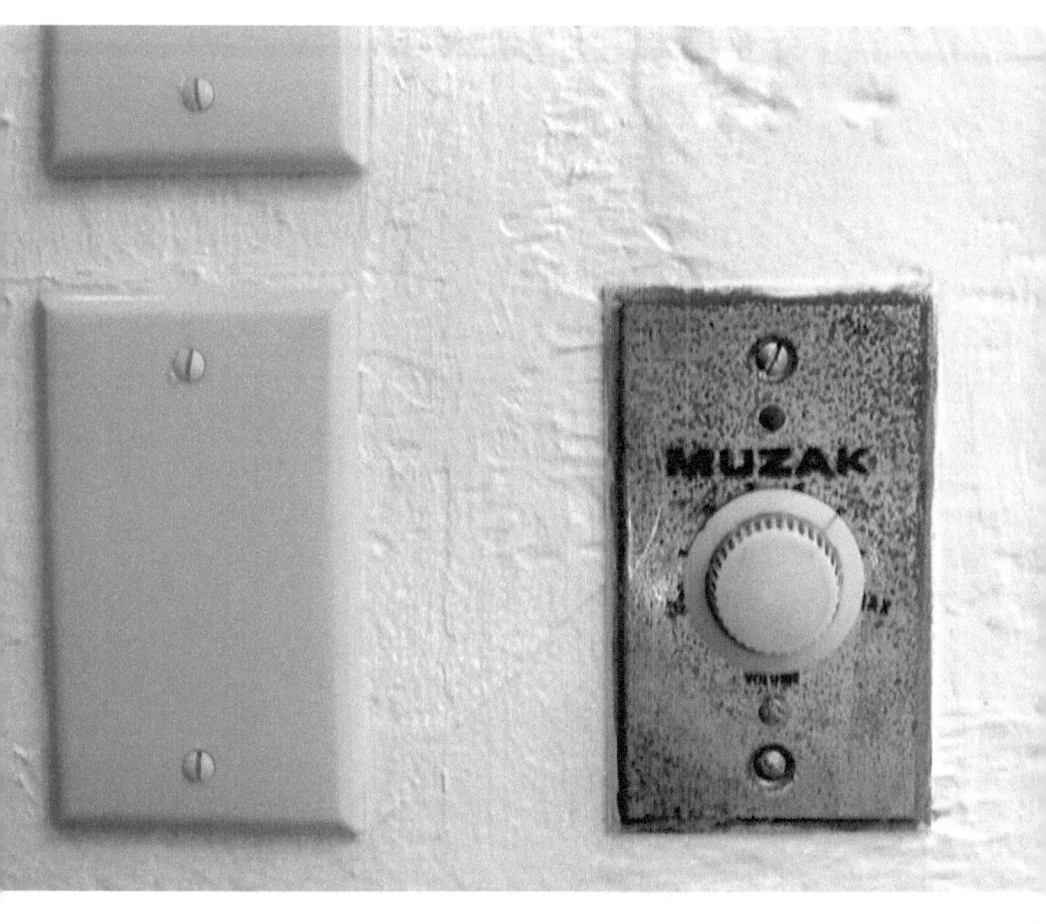

In early spring the sun in my Iowa house comes into the south-facing bedroom like a roaring tiger, with complete disregard to the beautiful play of light and shadow it creates on the cedar-clad walls.

After a swim turtles at Middleton Plantation ouside Charleston, South Carolina, tend to climb on floating logs and worship the sun. When there is more than one, they demonstrate sequential motion, and appear to diagram evolution as well.

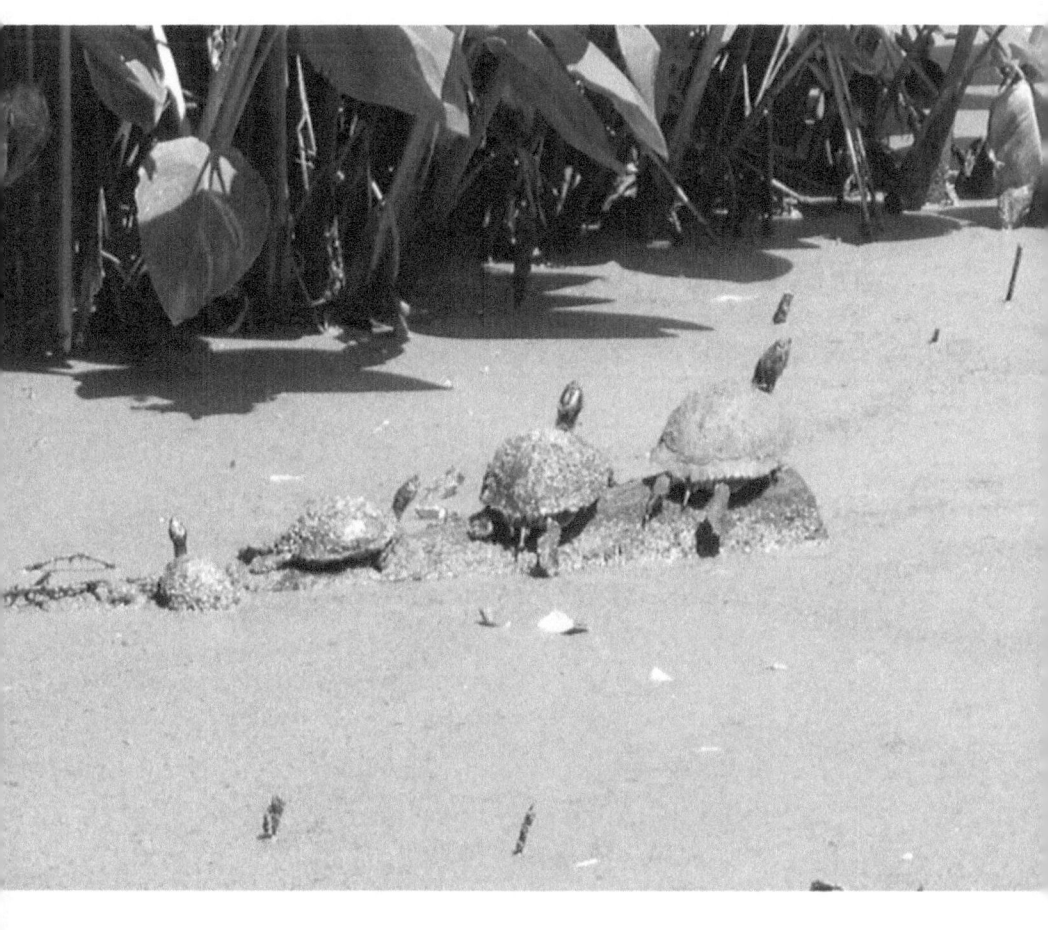

A few years back the Union Pacific Railroad announced that one of the largest steam locomotives in the world would come through Ames, Iowa. On the morning of the announced arrival a large group of railroad afficionados began to gather near the tracks and face west in anticipation. Not much happened until a large rain storm had everyone running for their cars that were parked nearby. The locomotive finally arrived many hours late.

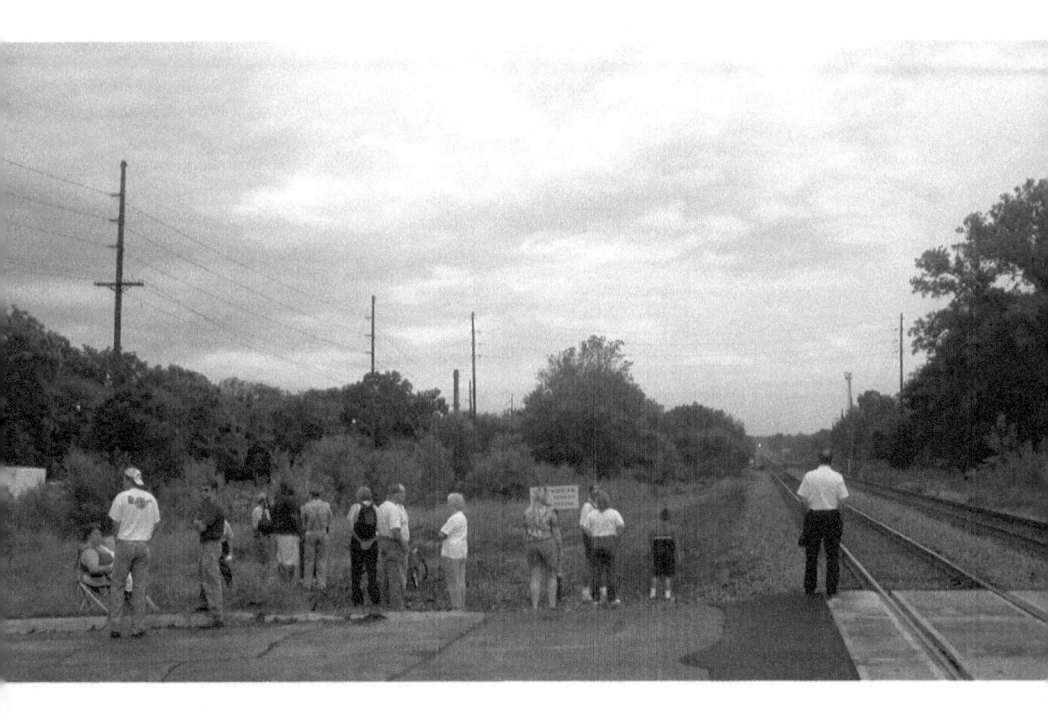

Snow is a blanket thrown over the world, reflecting the light evenly and muffling most sounds.

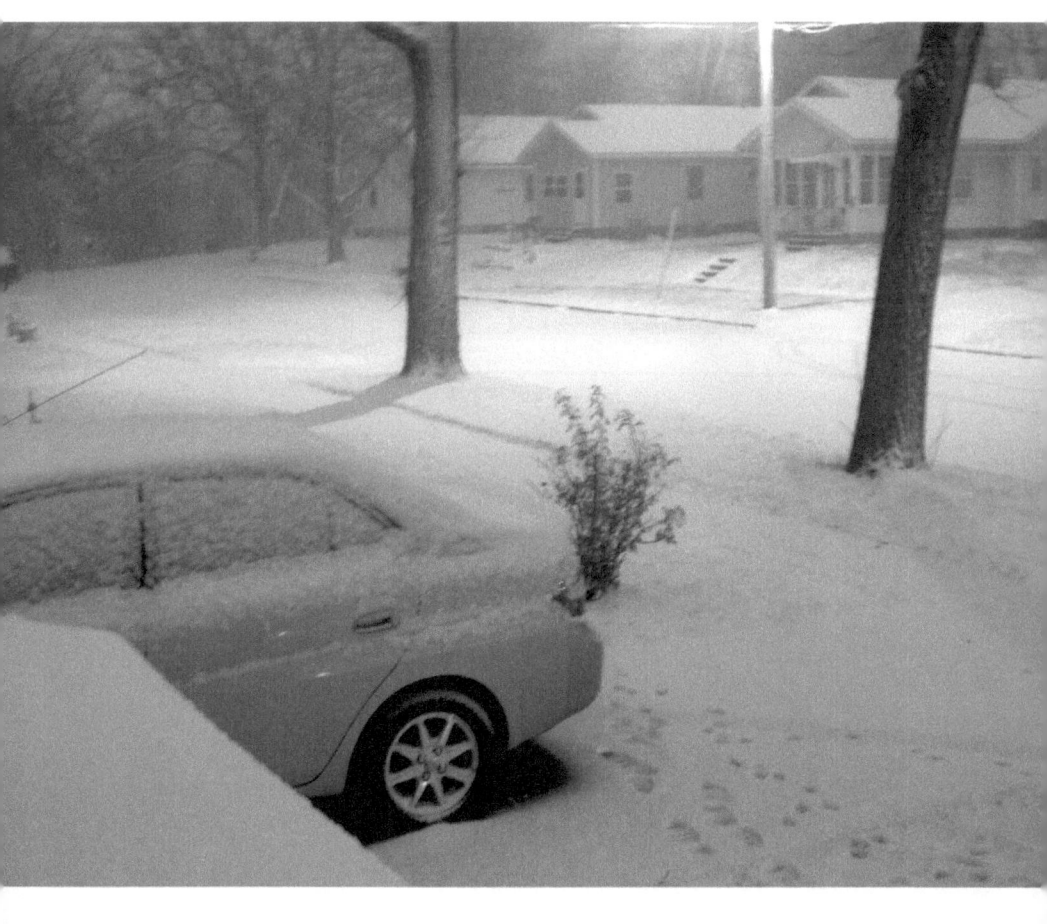

Scale

It's not enough that they build cute houses. The Swiss have to add even smaller cute houses on top of their chimneys.

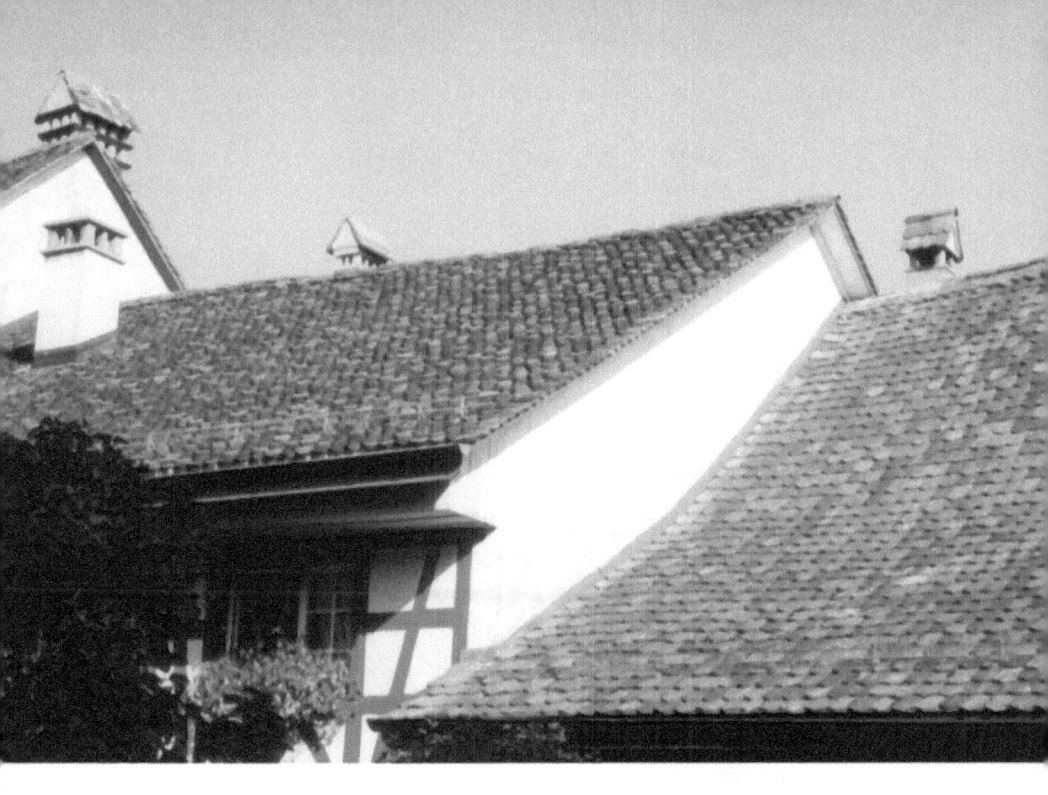

Scale 245

A spatial diagonal as a triad at the *documenta* in Kassel. From left, Hubertus Brand, Irma Mücke, Nina Mücke.

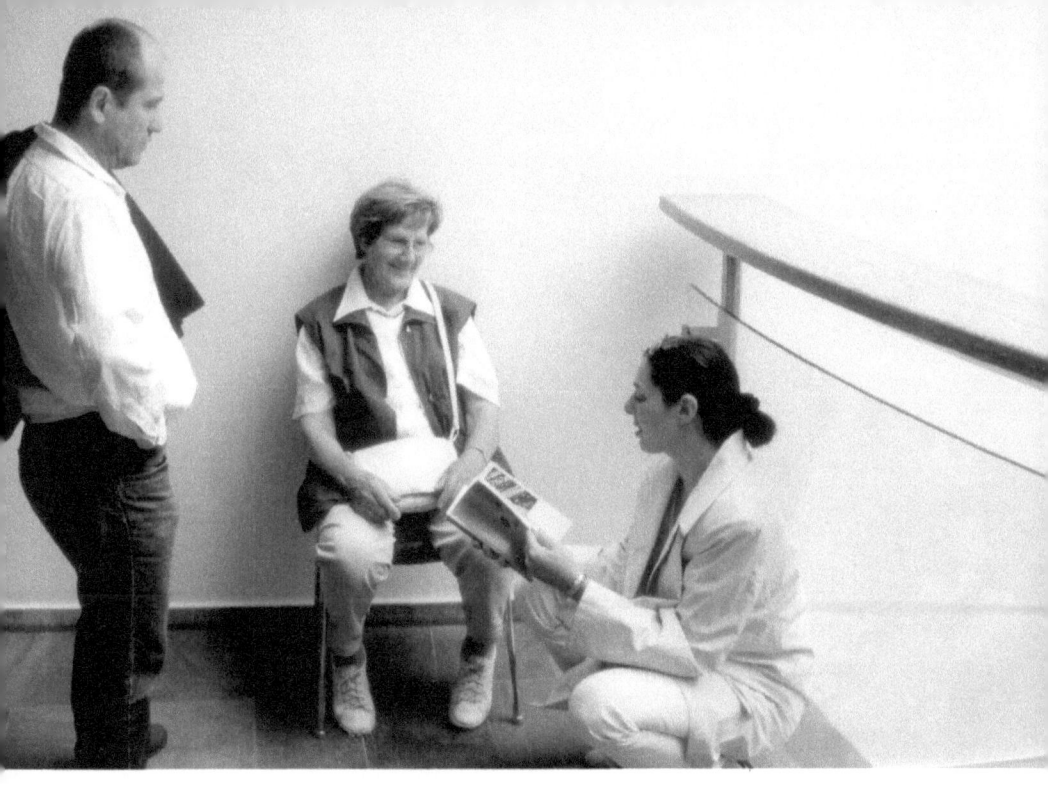

The Hoover Dam is a concrete landscape that weighs in at about 6,600,000 tons. It is overwhelming and supersized, like many other things in the USA.

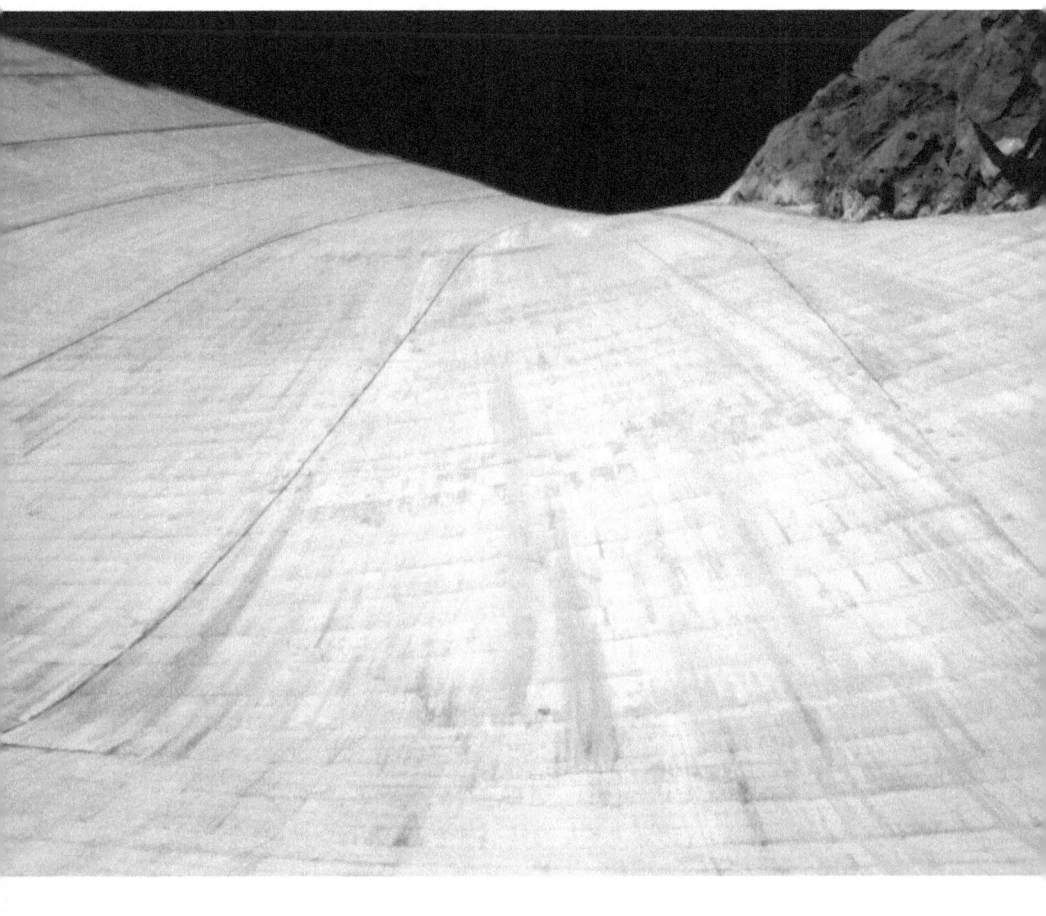

Scale 249

And all of a sudden I saw this bus-sized advertisement passing me in the street in Los Angeles, and I wondered: how did they do this? And then it turned out to be just another surface job that companies like *adsonwheels* and *buswrap* offer. Let's do this on static architecture!

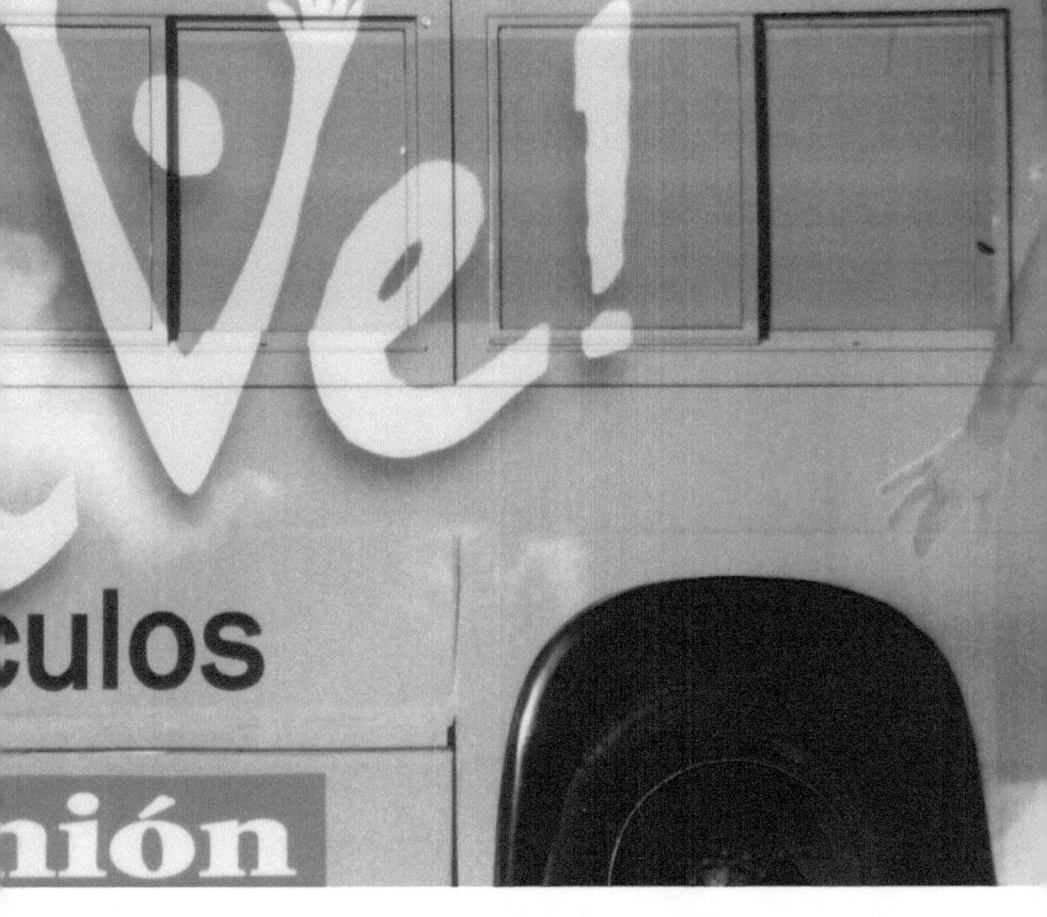

Rob Quigley's house in San Diego appears as a city *en miniature,* complete with tower and red-flashing marker lights for the far-too-low flying aircraft on final approach to SAN.

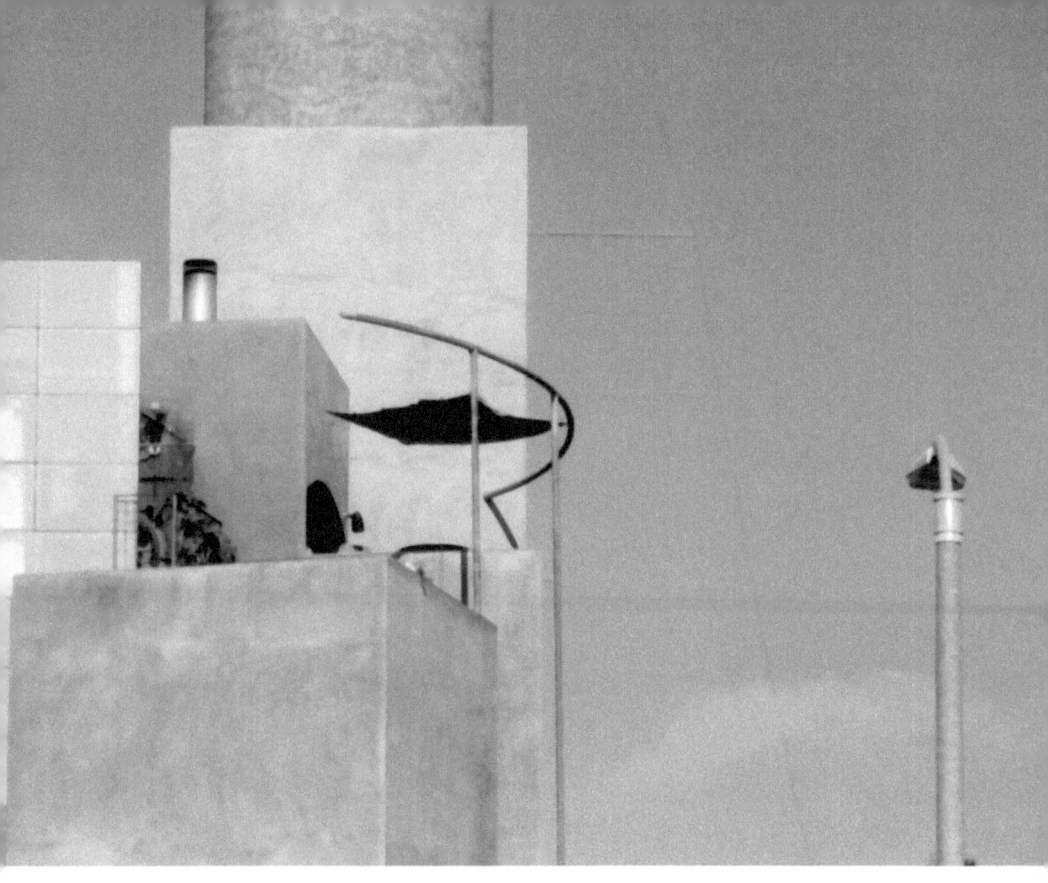

Scale 253

TEXTURES

In the mid 1990s we travelled for a few days to Key West, Florida where we came upon this palimpsest of corrugated metal.

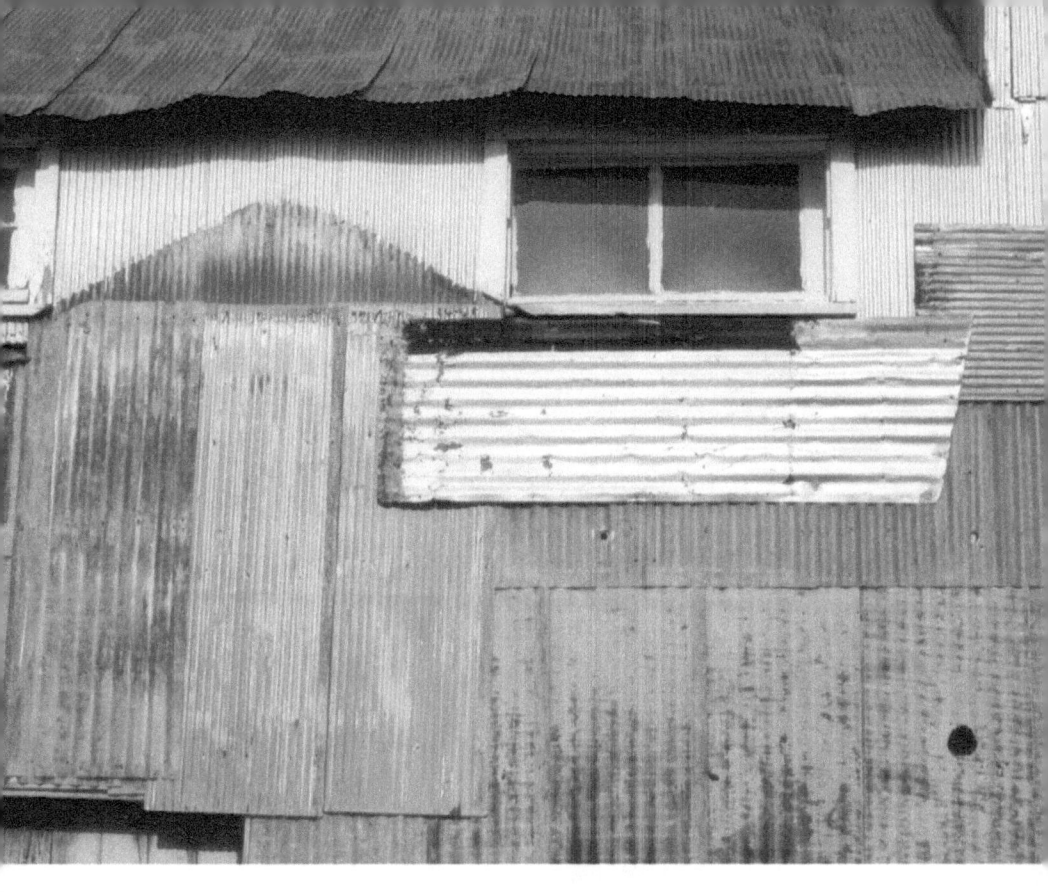

Vals, Switzerland.

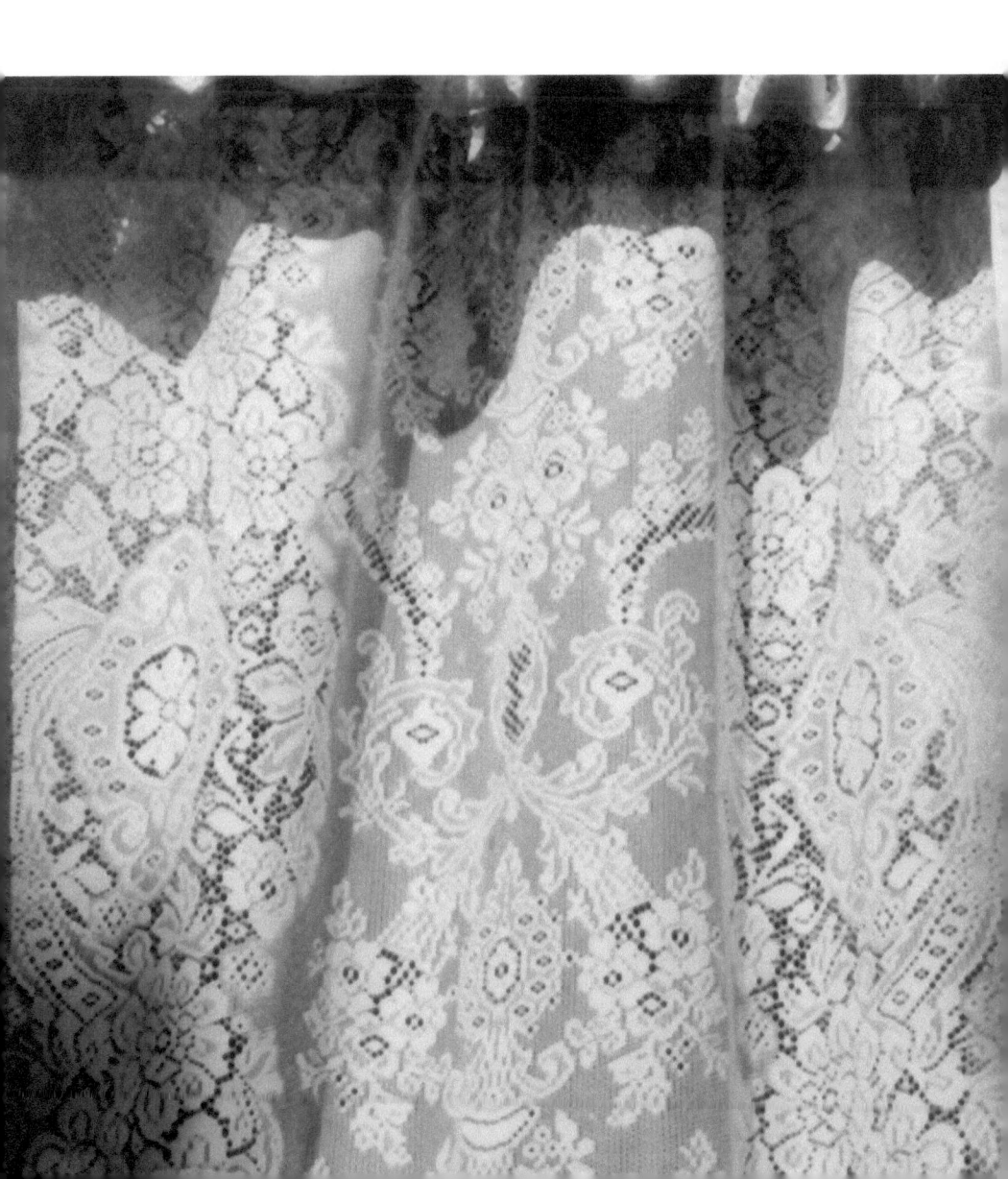

Freilichtmuseum (Open Air Museum) Detmold. Clay tiles, half-timbered construction, slate, stone, hay, mud, and paint on a warm, hazy summer day.

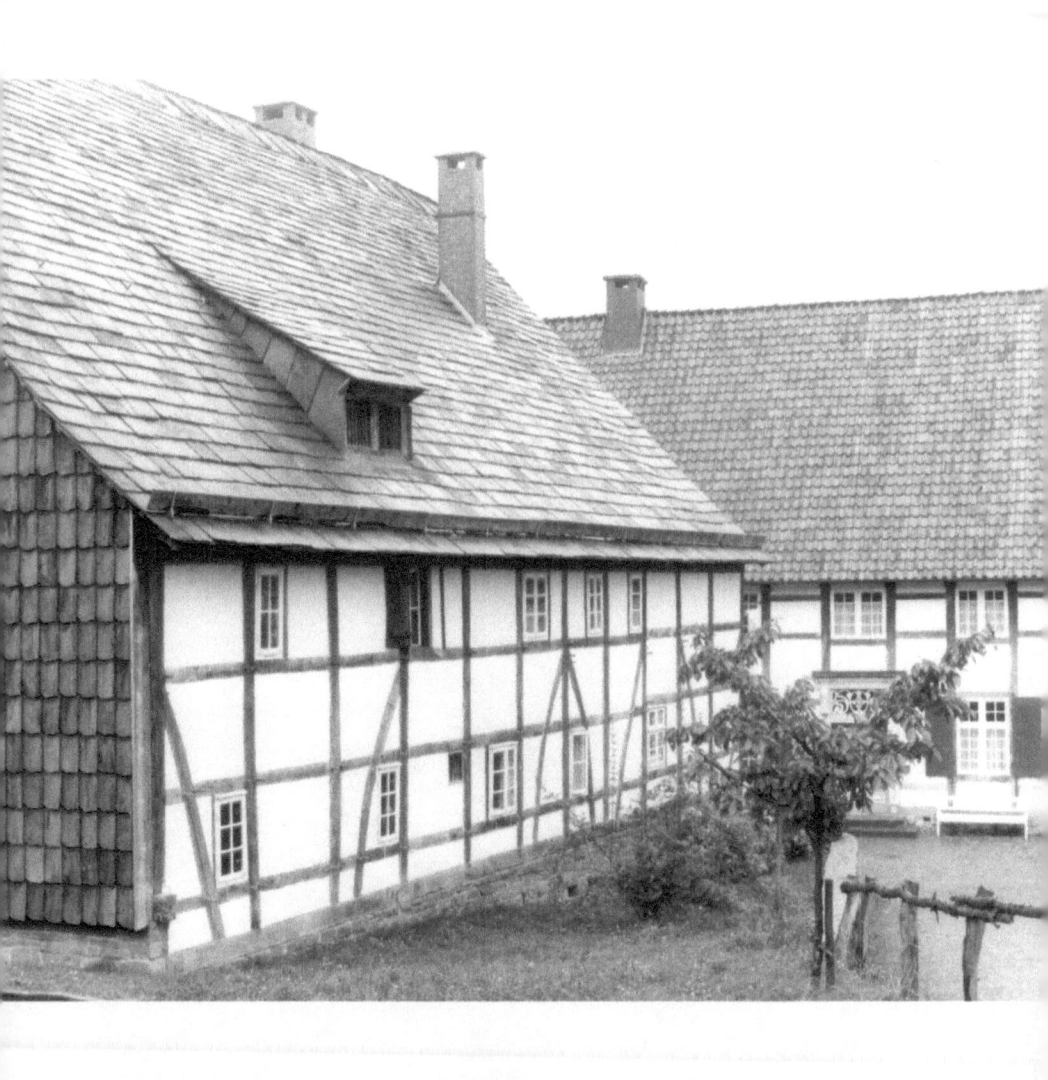

Mottled is a good word to describes this: light shining through a tree onto a house facade in Key West, Florida.

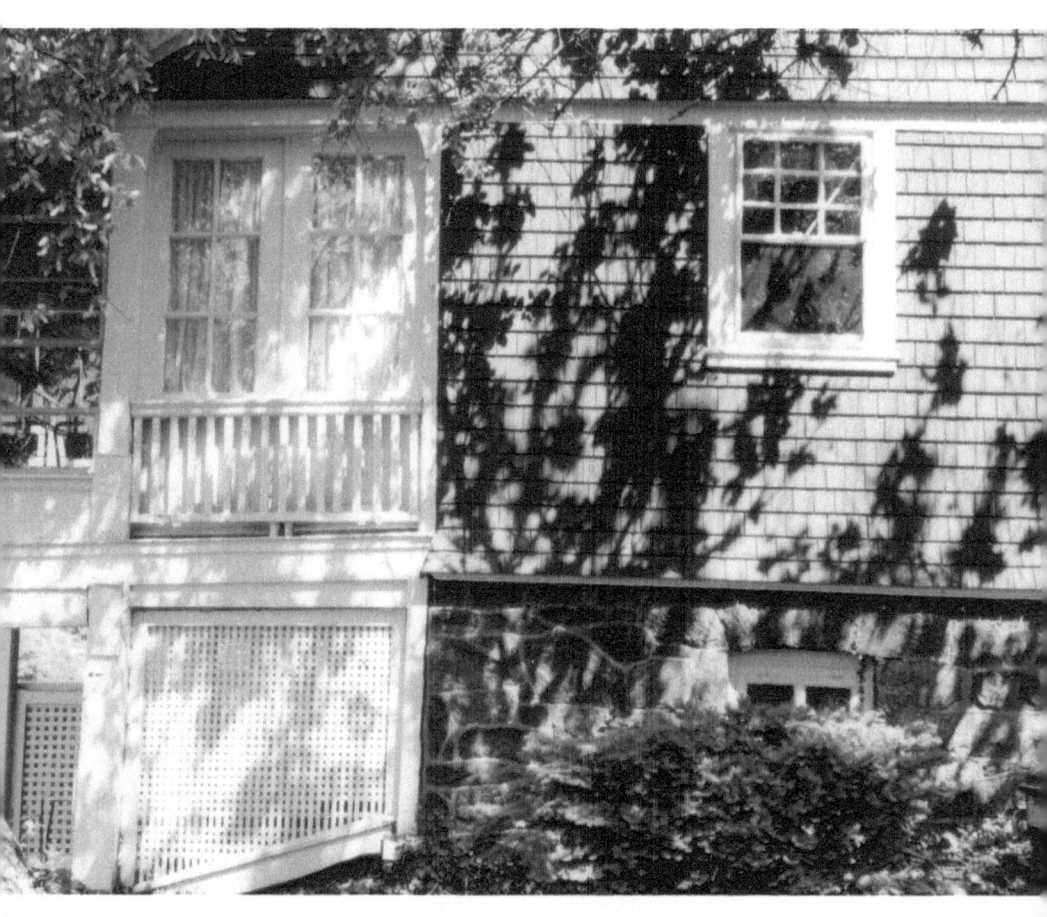

Freilichtmuseum (Open Air Museum) Detmold. Slate roof tile patterns on a half-timbered house from the 1800s.

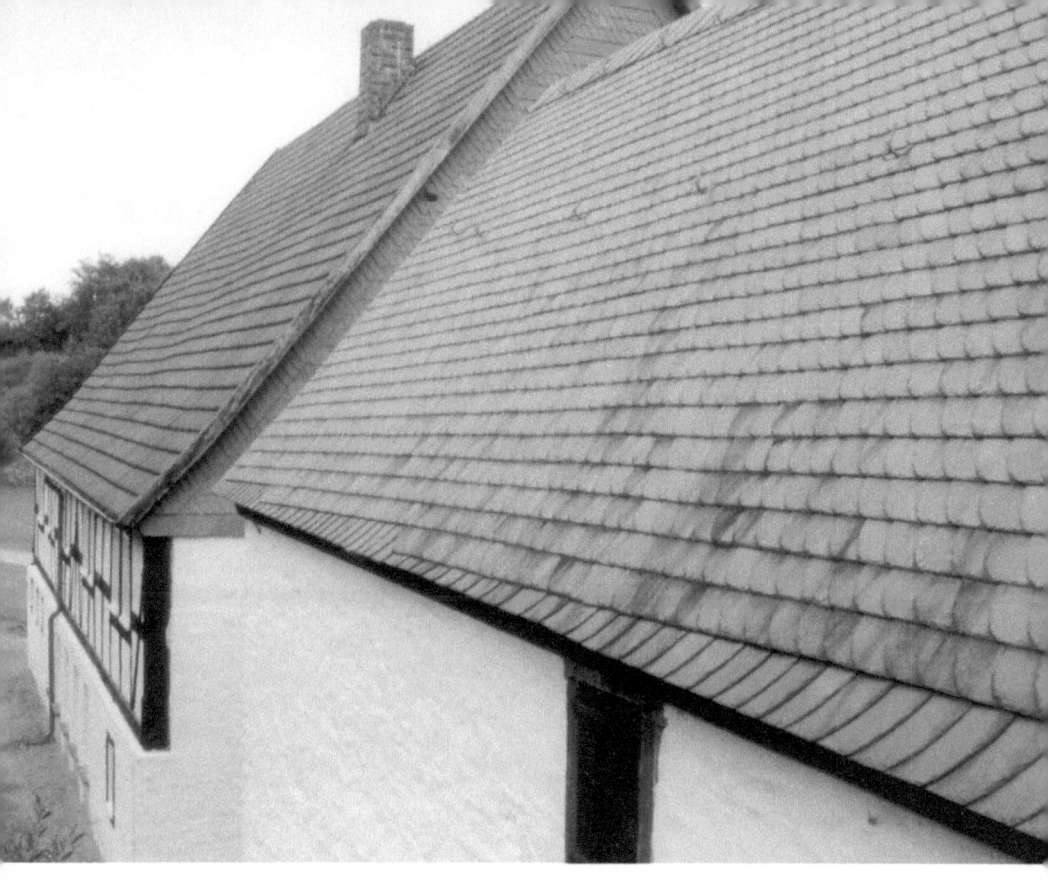

Two textures meeting in the sunlight, not saying hello to each other.

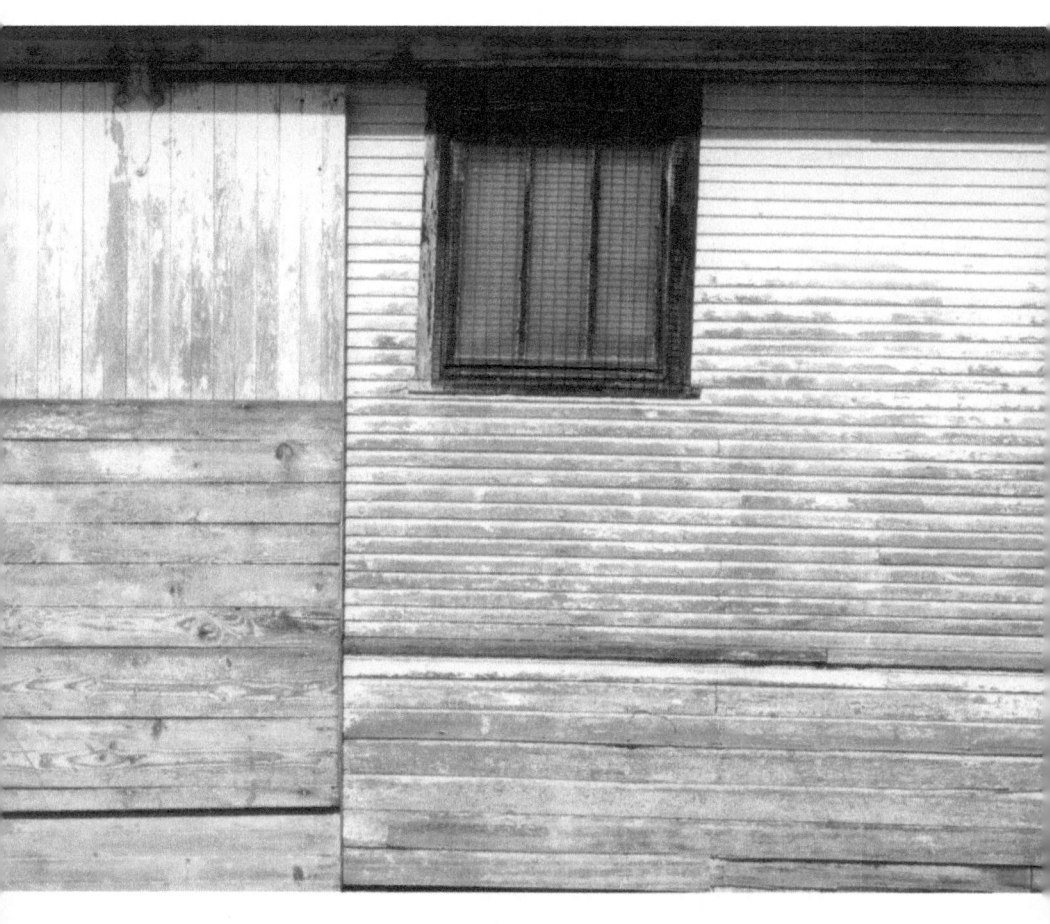

Until we visited Key West I didn't realize how many patterns can be made with parallel lines.

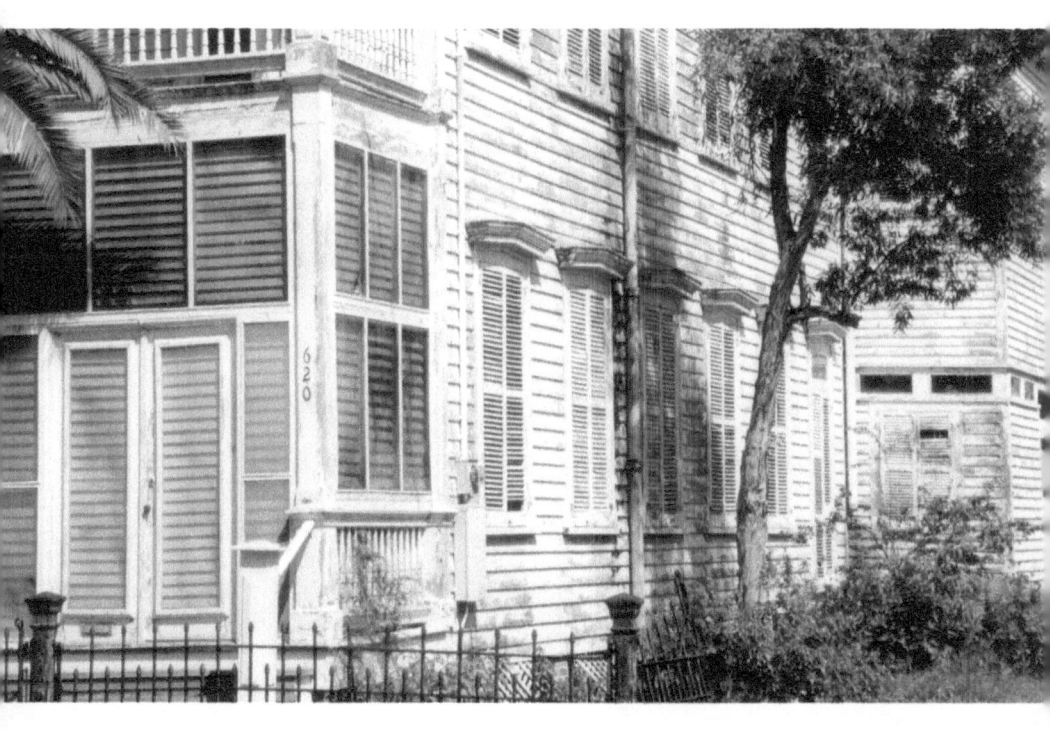

It was a cool September morning when we visited the sculpture garden of the Walker Arts Center in Minneapolis. The air was clear as the sun rose behind the pavilion holding Frank Gehry's fish sculpture, a 20'-tall-glass-skinned wood-and-metal-structured carp appearing to jump into the air.

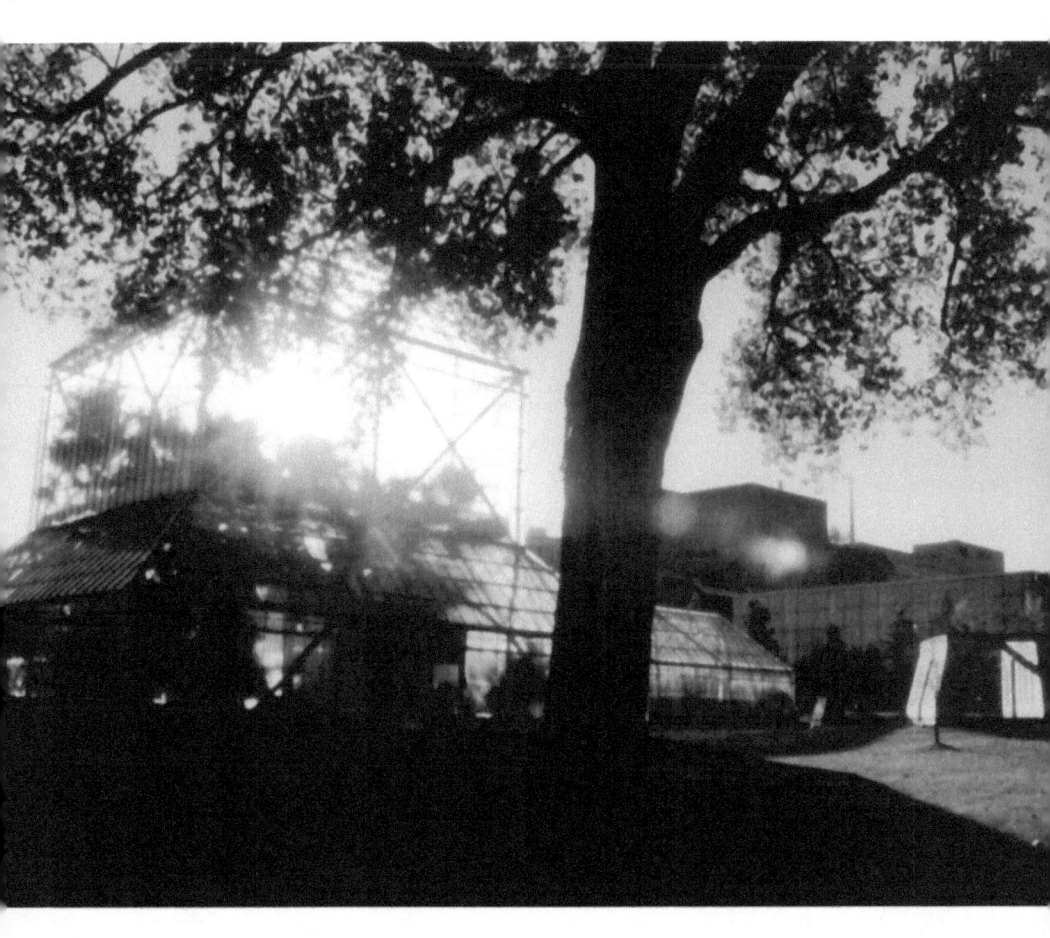

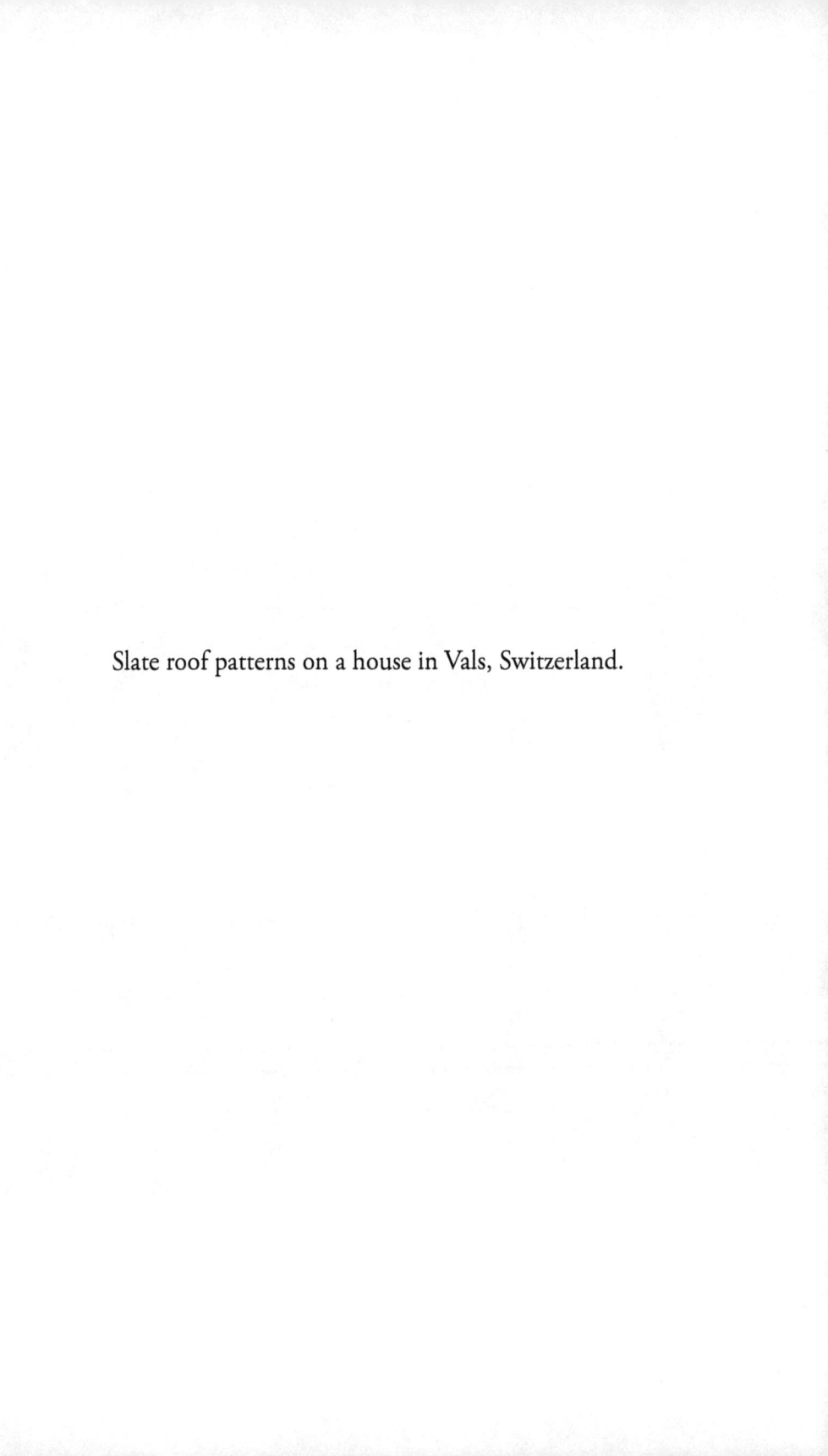

Slate roof patterns on a house in Vals, Switzerland.

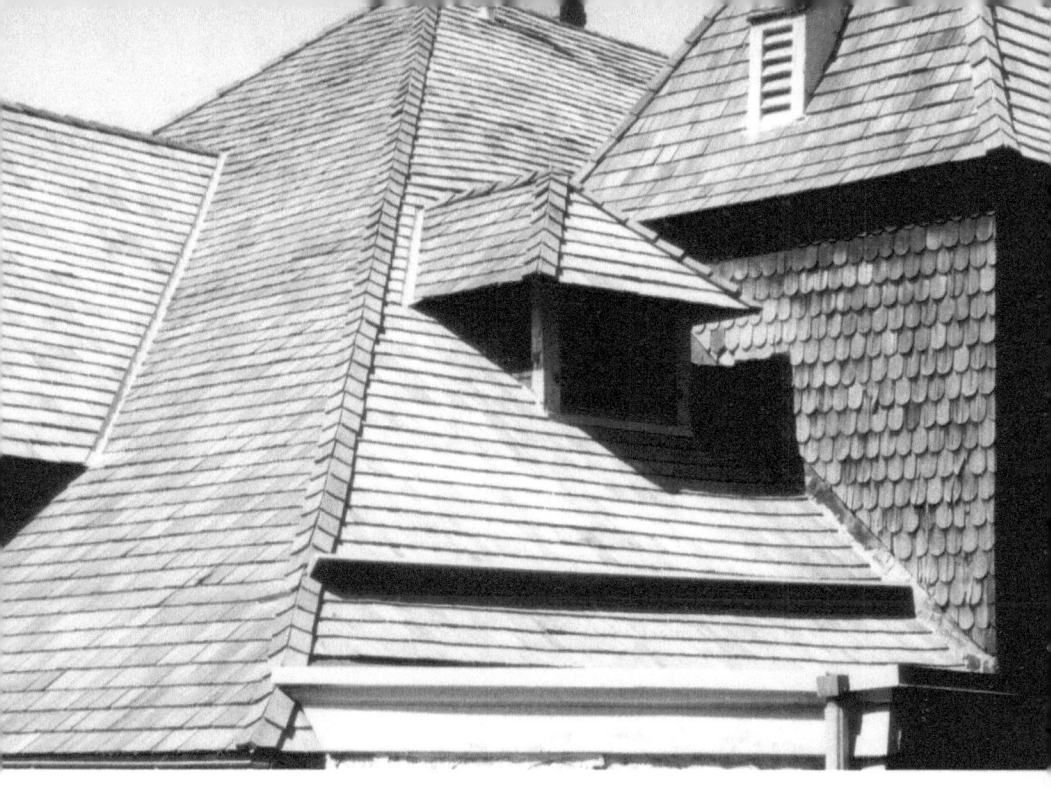

The rain gutter drain pipe on Old Point Loma lighthouse right after lunch in July.

Herzog and DeMeuron are masters in shaping and texturing, as here in the case of the pink-colored cast-concrete staircase of the Küppersmühle Museum - Grothe Collection in Duisburg, Germany.

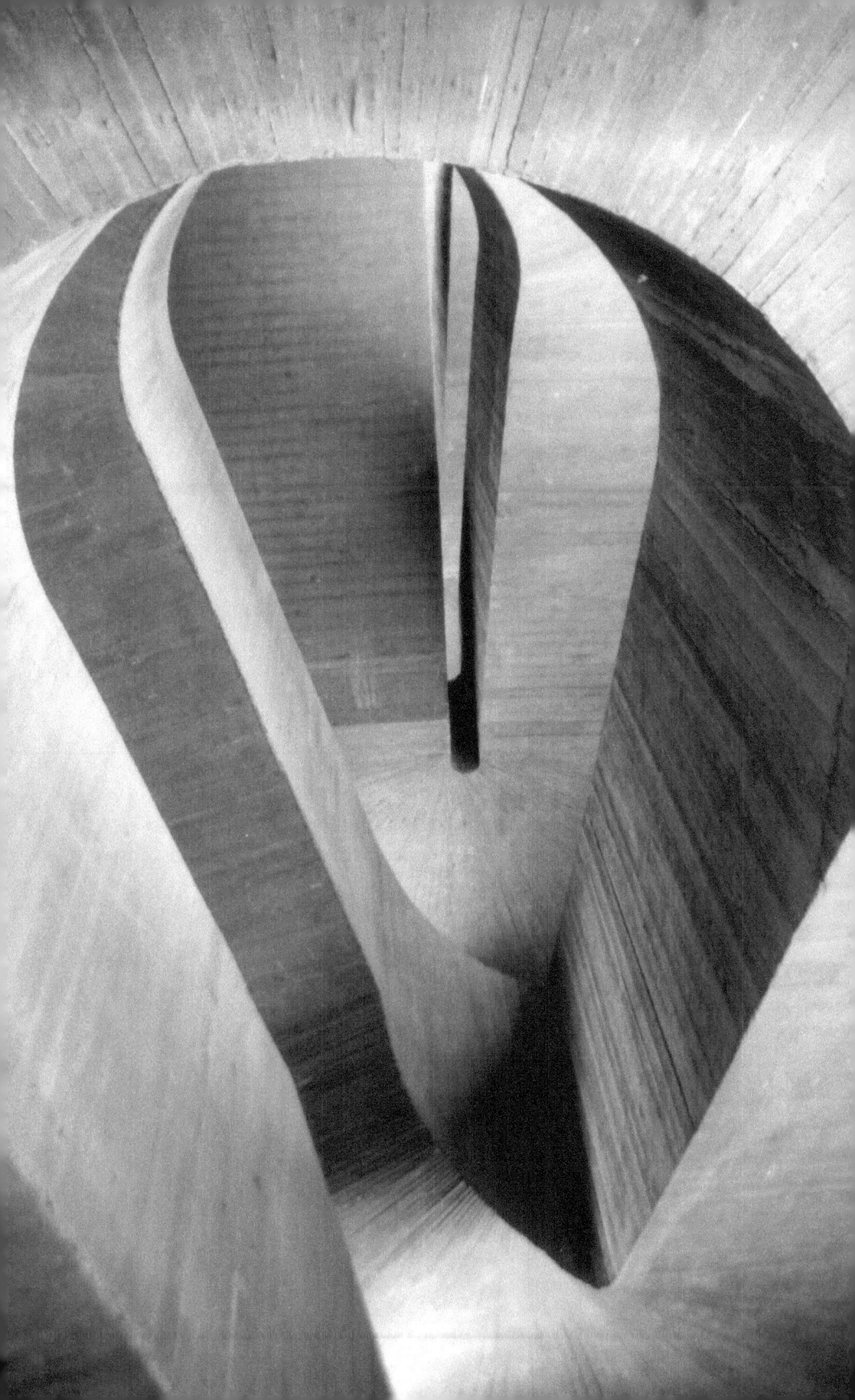

The San Diego sun throws sharp shadows that appear as *Scherenschnitte* on the facades of Quigley's humble but beautiful Single-Room-Occupancy hotels near the city center.

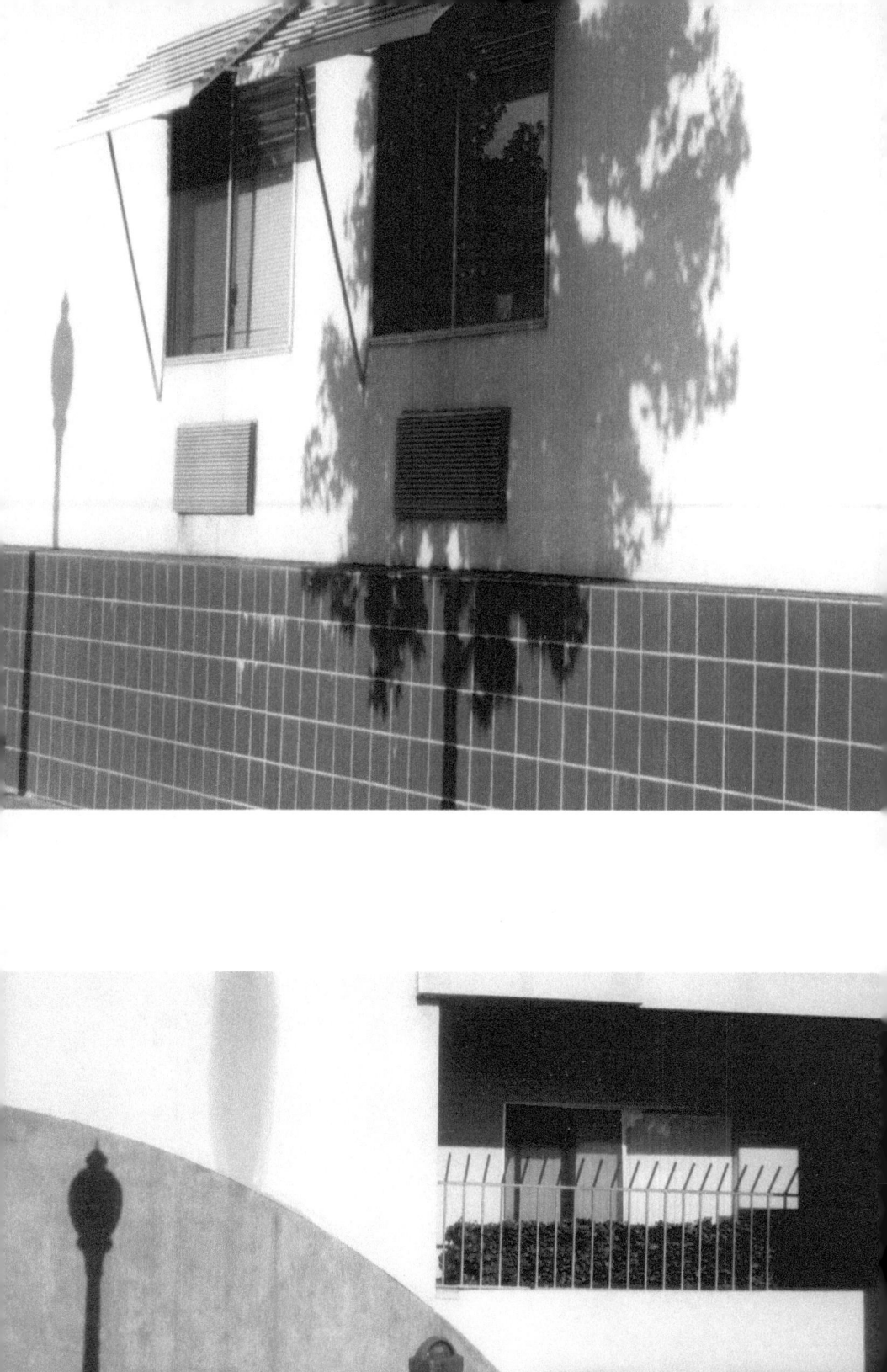

Many buildings in Vals, Switzerland, display a simple yet ingenious combination of load-bearing stone corners complemented by light-weight wooden infill panels, topped by heavy field stone or slate slab roofs. Durable architecture—in a slowly changing landscape.

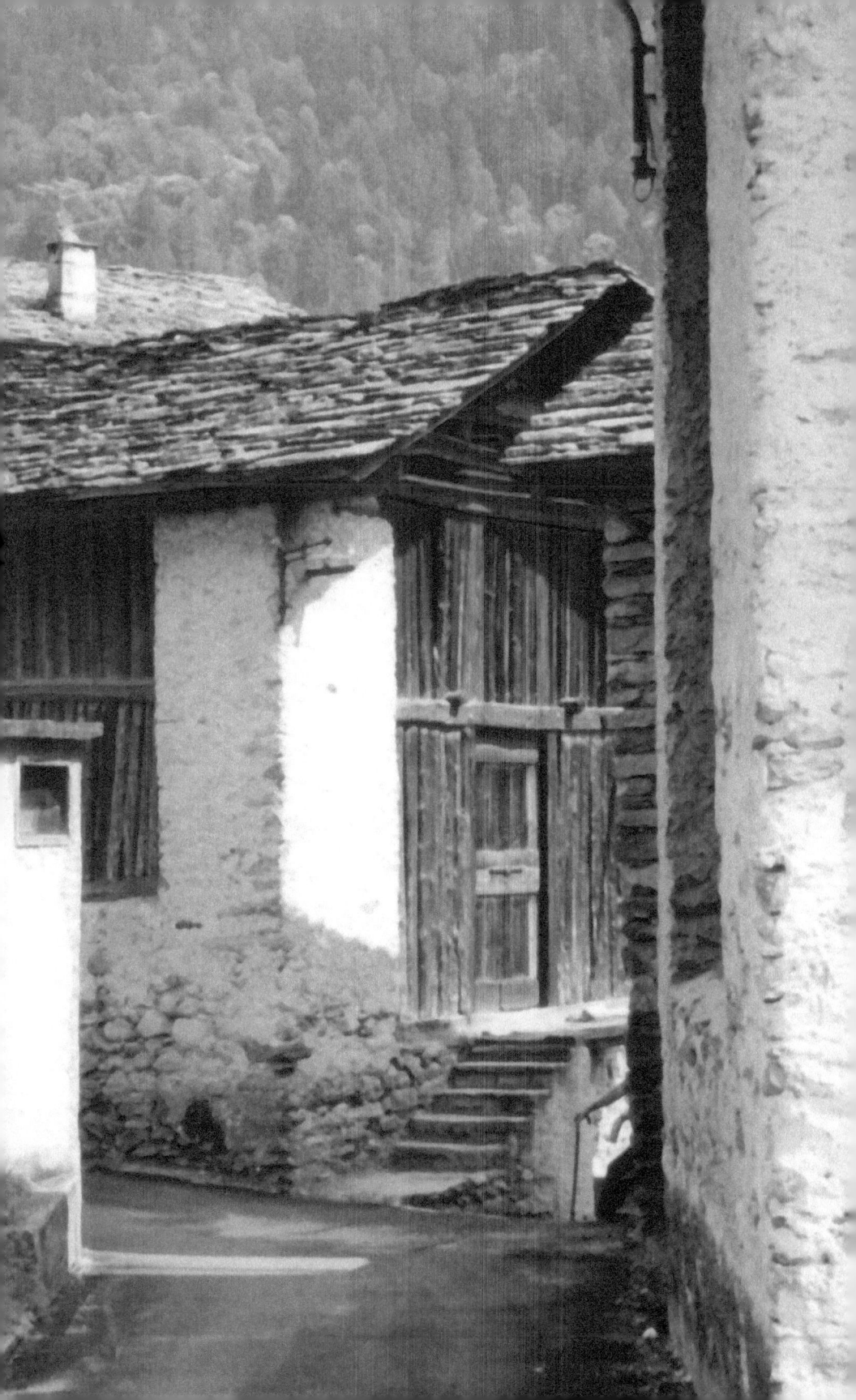

There are 219 steps that lead from the ground to the top-most platform of the old St. Augustine Lighthouse. The interior has a conical shape.

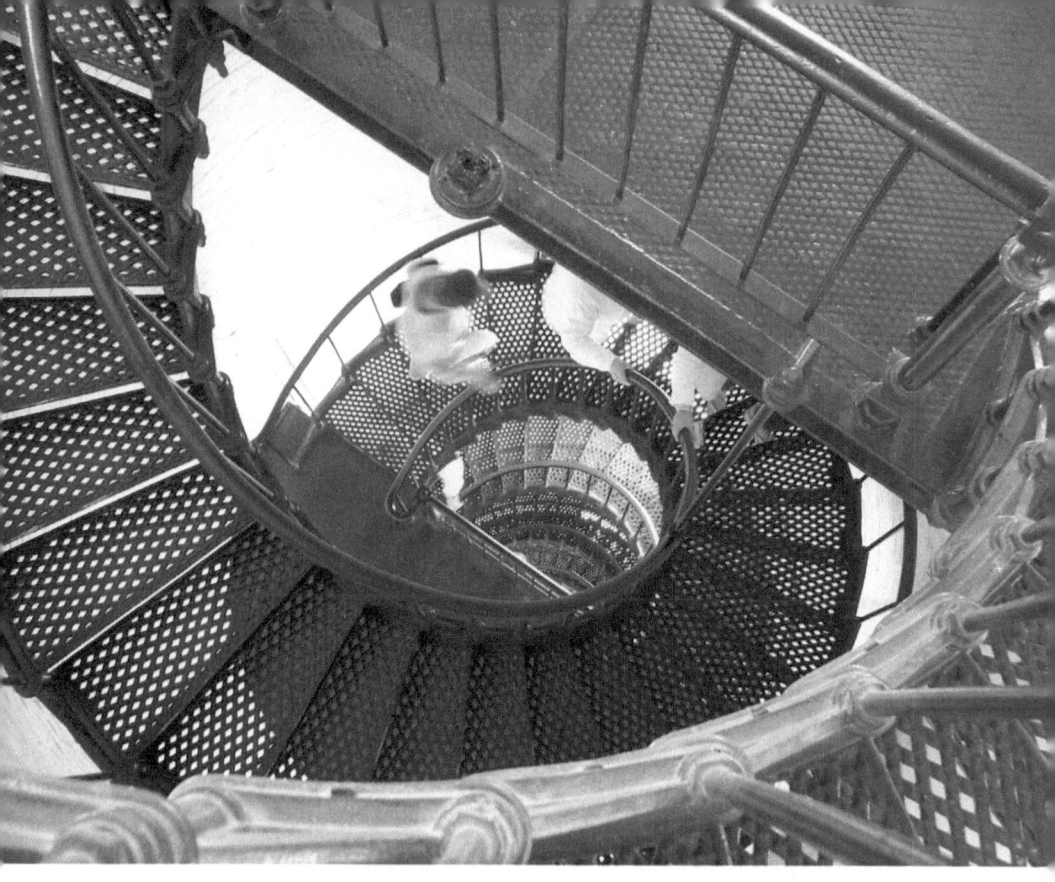

The painted wood skins of the houses in Vals, Switzerland, mimic those of fish. Scales shed water quite effectively.

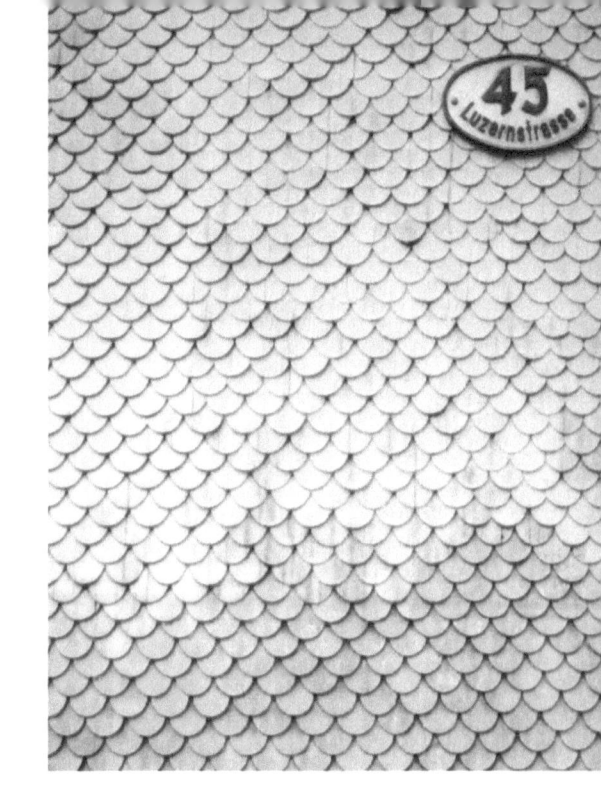

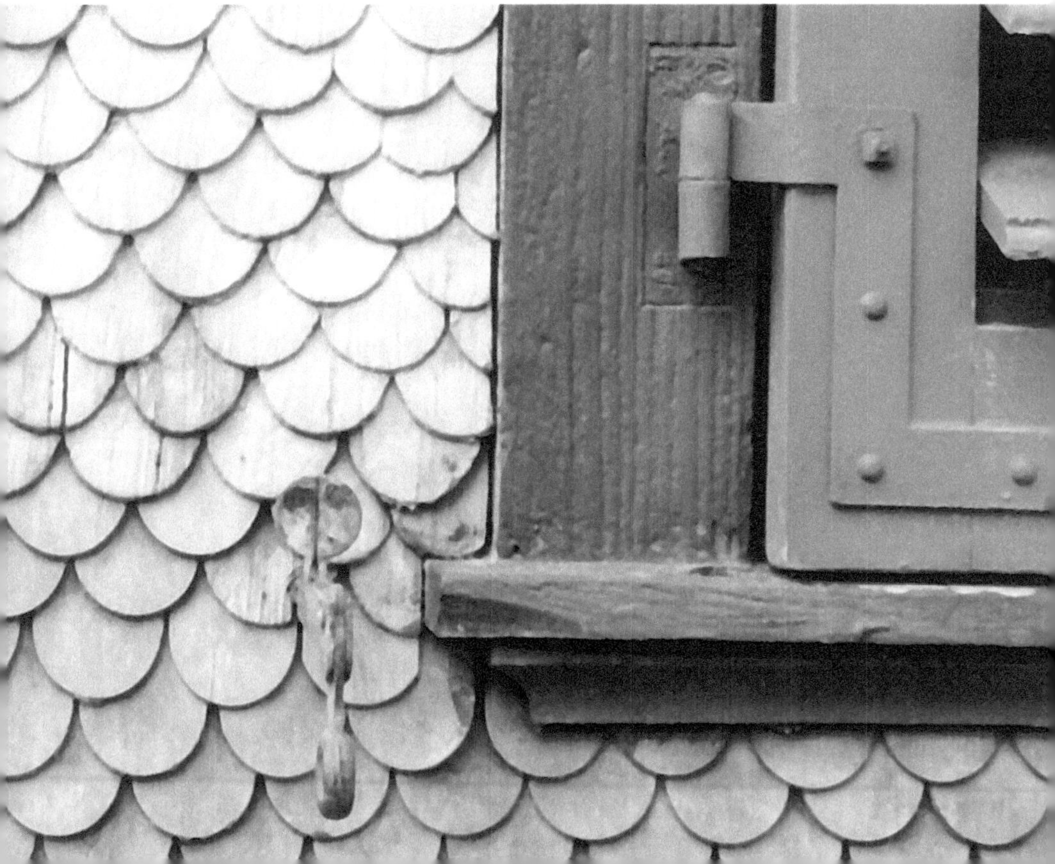

www.ingramcontent.com/pod-product-compliance
Lightning Source LLC
Chambersburg PA
CBHW031611210526
45464CB00004B/1519